ASCENT®

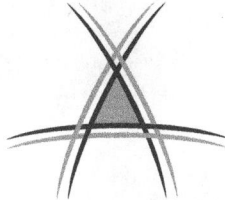

CENTER FOR TECHNICAL KNOWLEDGE

Creo Parametric 6.0
Introduction to Mechanism Design

Learning Guide
1st Edition

ASCENT - Center for Technical Knowledge®
Creo Parametric 6.0
Introduction to Mechanism Design
1st Edition

Prepared and produced by:

ASCENT Center for Technical Knowledge
630 Peter Jefferson Parkway, Suite 175
Charlottesville, VA 22911

866-527-2368
www.ASCENTed.com

Lead Contributor: Scott Hendren

ASCENT - Center for Technical Knowledge (a division of Rand Worldwide Inc.) is a leading developer of professional learning materials and knowledge products for engineering software applications. ASCENT specializes in designing targeted content that facilitates application-based learning with hands-on software experience. For over 25 years, ASCENT has helped users become more productive through tailored custom learning solutions.

We welcome any comments you may have regarding this guide, or any of our products. To contact us please email: feedback@ASCENTed.com.

AS-CRP6-MED1-SG // RS-CRP6-MED1-SG

Contents

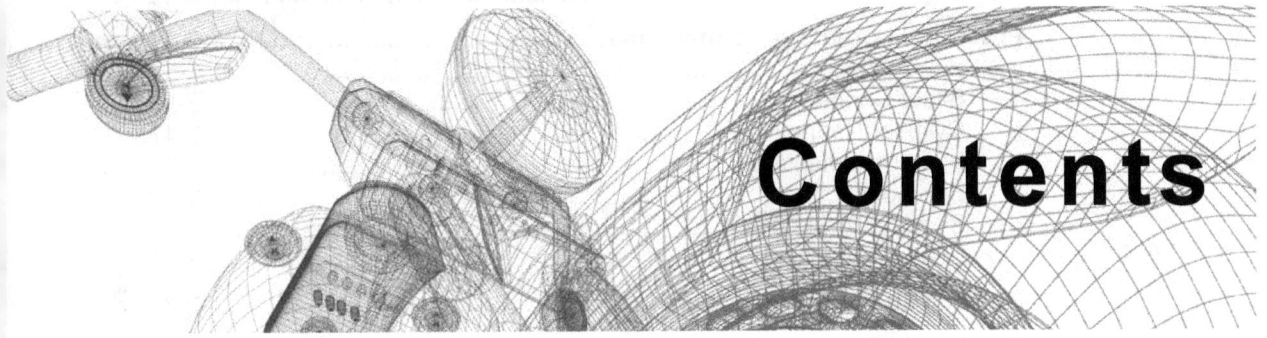

Preface

In the *Creo Parametric 6.0: Introduction to Mechanism Design* learning guide, you will learn how to simulate assembly motion in Creo Parametric using the Mechanism Design extension. You will also learn to set up your assemblies for motion, and create animations of the assembly using the Design Animation option. This hands-on learning guide contains numerous practices.

Topics Covered

- MDX interface
- Basic assembly connections
- Drag
- Snapshot configurations
- Joint axis settings
- Servo Motors
- Motion playback
- Basic Measure analysis
- Advanced connections
- Create movies and images
- Design Animation
- Key frame sequences
- Motion envelopes
- Trace curves
- Interference checks

Prerequisites

- Access to the Creo Parametric 6.0 software. The practices and files included with this guide might not be compatible with prior versions. Practice files included with this guide are compatible with the commercial version of the software, but not the student edition.

- It is highly recommended that you have completed the Creo Parametric: Introduction to Solid Modeling or Creo Parametric: Advanced Assembly Design and Management guides or have similar levels of prior experience using the Creo Parametric software.

Note on Software Setup

This guide assumes a standard installation of the software using the default preferences during installation. Lectures and practices use the standard software templates and default options for the Content Libraries.

This content was developed using Creo Parametric 6.0.4.0.

Lead Contributor: Scott Hendren

Scott Hendren has been a trainer and curriculum developer in the PLM industry for over 20 years, with experience on multiple CAD systems, including Pro/ENGINEER, Creo Parametric, and CATIA. Trained in Instructional Design, Scott uses his skills to develop instructor-led and web-based training products.

Scott has held training and development positions with several high profile PLM companies, and has been with the Ascent team since 2013.

Scott holds a Bachelor of Mechanical Engineering Degree as well as a Bachelor of Science in Mathematics from Dalhousie University, Nova Scotia, Canada.

Scott Hendren has been the Lead Contributor for *Creo Parametric: Introduction to Mechanism Design* since 2013.

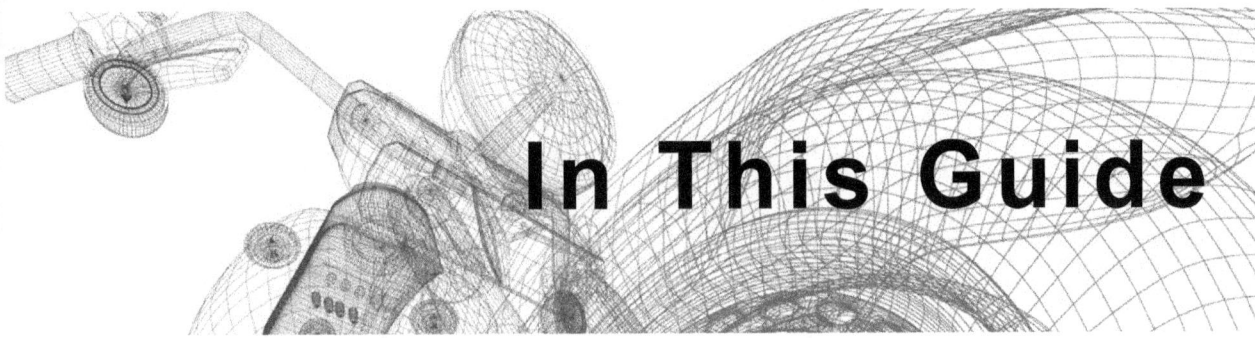

In This Guide

The following highlights the key features of this guide.

Feature	Description
Practice Files	The Practice Files page includes a link to the practice files and instructions on how to download and install them. The practice files are required to complete the practices in this guide.
Chapters	A chapter consists of the following - Learning Objectives, Instructional Content, Practices, Chapter Review Questions, and Command Summary.

- **Learning Objectives** define the skills you can acquire by learning the content provided in the chapter.
- **Instructional Content**, which begins right after Learning Objectives, refers to the descriptive and procedural information related to various topics. Each main topic introduces a product feature, discusses various aspects of that feature, and provides step-by-step procedures on how to use that feature. Where relevant, examples, figures, helpful hints, and notes are provided.
- **Practice** for a topic follows the instructional content. Practices enable you to use the software to perform a hands-on review of a topic. It is required that you download the practice files (using the link found on the Practice Files page) prior to starting the first practice.
- **Chapter Review Questions**, located close to the end of a chapter, enable you to test your knowledge of the key concepts discussed in the chapter.

Practice Files

To download the practice files for this guide, use the following steps:

1. Type the URL *exactly as shown below* into the address bar of your Internet browser, to access the Course File Download page.

   Note: If you are using the ebook, you do not have to type the URL. Instead, you can access the page simply by clicking the URL below.

   ## https://www.ascented.com/getfile/id/plattensis

   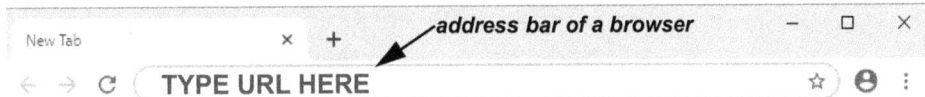

2. On the Course File Download page, click the **DOWNLOAD NOW** button, as shown below, to download the .ZIP file that contains the practice files.

3. Once the download is complete, unzip the file and extract its contents.

   The recommended practice files folder location is:
   C:\Creo Parametric Mechanism Design Practice Files

   Note: It is recommended that you do not change the location of the practice files folder. Doing so may cause errors when completing the practices.

   Stay Informed!

   To receive information about upcoming events, promotional offers, and complimentary webcasts, visit:

   www.ASCENTed.com/updates

MDX Capabilities

The Mechanism Design Extension, also known as MDX, enables you to communicate design intent when components in an assembly require movement (kinematic motion). Motion can be assigned using motors or by dragging components through their range of motion. These analyses enable you to examine the behavior of the mechanism.

Learning Objectives in this Chapter

- Learn what the Mechanism Design Extension (MDX) enables you to accomplish in the assembly.
- Gain a general understanding of connections, joint axis settings, servo motors, and analysis.
- Understand the basic design approach used when creating and analyzing a mechanism assembly.
- Learn how to activate subassemblies or top level assemblies while working in the Mechanism application.
- Learn how to access Mechanism mode, the general tools available in the application, and how to use the mechanism tree.

1.1 Mechanism Introduction

The Mechanism Design Extension (MDX) in Creo Parametric enables you to simulate kinematic motion in your assemblies. You can drag the mechanisms through their range of motion or apply Servo Motors to define predetermined animations. These analyses enable you to examine the behavior of the mechanism. You can observe and record the analysis or measure quantities, such as positions, velocities, or accelerations and graph the measurement. The velocity and acceleration measure data can be graphed or displayed as animated vector arrows during the playback of the analysis. You can also check for interference throughout the range of motion and create an envelope to account for the volume of swept motion. Different positions can easily be displayed in different drawing views.

You can use MDX with the Behavioral Modeling Extension (BMX) to evaluate important parameters throughout the mechanism's range of motion. You can also open mechanisms in Creo Simulate or use the Creo Mechanism Dynamics Extension to evaluate dynamic forces. If you need to make a presentation, you can create image files and movies.

1.2 Mechanism Components

While mechanisms can be designed and tested in many different ways, all mechanisms rely on the following:

- Connections
- Joint Axis Settings
- Servo Motors
- Analysis Definition

Connections

Connections are used instead of assembly constraints when creating an assembly. Basic mechanism connections are controlled in the Placement panel in the *Component Placement* dashboard, as shown in Figure 1–1.

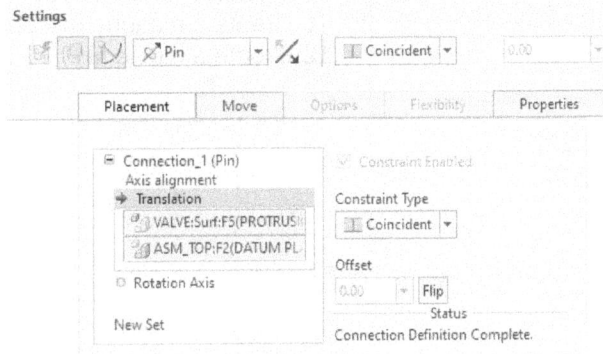

Figure 1–1

Joint Axis Settings

Joint Axis Settings are used to limit the range of motion. These limits are required because Creo Parametric enables you to assemble components that might interfere with other components. By limiting the range of motion of a component or body, you eliminate interference and can correctly mimic the motion.

Servo Motors

Servo motors force a specific type of motion to occur between assembled components.

Analysis Definition

Analyses create a motion definition using the applied Servo Motors. The total time is entered and the mechanism moves for the time allotted based on the servo motors.

1.3 Design Approach

Some of the steps might not be required depending on the type of motion or analysis.

How To: Create and Analyze a Mechanism Using MDX

1. Create the assembly and assemble the components using connections.
2. Create advanced cam-follower, belt, 3D contact, or gear connections.
3. Define the joint axis settings.
4. Move the assembly using the drag functionality.
5. Create servo motors.
6. Create the analysis definition.
7. Analyze the results.
8. Create measures.
9. Graph important measurements.
10. Check for interference.
11. Create a motion envelope part.
12. Create a movie file.

1.4 Mechanism Design & Subassemblies

When working with a top-level assembly that contains subassemblies, you can create, edit, or delete any mechanism entity defined in the top-level assembly or in any of its subassemblies. This functionality is very efficient and enables you to work with MDX consistent with Creo Parametric assemblies.

By default, the top-level assembly is always active and all modifications to the mechanism are made at this level. To make changes to a subassembly, select it in the Model Tree, and click

◇ (Activate) in the mini toolbar, as shown in Figure 1–2. Once active, 🔩 displays next to the component name.

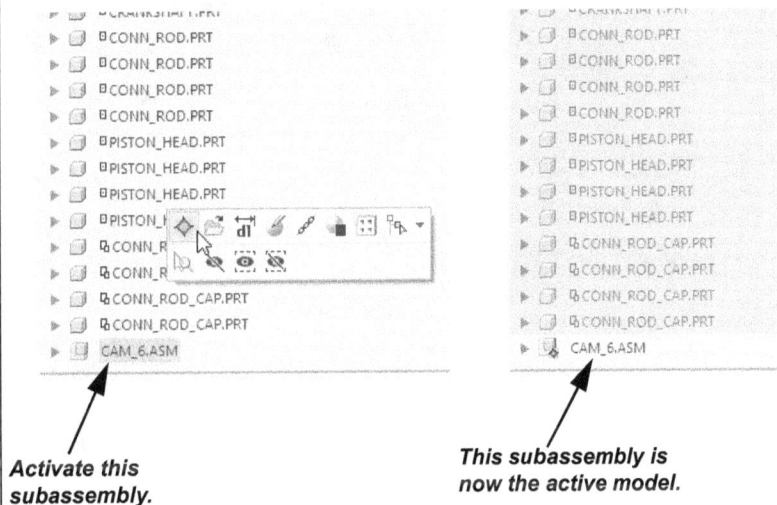

Activate this subassembly.

This subassembly is now the active model.

Figure 1–2

1.5 Mechanism Interface

Assemblies created with connections are manipulated in Mechanism mode. To access Mechanism mode, in the *Applications* tab, click 🛞 (Mechanism). The interface updates and the *Mechanism* tab activates, as shown in Figure 1–3.

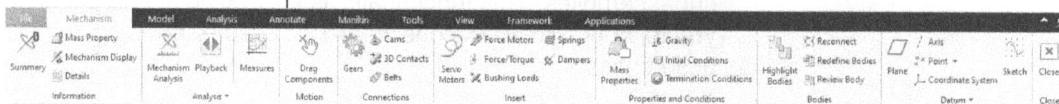

Figure 1–3

You can complete most Mechanism Design tasks using the options or icons on ribbon. Options are also available in the shortcut menus when selecting features on the model or Model Tree.

Some of the icons available in the Information, Analysis, and Motion groups in the *Mechanism* tab are described as follows:

Icon	Name	Description
	Summary	Displays a summary report in the browser window.
	Mechanism Display	Controls visibility of Mechanism icons in display window.
	Mechanism Analysis	Opens Analyses dialog box.
	Playback	Opens Playbacks dialog box.
	Measures	Opens Measure Results dialog box. Measurements throughout the range of motion can be graphed.
	Drag Components	Opens Drag dialog box, which enables interactive dragging.

The Connections and Insert group in the *Mechanism* tab has additional icons. These icons are described as follows:

Icon	Name	Description
	Cams	Displays Cam-Follower Connections dialog box.
	3D Contacts	Displays 3D Contact tab.

Icon	Name	Description
	Gears	Displays Gear Pairs dialog box.
	Belts	Displays Belt tab.
	Servo Motor	Displays Servo Motors dialog box.

The Bodies group in the *Mechanism* tab has additional icons. These icons are as follows.

Icon	Name	Description
	Highlight Bodies	Highlights bodies that can move relative to one another.
	Redefine Bodies	Displays how components were assembled using standard constraints.
	Reconnect	Locks and unlocks any bodies.
	Review Body	Displays body definitions.

You can click **File>Prepare>Model Properties** and click **change** next to Mechanism to open the Settings dialog box as shown in Figure 1–4. This dialog box enables you to specify the tolerance that Mechanism Design uses to assemble mechanisms, and to specify the action that Mechanism Design takes when an analysis run fails.

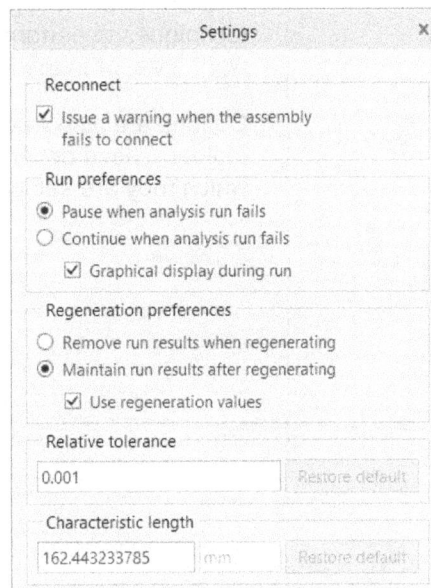

Settings

Reconnect

☑ Issue a warning when the assembly fails to connect

Run preferences

◉ Pause when analysis run fails
○ Continue when analysis run fails
   ☑ Graphical display during run

Regeneration preferences

○ Remove run results when regenerating
◉ Maintain run results after regenerating
   ☑ Use regeneration values

Relative tolerance

0.001   Restore default

Characteristic length

162.443233785   mm   Restore default

Figure 1–4

The mechanism items are listed in the mechanism tree, as shown in Figure 1–5. It provides easy access to creating new mechanism items (e.g., a cam connection) and to editing, deleting and copying items (e.g., servo motors). You can also open the Playbacks dialog box and play previously run analyses. It also lists any assembly connections. To highlight connections on the model, select them in the mechanism tree.

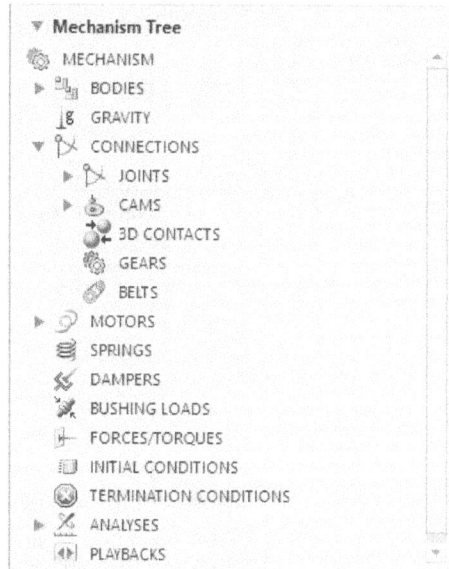

Figure 1–5

In Creo Parametric Mechanism, you can use object-action techniques to perform an action on an object selected in the work area, or in the Model Tree.

Options are also available in the shortcut menus and mini toolbar. These options will vary depending on the context in which they are selected.

Chapter Review Questions

1. What function is used to limit the range of motion along a connection axis?

   a. Analysis Definition

   b. Suppress

   c. Playback

   d. Joint Axis Settings

2. What can be used to drive or force motion between components in a mechanism?

   a. Joint Axis Settings

   b. Analysis Definition

   c. Servo Motor

   d. Playback

3. What is set up to define a motion study by running the servo motors for a given period?

   a. Joint Axis Settings

   b. Analysis Definition

   c. Servo Motor

   d. Playback

4. While using the Assemble command to add a component to the assembly, you will have access to both Connections and Constraints.

   a. True

   b. False

5. The Mechanism application and the Behavioral Modeling Extension can be used in combination to study parameters throughout the mechanism's range of motion

   a. True

   b. False

Answers: 1d, 2c, 3b, 4a, 5a

Creating Assemblies

In standard Assembly mode, components are assembled using assembly constraints to fix the components to each other. Motion can be simulated using offset constraints and relations to change a component's position with each regeneration. In MDX, connections are used to eliminate fixed constraints. This enables degrees of freedom between bodies.

Learning Objectives in this Chapter

- Understand the reasons a connection is used and where they are located in the Component *Placement* tab.
- Understand the different connection types, the remaining degrees of freedom, and the standard assembly constraint types required to complete the connection.
- Learn the general steps to assemble a component with connections in the Component *Placement* tab.
- Understand the rotation and translation degrees of freedom for each connection type.

2.1 Types of Connections

Connections serve two purposes. First, Creo Parametric uses connections to locate the component in the assembly. Second, the connection limits the range of motion of the component with respect to other components.

Since the components are not fully constrained, they display as packaged in the Model Tree.

Before a connection type is selected, you should decide which type of movement is required. Each connection type has a unique set of placement constraints based on the existing constraints used in Assembly mode. Each connection type also has a unique Degree of Freedom (DOF) for both translation and rotation.

Creo Parametric currently has many available connection types, which are available in the Placement panel, as shown in Figure 2–1. Once you select the connection type, the *Constraints* area displays the types of constraints required.

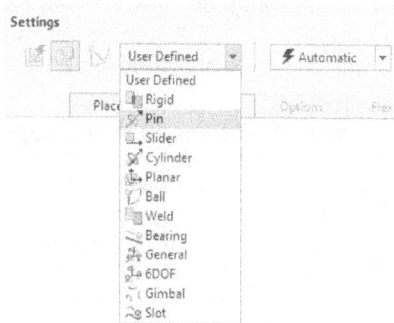

Figure 2–1

Each connection type, with the exception of Rigid, displays a specific icon on the mechanism. These icons display when the Mechanism mode is active and enable you to identify how the component was connected.

Rigid Connection

Use the rigid connection to assemble a component using standard assembly constraints to fully constrain the component in all degrees of freedom. With the rigid connection, relative motion between the new component and the referenced assembly components is not permitted. The rigid connection defines the ground for the mechanism and does not move with respect to other components. As shown in Figure 2–2, a connection icon is not displayed to identify a rigid component.

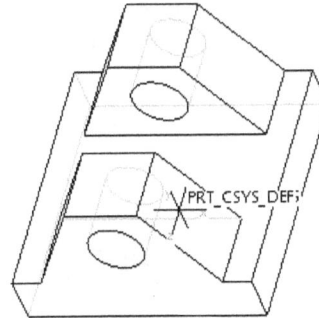

Figure 2–2

Pin Connection

Use the pin connection to assemble a component that can rotate about an axis. Two constraints are required for this type of connection: the axis alignment and the translation constraint.

The axis alignment is the axis about which rotation occurs. An axis or cylindrical surface can be selected. The translation constraint locates the component along the axis as shown in Figure 2–3, and is similar to a coincident or distance constraint. The linkage can rotate about the selected axis. Figure 2–3 also shows the **Pin connection** icon.

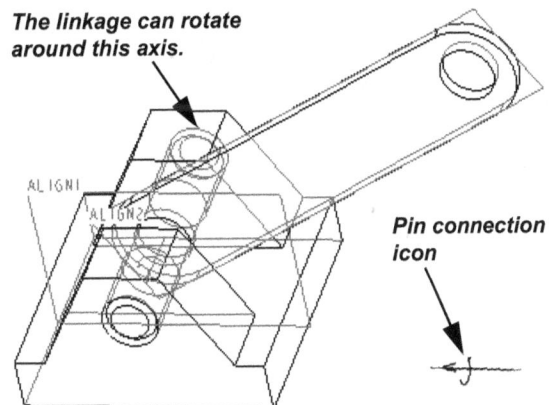

The linkage can rotate around this axis.

Pin connection icon

Figure 2–3

Slider Connection

A component assembled with a slider connection can translate along an axis. Two constraints are required for this type of connection: the axis alignment and the rotation constraint.

The axis alignment dictates the axis along which translation occurs. An axis or cylindrical surface can be selected. The rotation constraint is a coincident or distance constraint and restricts the rotation about the axis. In the example shown in Figure 2–4, the inner cylinder can travel along the axis but rotation cannot occur. Figure 2–4 also shows the **Slider connection** icon.

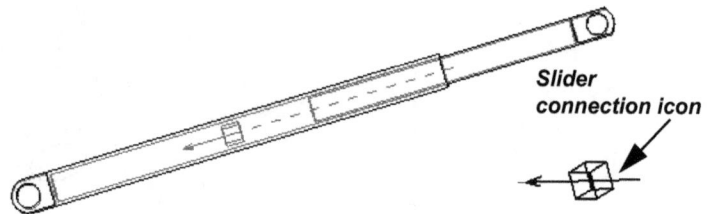

Slider connection icon

Figure 2–4

Cylinder Connection

The cylinder connection is a combination of the pin connection and the slider connection. A component assembled using a cylinder connection can translate and rotate about a specific axis. Only the axis alignment constraint is required for this type of connection.

The axis alignment constraint specifies the axis for rotation and translation. An axis or cylindrical surface can be selected to specify this constraint. An example of a cylinder connection is shown in Figure 2–5. The handle can rotate about the cylinder and translate along the axis. Figure 2–5 also shows the **Cylinder connection** icon.

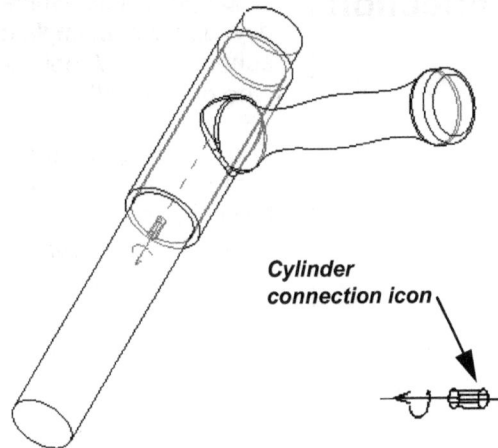

Figure 2–5

Planar Connection

A component assembled with the planar connection can move in a plane. One constraint is required for this type of connection: a planar placement plane.

This connection is similar to a coincident constraint between two planar surfaces. The new component can now translate in both directions in the plane and can rotate about an axis that is normal to the plane. An example of a planar connection is shown in Figure 2–6. As the disk slides across the planar surface, it can rotate about its axis. Figure 2–6 also shows the **Planar connection** icon.

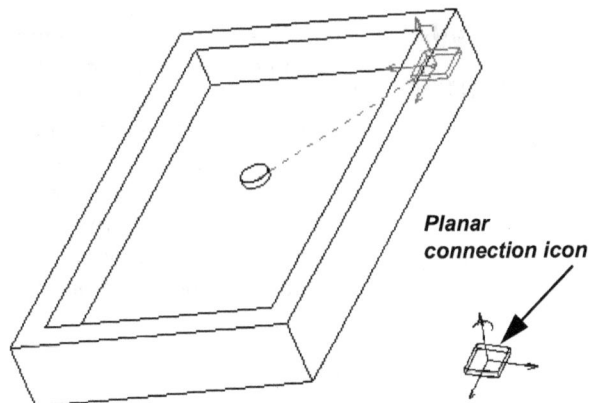

Figure 2–6

Ball Connection

A component assembled with a ball connection can rotate in any direction. An example of this is a joint consisting of a ball in a spherical cup. A point alignment constraint is required for this type of connection.

The point alignment constraint requires the selection of a point or vertex, which becomes the center of rotation. An example of a ball connection is shown in Figure 2–7. The ball can rotate in all directions in the cup. Figure 2–7 also shows the **Ball connection** icon.

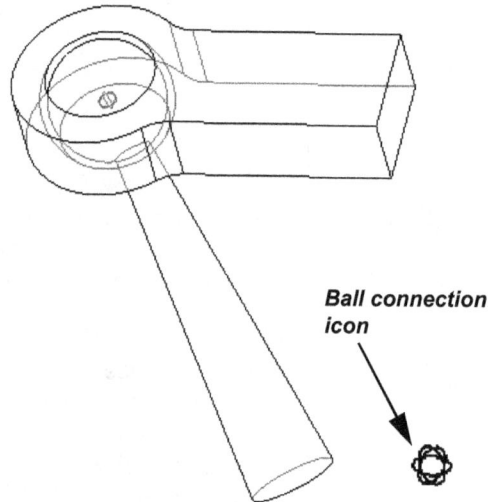

Ball connection icon

Figure 2–7

Weld Connection

Subassemblies can be mechanisms in themselves, which may require a loop connection back to the component. A weld connection enables the subassembly to be adjusted based on the open degree of freedom to satisfy multiple coincident constraints between two coordinate systems in the top-level assembly. Using a Rigid connection to assemble a subassembly that has mechanism connections may cause the subassembly to lose its ability to move. To avoid this, use a Weld connection so that movement can be maintained.

To use a weld connection, coordinate systems are selected on the subassembly and in the top-level assembly. Figure 2–8 shows the **Weld connection** icon.

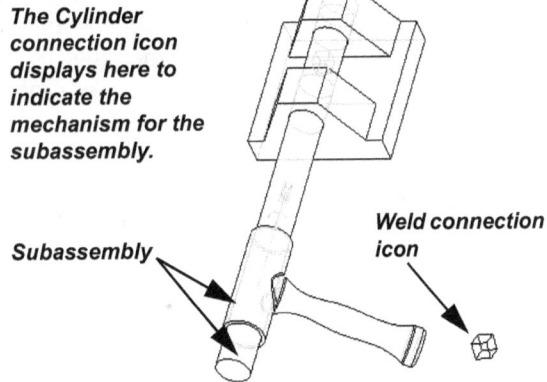

The Cylinder connection icon displays here to indicate the mechanism for the subassembly.

Subassembly

Weld connection icon

Figure 2–8

Bearing Connection

A bearing connection is a combination of a ball joint and slider connection. The connection is specified by selecting two references: a point or vertex on one component and an axis or linear edge on the other component. The new component rotates in all three directions about the selected point and translates along the axis connection. An example of a bearing connection is shown in Figure 2–9. The ball can travel along the axis of the tube and can rotate in any direction about the selected reference point. Figure 2–9 also shows the **Bearing connection** icon.

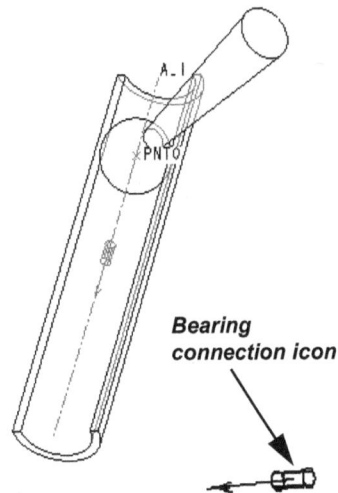

Bearing connection icon

Figure 2–9

General Connection

A general connection enables you to assemble a component using one or two standard assembly constraints. The number of degrees of freedom for this general connection depends on the assembly constraints that you specify. An example of a general connection is shown in Figure 2–10. The assembly constraints to place the linkage involve an aligned axis in the base and in the linkage components as well as an aligned datum. Figure 2–10 also shows the **General connection** icon.

The linkage can rotate around this axis.

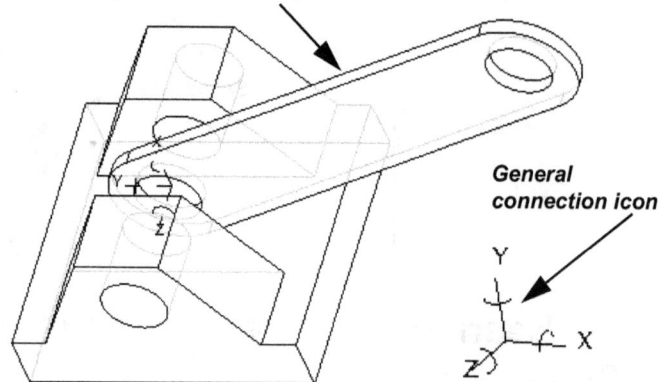

General connection icon

Figure 2–10

6DOF Connection

A 6DOF connection enables you to assemble a component so that it has three rotational and three translational degrees of freedom.

To use a 6DOF connection, coordinate systems are selected on the component and in the assembly. Translational distance limits can be specified along the X, Y, and Z axes. Figure 2–11 shows the **6DOF connection** icon.

A servo motor can be applied to an axis of a 6DOF connection.

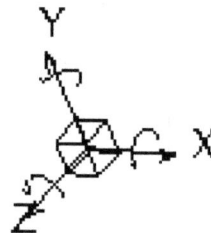

Figure 2–11

Gimbal Connection

A Gimbal connection enables you to assemble a component so that it has three rotational degrees of freedom similar to the Ball connection, but coordinate systems are selected instead of points or vertices.

To use the Gimbal connection, the centered constraint is used and coordinate systems are selected on both the component and the assembly. This aligns the centers (origins) of the two coordinate systems. Figure 2–12 shows the **Gimbal connection** icon.

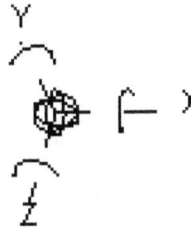

Figure 2–12

Slot Connection

A slot connection enables you to assemble a component using a point or vertex on the component or the assembly for the first reference. That point is constrained coincident to a linear or non-linear set of curves or edges. You can constrain the point to stay between specified endpoints. Those curve or edge endpoints are set when the connection is configured. A Slot connection aligns a single point to single or multiple edges or curves. Figure 2–13 shows the **Slot connection** icon.

Figure 2–13

2.2 Assembling a Component with Connections

How To: Assemble a Component with Connections

1. Click 🖳 (Assemble). The Open dialog box opens.
2. Select the component and click **Open**. The *Component Placement* dashboard opens.
3. Activate the Placement panel, as shown in Figure 2–14.

It is not required that you open the Placement panel, but it is helpful when first using Mechanisms, so you can see the required references as you create connections.

By default, Creo Parametric automatically assumes you want to create constraints and not connections.

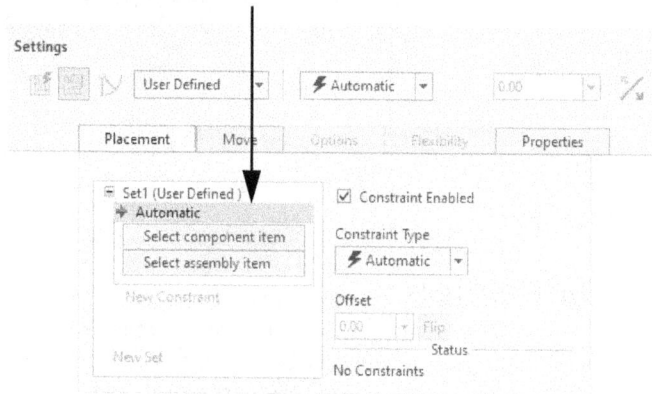

Figure 2–14

4. Select the required connection type in the Connection Type drop-down list, as shown in Figure 2–15.

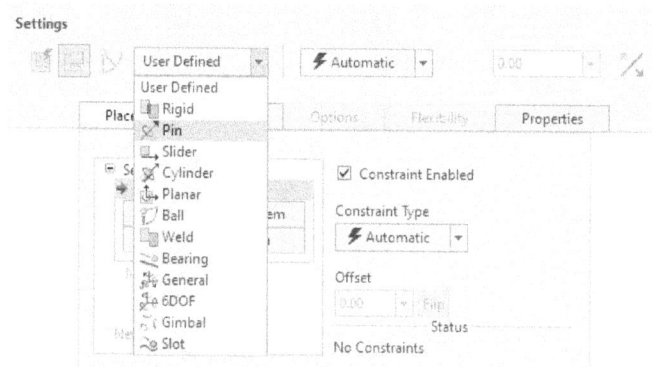

Figure 2–15

5. Specify the placement references.

6. If additional connections are required, click **New Set** and repeat Steps 4 and 5, as shown in Figure 2–16.

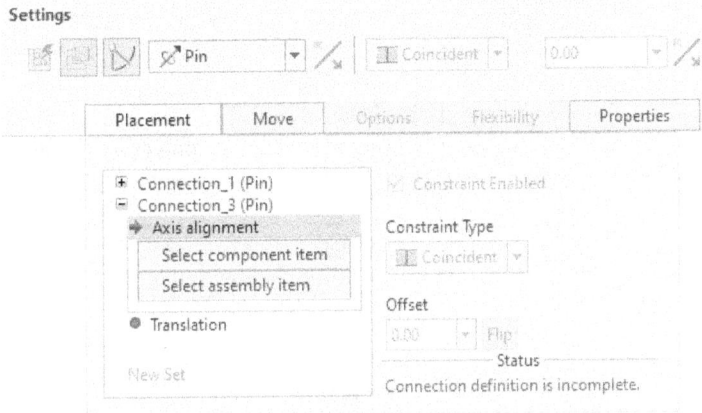

Figure 2–16

7. Click ✓ (OK) to place the component.

Constraint Conversion

You can convert mechanism connections to assembly constraints and vice-versa by clicking ⌇ (Convert Constraints) in the *Component Placement* dashboard. You can find this tool's icon next to the Connection Type drop-down list in the *Component Placement* dashboard.

2.3 Degrees of Freedom

A specific rotation and translation degree of freedom has been assigned to each connection type. The connection types and their rotation and translation degrees of freedom are described as follows:

Connection Type	Connection Icon	Degrees of Freedom		Description
		Rotation	Translation	
Rigid		0	0	Component does not have any motion relative to the other component.
Pin		1	0	Component rotates about an axis.
Slider		0	1	Component translates along an axis.
Cylinder		1	1	Component translates along and rotates about an axis.
Planar		1	2	Component can move in a plane and rotate about an axis normal to the plane.
Ball		3	0	Component rotates about a point.
Weld		0	0	Component has no motion relative to the other component.
Bearing		3	1	Component rotates about a point and translates along an axis.
General		up to 3	up to 2	Component motion depends on specified constraints.

6DOF (6 degrees of freedom)		3	3	Component rotates and translates in any direction.
Gimbal		3	0	Component rotates about the center of the coordinate systems.
Slot		3	1	Component follows a point that moves along a non-linear trajectory

Practice 2a

Creating Connections

Practice Objective

- Create various types of connections such as: rigid, pin, slider, cylinder, planar, ball, bearing, and weld.

In this practice, you will create seven simple assemblies that will enable you to practice assembling models using different connection types. You will start each assembly by assigning a Rigid connection, assign specific connections to each assembly, and select any required references. The notes in the margin provide review information on the potential use for each connection.

Pin Connection

Task 1 - Create a new assembly and assemble the first component using a Rigid connection.

1. Set the working directory to the *Creating_Connections* folder.

2. Create a new assembly using the default template and set the *Name* to **pin**.

3. Set the model display as follows:

    - ⌖ *(Datum Display Filters)*: All Off

    - ⤚ *(Spin Center)*: Off

    - ⬚ *(Display Style)*: ⬚ (Shading With Edges)

4. In the *Model* tab, click ⬚ (Assemble).

5. Double-click on **pin_base.prt** to assemble this component.

6. Note that the default connection type is **User Defined**. Select **Rigid** in the Connection Type drop-down list, as shown in Figure 2–17.

The rigid connection is used to assemble a component using standard assembly constraints. The rigid connection defines ground for the mechanism and does not move with respect to other components.

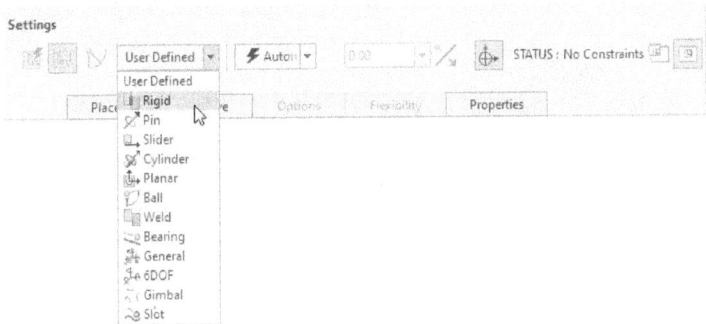

Figure 2–17

7. The constraint type drop-down list currently indicates Automatic. Select **Coincident** in the constraint type drop-down list and select the **PRT_CSYS_DEF** and **ASM_DEF_CSYS** coordinate systems in the Model Tree.

8. Click ✔ (OK) to complete the component placement.

Task 2 - Assemble the second component using a pin connection.

---

1. In the *Model* tab, click 🖳 (Assemble).

2. Double-click on **link-a.prt**.

3. Activate the Placement panel in the *Component Placement* tab.

4. Select the **Set1 (User Defined)** row, as shown in Figure 2–18.

Naming connections is not a requirement, but can make the mechanism easier to understand.

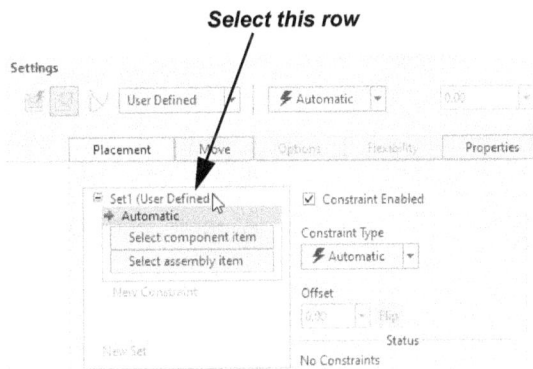

Figure 2–18

5. Enter **link_to_base** in the *Set Name* field as the new name and press <Enter>. The new connection name displays.

Use the pin connection to assemble a component that can rotate about an axis. Two constraints are required for this type of connection: the axis alignment and the translation constraint.

6. Note that the default connection type is **User Defined**. Select **Pin** in the Set Type drop-down list, in the Placement panel.

7. In the In-graphics toolbar, enable ⨍₀ (Axis Display).

8. The pin connection requires two constraints as shown in the Placement panel in the dashboard. Select the axis in the left hole (as viewed in the preview position) in the **link-a** part and axis on the hole in the **pin_base** part to specify the axis of rotation.

9. The link now needs to be positioned along the axis. In the mode tree, select the datum plane **ALIGN2** in the **link-a** part and the datum plane **ALIGN1** in the **pin_base** part.

10. Verify that the placement status is complete in the *Placement Status* area in the tab. Click ✔ (OK). The model displays similar to that shown in Figure 2–19.

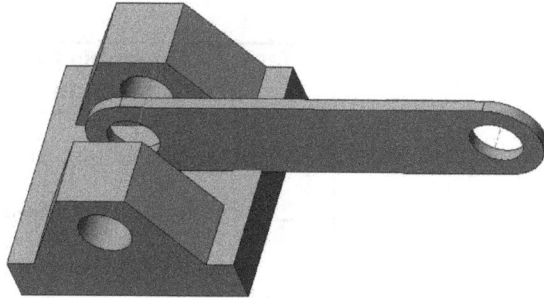

Figure 2–19

11. Save the assembly and erase it from memory.

Slider Connection

Task 3 - Create a new assembly and assemble the first component using a Rigid connection.

1. Create a new assembly using the default template and set the *Name* to **slider**.

2. Assemble **shock-1.prt**.

3. Select **Rigid** in the Connection Type drop-down list.

4. Select the **PRT_CSYS_DEF** and **ASM_DEF_CSYS** coordinate systems. Note that constraint is automatically set to **Coincident**.

5. Click ✔ (OK) to complete the component placement.

Task 4 - Assemble the shock-2.prt using the slider connection.

1. Assemble **shock-2.prt**.

2. Select **Slider** in the Connection Type drop-down list.

3. Activate the Placement panel in the *Component Placement* tab.

4. Select the axis running the length of **shock-2.prt**. Select the axis running the length of **shock-1.prt**. These are the axes along which the part can translate.

5. Select datum plane **RIGHT** on both components as the rotation references.

6. If the assembly does not correspond with Figure 2–20, select the Axis alignment rule in the *Constraint Type* area and click **Flip** to flip the axis alignment.

A component assembled with a slider connection can translate along an axis. Two constraints are required for this type of connection: the axis alignment and the rotation constraint.

Note that you do not have to expand the Placement panel, but we will do so in this practice so you can see the required connections.

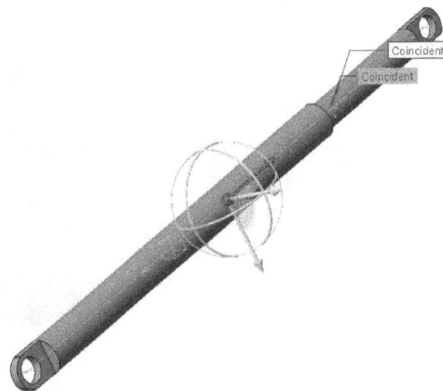

Figure 2–20

7. Click ✓ (OK) to complete the component placement.

8. Save the assembly and erase it from memory.

Cylinder Connection

Task 5 - Create a new assembly and assemble the first component using a Rigid connection.

1. Create a new assembly using the default template and set the *Name* to **cylinder**.

2. Assemble **shaft.prt** using a Rigid connection. Use the Coincident constraint and select the **PRT_CSYS_DEF** and **ASM_DEF_CSYS** coordinate systems.

Task 6 - Assemble the handle.prt using the cylinder connection.

1. Assemble **handle.prt**.

The cylinder connection is a combination of the pin connection and the slider connection. A component assembled using a cylinder connection can translate and rotate about a specific axis. Only the axis alignment constraint is required for this type of connection.

2. Assign **Cylinder** in the Connection Type drop-down list. Select the axis in **shaft.prt** and the axis in the cylindrical section of **handle.prt**.

3. Click ✓ (OK) to complete the component placement. The model displays as shown in Figure 2–21.

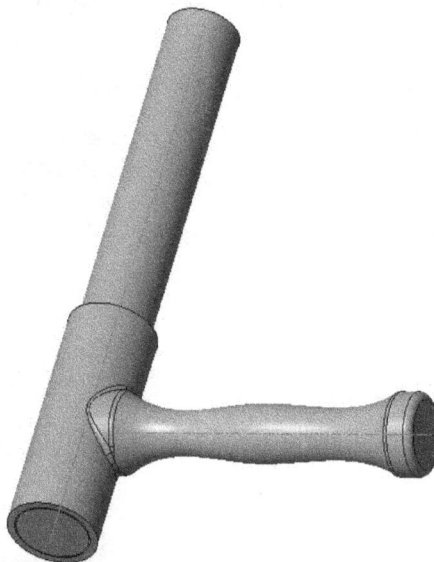

Figure 2–21

4. Save the assembly and erase it from memory.

Planar Connection

Task 7 - Create a new assembly and assemble the first component using a Rigid connection.

1. Create a new assembly using the default template and set the *Name* to **planar**.

2. Assemble **rink.prt** using a Rigid connection. Use the Coincident constraint and select the **PRT_CSYS_DEF** and **ASM_DEF_CSYS** coordinate systems.

Task 8 - Assemble the puck.prt using the planar connection.

1. Assemble **puck.prt**.

A component assembled with the planar connection can move in a plane. One constraint is required for this type of connection: a planar placement plane.

2. Select **Planar** in the Connection Type drop-down list. Select the flat planar surface of the puck and select the surface labeled **ICE**.

3. Reorient the assembly using the saved **FRONT** view. Click **Flip** for the correct surface alignment (if required) as shown on the left of Figure 2–22.

4. Reorient the assembly using the saved Default Orientation. Click ✔ (OK) to complete the component placement. The model displays as shown on the right of Figure 2–22.

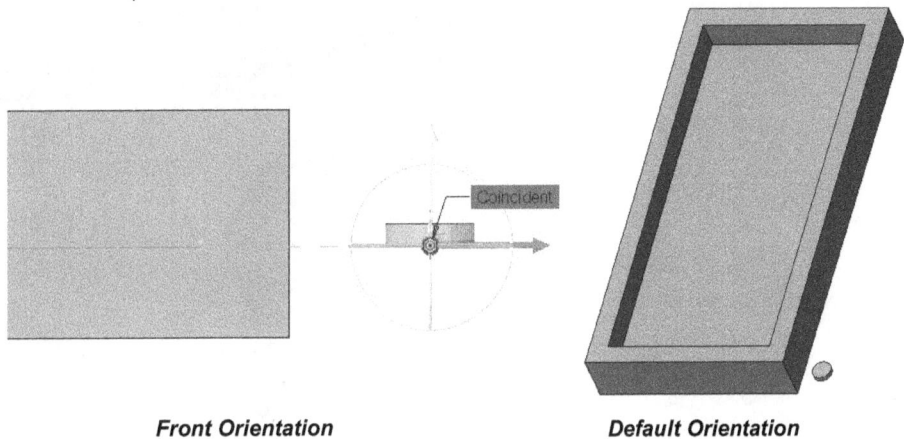

Front Orientation   *Default Orientation*

Figure 2–22

5. Save the assembly and erase it from memory.

Ball Connection

Task 9 - Create a new assembly and assemble the first component using a Rigid connection.

1. Create a new assembly using the default template and set the *Name* to **ball**.

2. Assemble **cup.prt** using a Rigid connection. Use the Coincident constraint and select the **PRT_CSYS_DEF** and **ASM_DEF_CSYS** coordinate systems.

A component assembled with a ball connection can rotate in any direction. A point alignment constraint is required for this type of connection.

Task 10 - Assemble the ball1.prt using the ball connection.

1. In the In-graphics toolbar, enable ⅹⅹ⊙ (Point Display).

2. Assemble **ball1.prt**.

3. Select **Ball** in the Connection Type drop-down list.

4. In the Model Tree, select **PNT0** in **ball1.prt** and **PNT0** in **cup.prt**.

5. Click ✓ (OK) to complete the component placement. The model displays as shown in Figure 2–23.

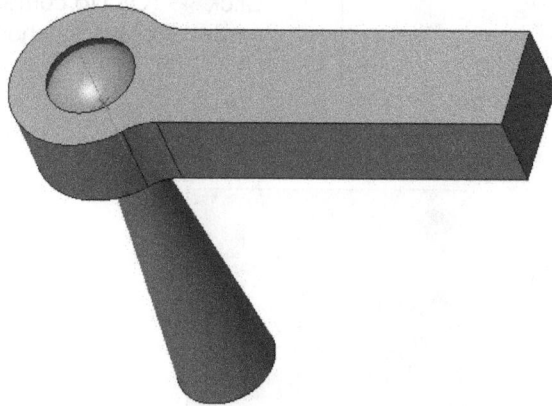

Figure 2–23

6. Save the assembly and erase it from memory.

Bearing Connection

Task 11 - Create a new assembly showing the bearing connection.

1. Create a new assembly using the default template and set the *Name* to **bearing**.

2. Assemble **channel.prt** using a Rigid connection. Use the Coincident constraint and select the **PRT_CSYS_DEF** and **ASM_DEF_CSYS** coordinate systems.

Task 12 - Assemble the ball1.prt.

1. Assemble **ball1.prt**.

2. Select **Bearing** in the Connection Type drop-down list.

3. In the Model Tree, select **PNT0** on **ball1.prt** and **A_1** on the **channel.prt**.

4. Click ✅ (OK). The model displays as shown in Figure 2–24.

A bearing connection is a combination of a ball joint and a slider connection. The point alignment is specified by selecting two references: a point or vertex on one component and an axis or linear edge on the other component.

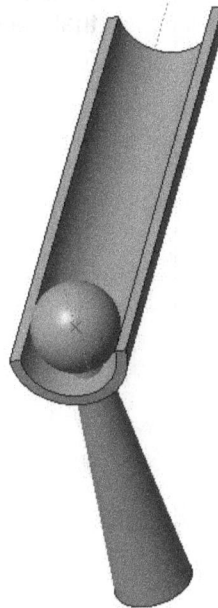

Figure 2–24

5. Save the assembly and erase it from memory.

Weld Connection

Task 13 - Create a new assembly and assemble the first component using a Rigid connection.

1. Create a new assembly using the default template and set the *Name* to **weld**.

2. In the In-graphics toolbar, disable ˣˣₓₒ (Point Display) and ╱ₒ (Axis Display).

3. Assemble **weld_base.prt** using a Rigid connection. Use the Coincident constraint and select the **PRT_CSYS_DEF** and **ASM_DEF_CSYS** coordinate systems.

Task 14 - Assemble the weld_cylinder.asm using the weld connection.

1. Assemble **weld_cylinder.asm**.

2. Select **Weld** in the Connection Type drop-down list.

3. In the Model Tree, select the **SHOCK1-BOLT** coordinate system from the **cylinder_mount.prt** (the **cylinder_mount** part is in the **weld_cylinder** subassembly) and the **BASE1-BOLT** coordinate system from **weld_base.prt**. Note that the cylinder is currently too short to reach the top mounting holes as shown inFigure 2–25.

A weld connection enables the subassembly to be adjusted based on the open degree of freedom to fit the top-level assembly.

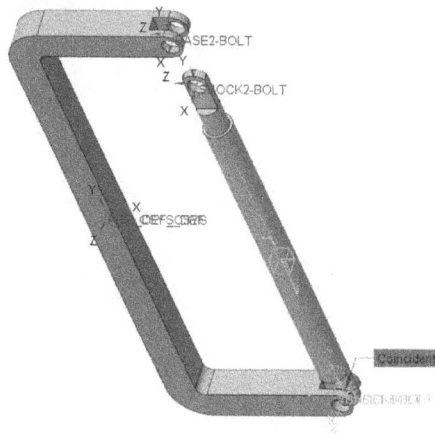

Figure 2–25

4. In the *Placement* tab, select **New Set** as shown in Figure 2–26.

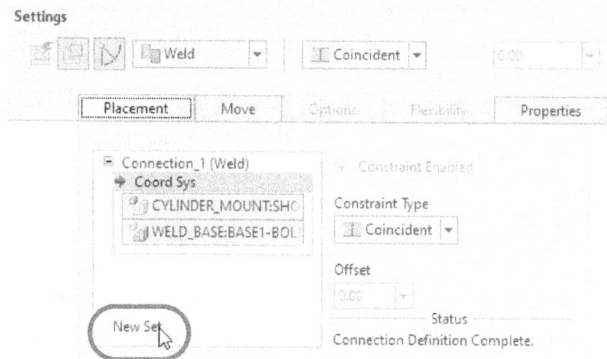

Figure 2–26

5. Select the **SHOCK2-BOLT** coordinate system from **cylinder_housing.prt** (the **cylinder_housing** part is in the **weld_cylinder** subassembly) and the **BASE2-BOLT** coordinate system from **weld_base.prt**.

6. Click ✔ (OK). The model displays as shown in Figure 2–27.

Figure 2–27

7. In the Model Tree, expand **WELD_BASE.PRT** and click on **Extrude 1**.

8. Click $\overset{\longleftrightarrow}{\text{d1}}$ (Edit Dimensions) in the mini toolbar, as shown in Figure 2–28.

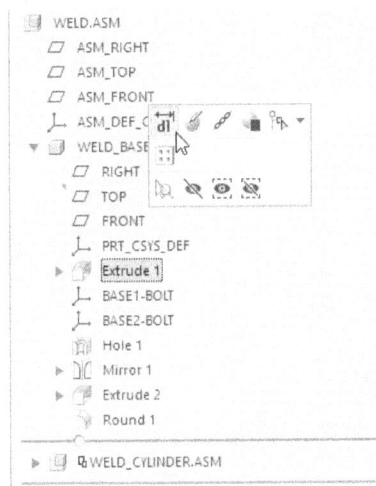

Figure 2–28

9. Change the height dimension from 22.00 to 27.00 and Regenerate the assembly. Note that the subassembly expands along its axis to keep both Weld connections connected as shown in Figure 2–29.

Figure 2–29

10. Save the assembly and erase it from memory.

Practice 2b | Four-Bar Linkage

Practice Objective

- Model a three-bar linkage using pin and cylinder connections.

In this practice, you will add additional links to an existing assembly to create a four-bar linkage. The Link-B component that is assembled requires two connections. One with the original Link-A and one with Link-C. The final assembly displays as shown in Figure 2–30.

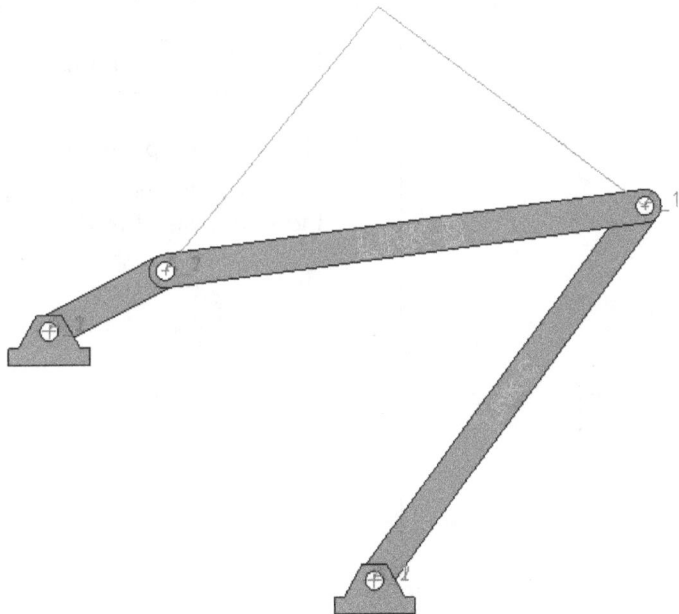

Figure 2–30

Task 1 - Open an assembly and assemble the next component.

1. Set the working directory to the *Four_Bar* folder.

2. Open **pin_1.asm**.

3. Set the model display as follows:

   - ⤢ *(Datum Display Filters)*: All Off
   - ⤡ *(Spin Center)*: Off
   - ⬚ *(Display Style)*: ⬚ (Shading With Edges)

4. Click ⬚ (Assemble) and double-click on **pin_base.prt**.

5. Select **Rigid** from the Connection Type drop-down list.

6. Select **Coincident** in the Constraint Type drop-down list. In the Model Tree, select the datum plane **ALIGN1** in both **pin_base** components.

7. In the *Placement* panel. click **New Constraint** and select **Distance** as the constraint type. Select datum plane **TOP** in both **pin_base** components. Set the *Offset* value to **-15**. Press <Enter>.

8. Click **New Constraint** in *Placement* panel and select **Distance** as the constraint type and select datum planes **RIGHT** in both **pin_base** components. Set the *Offset* value to **20** and press <Enter>.

9. Once the component has been fully constrained, click

   ✔ (OK). The model displays as shown in Figure 2–31, using the saved view **FRONT**.

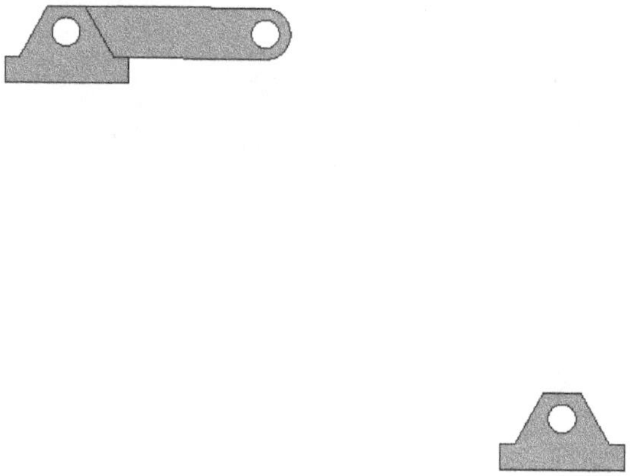

Figure 2–31

Task 2 - Assemble the output link.

1. Select the *View* tab and enable ⬚ (Axis Display) and ⬚ (Axis Tag Display).

2. Select the *Model* tab and assemble **link-c.prt**.

3. Assign a **Pin** connection.

4. For the axis alignment, select **axis A_2** in **LINK-C** and **axis A_1** from the newly assembled **pin_base** component.

5. In the Model Tree, select datum plane **FRONT** in **LINK-C** and datum plane **ALIGN1** in **pin_base** as the translation requirement.

6. If the text on **LINK-C** is facing the other side, select the axis alignment constraint, and click **Flip**. Reorient the model to the **FRONT** view, which displays as shown in Figure 2–32.

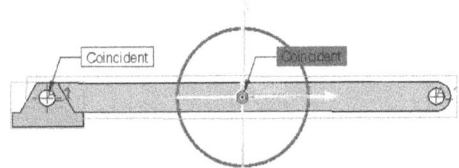

Figure 2–32

*You can also activate the Move panel in the Component Placement tab and select **Rotate** in the Motion Type drop-down list.*

7. Use the 3D dragger to rotate the **LINK-C** part as shown in Figure 2–33. Click ✓ (OK).

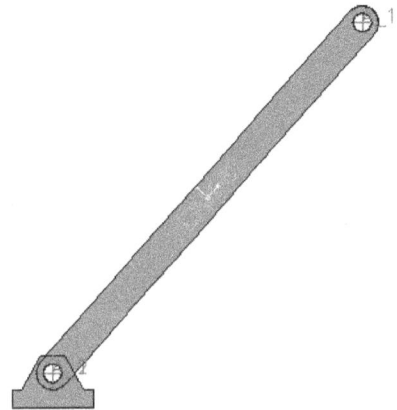

Figure 2–33

As an alternative to using the *Component Placement* tab or the 3D dragger, you can press <Ctrl>+<Alt> and drag the component using the left mouse button.

Task 3 - Assemble the connecting link.

1. Assemble **link-b.prt**.

2. Select **Pin** in the Connection Type drop-down list.

3. In the *Placement* panel, select **Connection_7 (Pin)** and enter **a-b** in the *Set Name* field and press <Enter>. The connection name updates.

4. Select **Axis alignment** in the *Placement* panel and select **axis A_2** in **LINK-B** and **axis A_1** in **LINK-A**.

5. Select **Coincident** and select the surfaces on both links for the translation references, as shown in Figure 2–34.

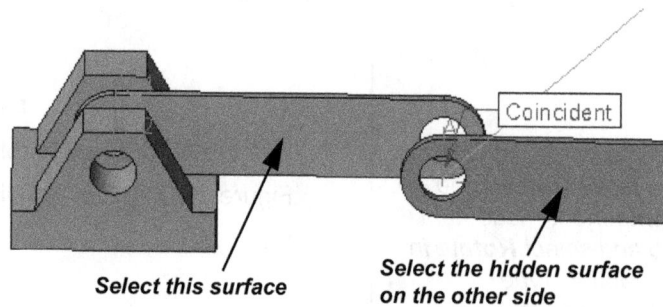

Select this surface

Select the hidden surface on the other side

Coincident

Figure 2–34

6. The model displays as shown in Figure 2–35. Note that **LINK-B** cannot reach the current position of **LINK-C**. Another connection must be added to connect **LINK-B** and **LINK-C**.

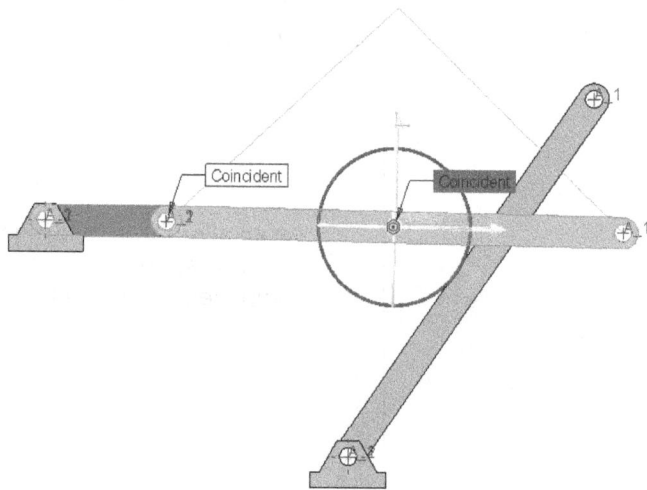

Coincident

Coincident

Figure 2–35

7. In the Placement panel, click **New Set**.

8. Select **Cylinder** in the Connection Type drop-down list.

9. Select **Connection_8(Cylinder)** and enter **b-c** in the *Set Name* field and press <Enter>. The connection name updates.

10. Select Axis alignment and select **axis A_1** in **LINK-B** and **axis A_1** in **LINK-C** for the axis alignment.

11. Click ✔ (OK). The links are connected. Press <Ctrl>+<Alt> and drag LINK-B until it displays similar to that shown in Figure 2–36. Creo Parametric moves components to satisfy the connections.

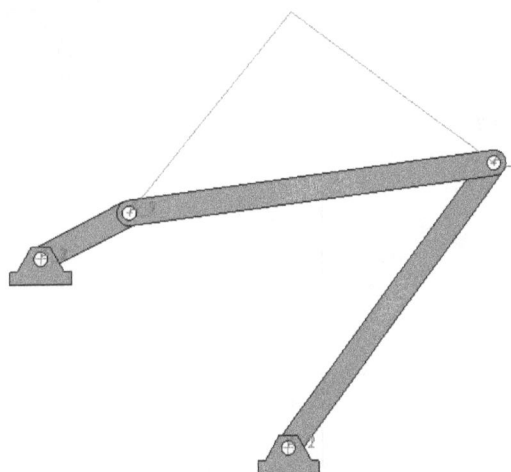

Figure 2–36

Design Considerations

For the last connection in step 8 why was the pin type connection not used? For the first pin connection, the translation along the axis was defined. If a second pin connection were used, translation along the axis would have to be defined again and might cause conflicts with the initial connection. To prevent having this conflict in a mechanism, the second connection type is usually a cylinder connection.

12. Press and hold <Ctrl>+<Alt> and drag the components using the left mouse button to show their range of motion.

13. Save the assembly and erase it from memory.

You can also click

🖑 *(Drag Components) and select the component that you want to move. Click the left mouse button to place the component.*

Practice 2c | Track Slider

Practice Objective

- Create an assembly of a sliding carriage on a track.

In this practice, you will build an assembly of a sliding carriage on a linear track. The carriage will be connected to a rotating crank arm through 3 linking arms. The geometry will create a sliding motion in the carriage that stops for a few moments as the input crank continues to rotate a constant angular velocity. the final assembly displays as shown in Figure 2–37.

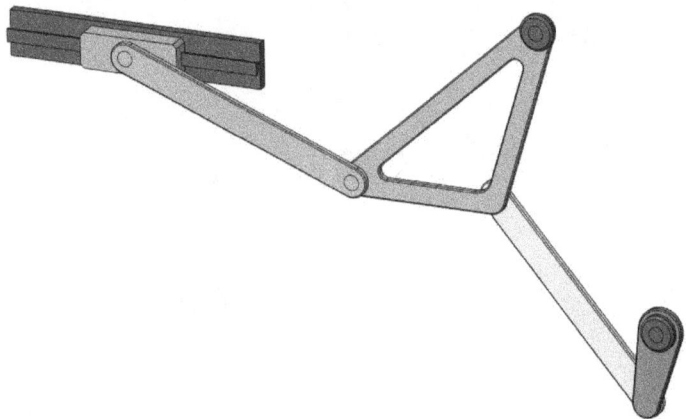

Figure 2–37

Task 1 - Open an existing assembly and assemble components.

1. Set the working directory to the *Track_Slider* folder.

2. Open **pause_slider.asm**.

3. Set the model display as follows:

   - *(Datum Display Filters):* (Axis Display)

   - *Datum Tag Display:* (Plane Tag Display), (Axis Tag Display), (Csys Tag Display)

   - *(Spin Center):* Off

   - *(Display Style):* (No Hidden)

4. In the *Model* tab, click (Assemble).

5. Double click on **sliding_block.prt**.

6. Select **Slider** as the connection type as shown in Figure 2–38.

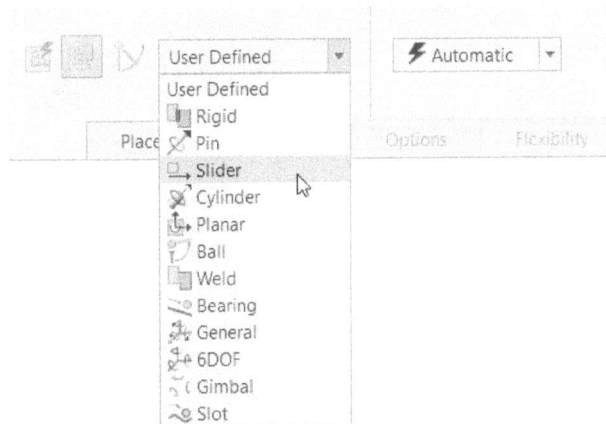

Figure 2–38

7. Select axis **A_1** in track part and axis **A_2** in **sliding_block** part as the axis alignment, as shown in Figure 2–39.

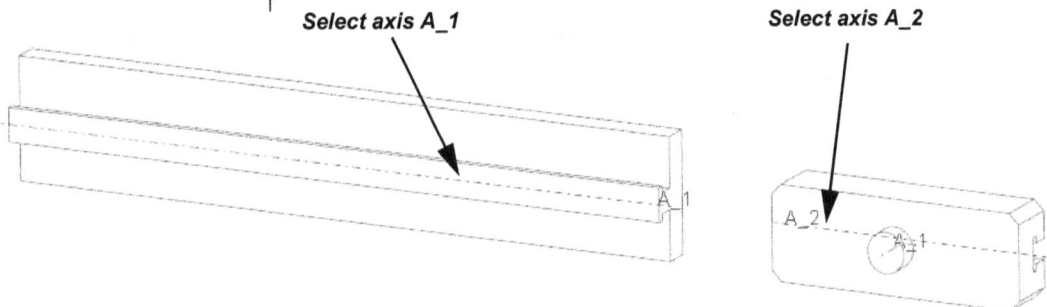

Select axis A_1

Select axis A_2

Figure 2–39

8. In the Model Tree, select datum plane **RIGHT** from **TRACK.PRT** and datum plane **TOP** from **SLIDING_BLOCK.PRT** as the Rotation references.

9. Drag the **sliding_block** to the center of the track. Click ✓ (OK).

10. In the In-Graphics toolbar, click ⬜ (Shading With Edges). The assembly updates as shown in Figure 2–40.

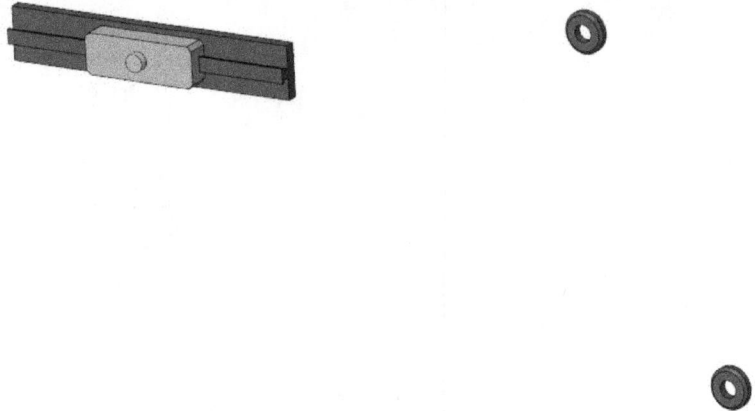

Figure 2–40

11. In the *Model* tab, click ⬛ (Assemble).

12. Double click on **link_b.prt**.

13. Select **Pin** as the connection type as shown in Figure 2–41.

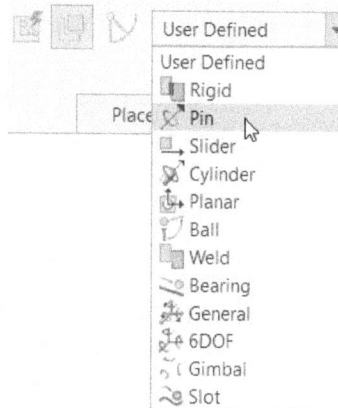

Figure 2–41

14. Select axis **MOUNT-2** in **link_b.prt** and axis **MOUNT-2** in **mount-2.prt**, as shown in Figure 2–42.

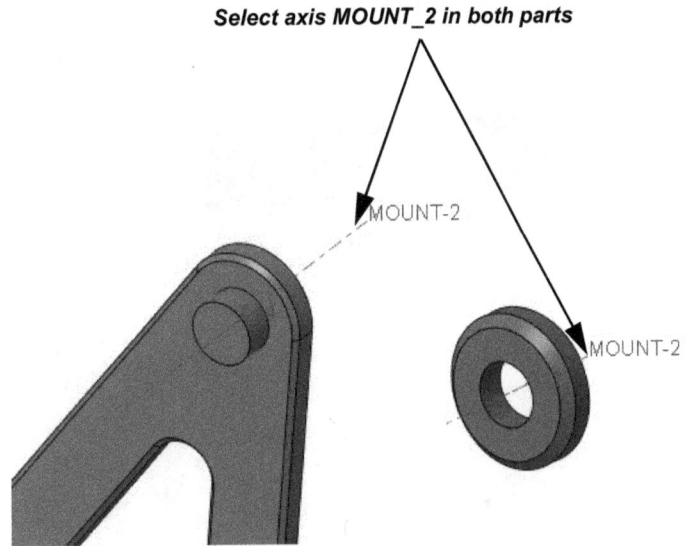

Select axis MOUNT_2 in both parts

MOUNT-2

MOUNT-2

Figure 2–42

15. Select the two planar surfaces shown in Figure 2–43, as the Translation references.

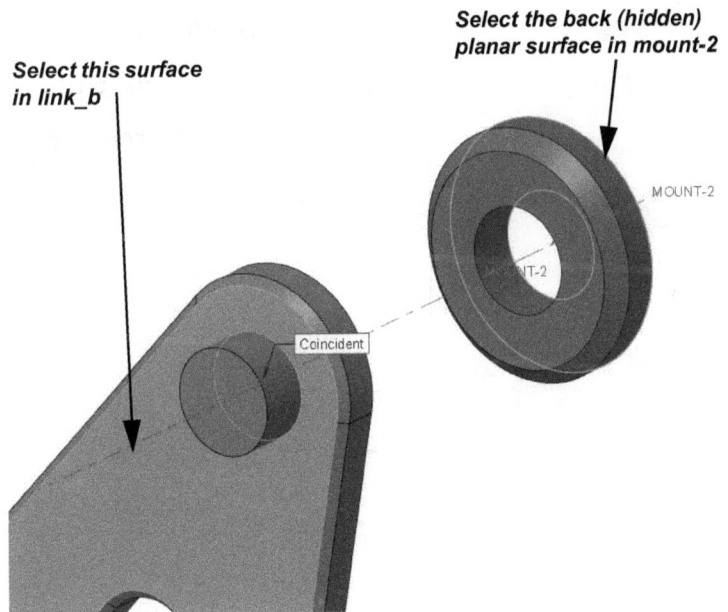

Select the back (hidden) planar surface in mount-2

Select this surface in link_b

MOUNT-2

NT-2

Coincident

Figure 2–43

16. Drag **link_b** to the position shown in Figure 2–44. Click ✓ (OK).

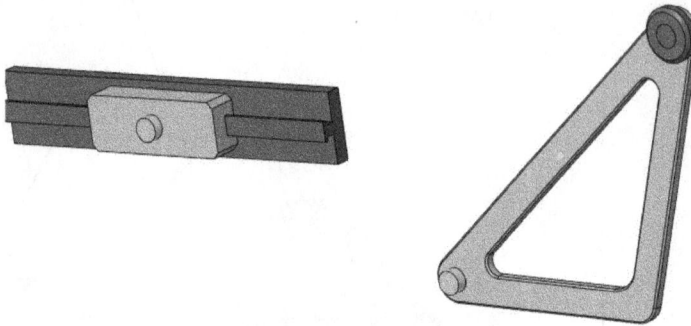

Figure 2–44

17. Save the assembly.

18. In the *Model* tab, click 🖳 (Assemble).

19. Double click on **link_d.prt**.

20. Select **Pin** as the connection type, as shown in Figure 2–45.

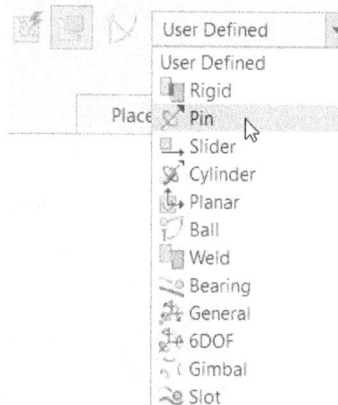

Figure 2–45

21. Select the two cylindrical surfaces shown in Figure 2–46, as the axis alignment.

Select these cylindrical surfaces

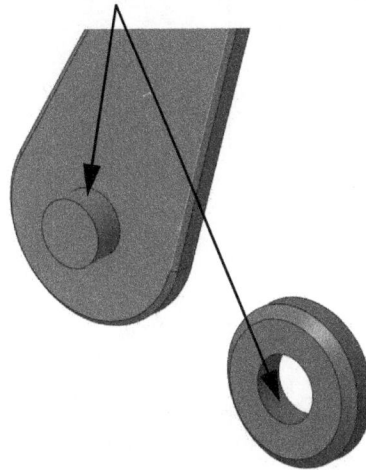

Figure 2–46

22. Select the two planar surfaces shown in Figure 2–47, as the Translation references.

Select this surface in link_d

Select the back (hidden) planar surface in mount-1

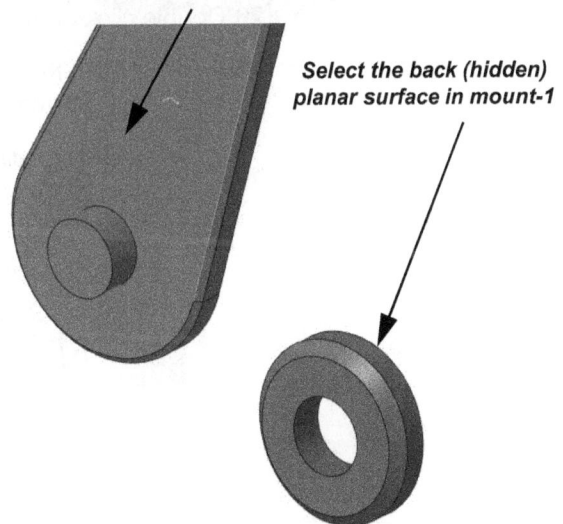

Figure 2–47

23. Drag **link_d** to the position shown in Figure 2–48. Click ✓ (OK).

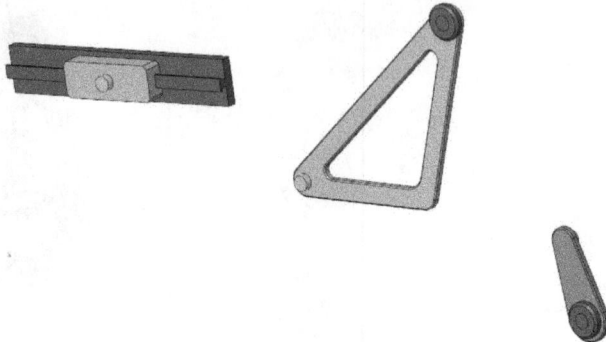

Figure 2–48

24. Save the assembly.

Observe the two green cylinders on the **sliding_block** and **link_b** parts. The surfaces of those cylinders will used as the references to assembly **link_a**.

25. In the *Model* tab, click 🗗 (Assemble).

26. Double click on **link_a.prt**.

27. Select **Pin** as the connection type and, select the two cylindrical surfaces shown in Figure 2–49.

Select these 2 cylindrical surfaces

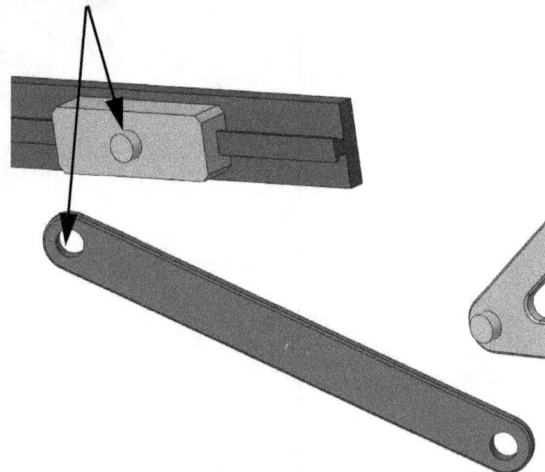

Figure 2–49

28. Select the front planar face of **link_a** and front planar face of the cylinder in **sliding_block**, as shown in Figure 2–50.

Select these 2 planar surfaces

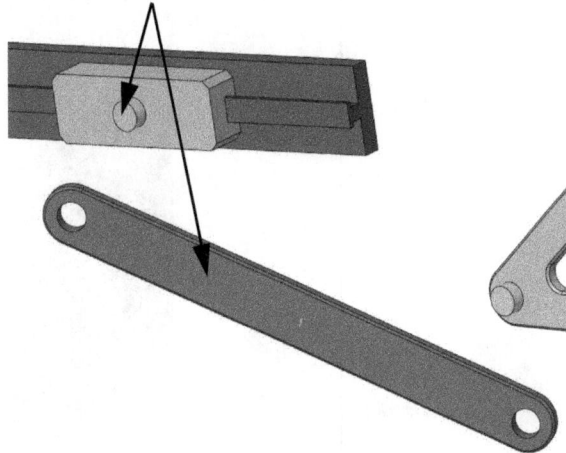

Figure 2–50

29. In the *Placement* tab, select **New Set** to add a second connection. Click on the second connection in the list and change the second connection type to Cylinder, as shown in Figure 2–51.

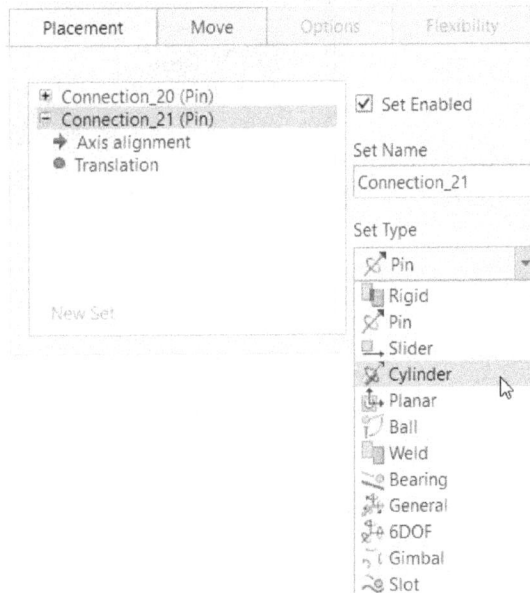

Figure 2–51

30. Select the two cylindrical surfaces shown in Figure 2–52.

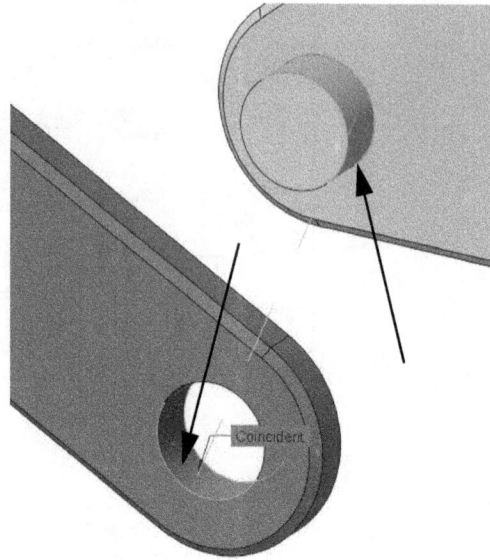

Figure 2–52

31. Click ✓ (OK). The assembly updates as shown in Figure 2–53.

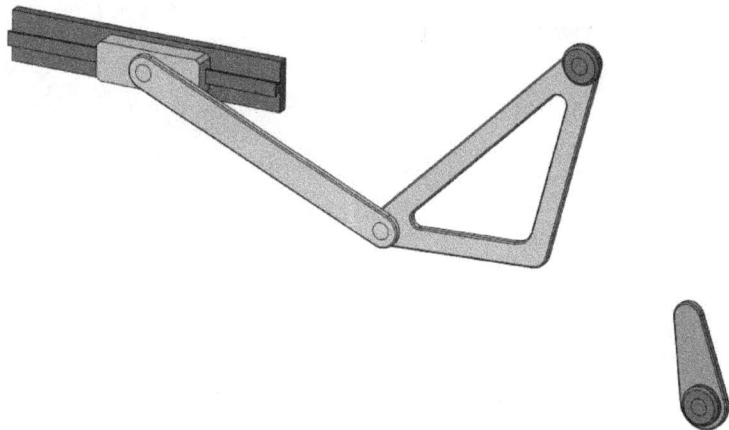

Figure 2–53

32. Spin the assembly to a view similar to shown in Figure 2–54.

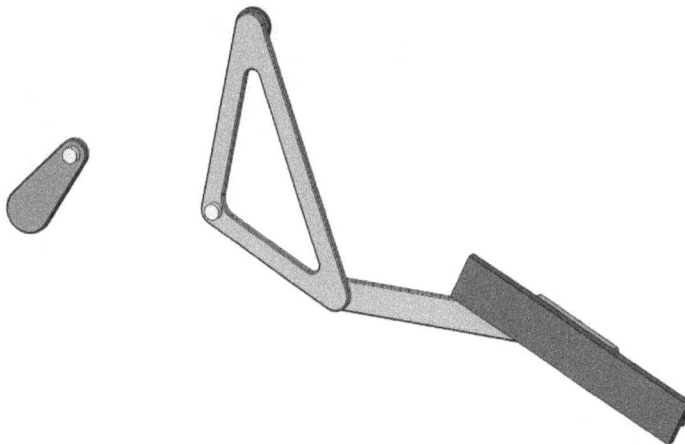

Figure 2–54

Observe the two yellow cylinders on the **link_d** and **link_b** parts. The surfaces of those cylinders will be used as the references to assembly **link_c**.

33. Assemble **link_c**. Select **Pin** as the type of connection and, select the two cylindrical surfaces shown in Figure 2–55.

Select these 2 cylindrical surfaces

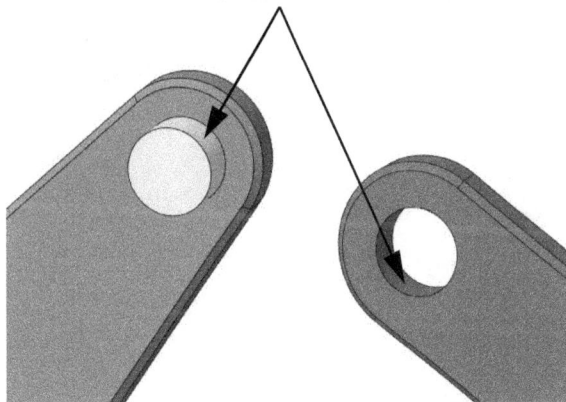

Figure 2–55

34. Select the planar front face of **link_c** and the planar top face of the cylinder on **link_b**, as shown in Figure 2–56.

Select these 2 planar surfaces

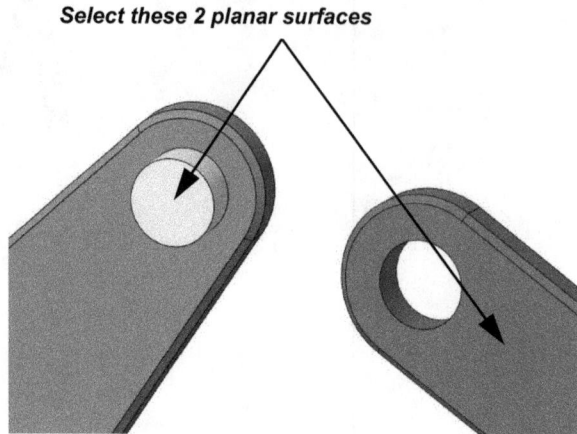

Figure 2–56

35. In the *Placement* tab, select **New Set** to add a second connection. Click on the second connection in the list and change the second connection type to **Cylinder**, as shown in Figure 2–57.

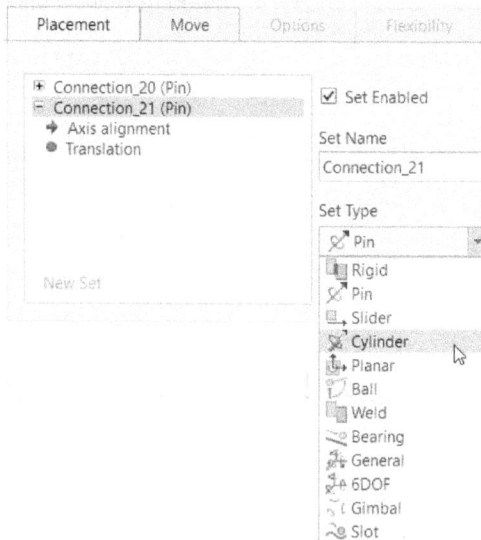

Figure 2–57

36. Select the two cylindrical surfaces shown in Figure 2–58.

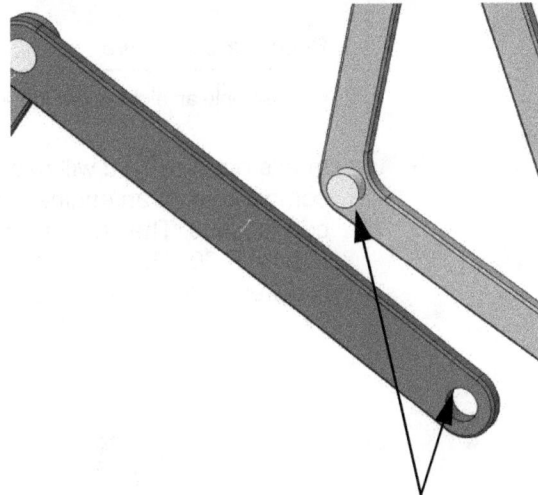

Select these 2 cylindrical surfaces

Figure 2–58

37. Click ✔ (OK). Return to the Standard view. The assembly updates as shown in Figure 2–59.

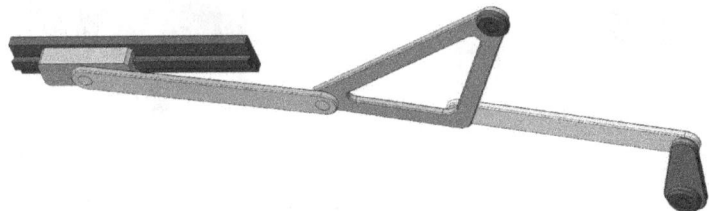

Figure 2–59

38. Click 🖑 (Drag) and select a point on **link_d**. Drag **link_d** around to view the motion of the assembly. Note that the **sliding_block** will pause at its left hand potion as it changes directions while rotating **link_d**. After dragging, click **Close** in the Drag dialog box.

39. Save the assembly and erase from memory.

Practice 2d | Project - Engine

Practice Objective

- Assemble an eight-valve, four-cylinder engine in an in-line configuration.

In this practice, you will begin assembling the internal components of an engine assembly using mechanism connections. The final assembly displays as shown in Figure 2–60. This assembly is used again in subsequent chapters. When complete, this engine becomes an eight-valve, four-cylinder engine with an in-line configuration.

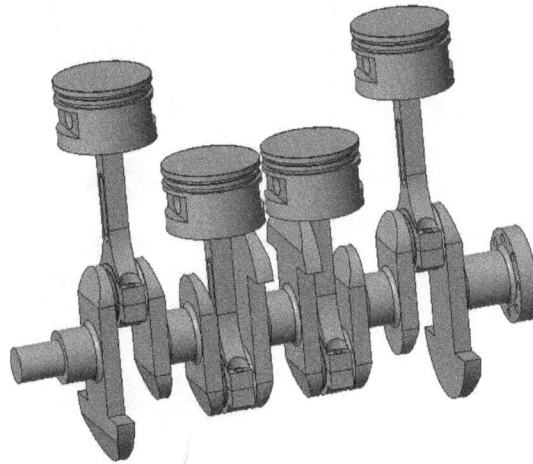

Figure 2–60

Task 1 - Open an existing assembly and investigate its contents.

1. Set the working directory to the *MDX_Engine_I* folder.

2. Open **engine.asm**.

3. Set the model display as follows:

- *(Datum Display Filters)*: All On
- *Datum Tag Display:* (Plane Tag Display), (Axis Tag Display), (Csys Tag Display)
- *(Spin Center)*: Off
- *(Display Style)*: (Shading With Edges)

4. Examine the assembly, which displays as shown in Figure 2–61.

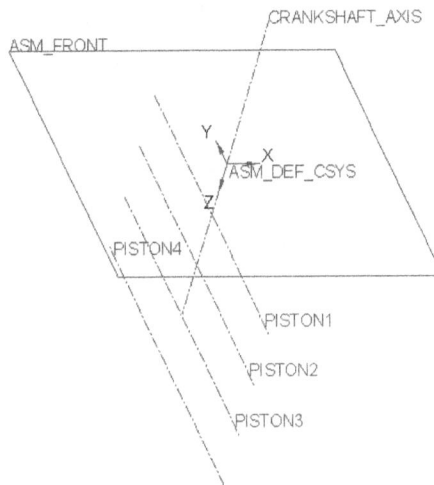

Figure 2–61

Design Considerations

Several datum features have been created for you in the assembly. This forms the skeleton to which you will assemble and place the mechanism components. By using a skeleton of datum features you can ensure that the assembly connection references are made to the datum references instead of to other components, which helps to create the required parent-child relationships in the model.

Task 2 - Assemble crankshaft.prt using connections.

Design Considerations

Unlike the first components assembled in the previous practices, the first component in this practice is not required to be assembled with a rigid constraint.

1. Assemble **crankshaft.prt**.

2. Select **Pin** in the Connection Type drop-down list.

3. In the Placement panel, select **Connection_1 (Pin)** and enter **crank** in the *Set Name* field and press <Enter>. The connection name updates.

4. Select **Axis alignment**.

5. Select **CRANKSHAFT_AXIS** in both the crankshaft and the assembly for the axis alignment.

6. Select the Translation references. In the Model Tree, select datum plane **FRONT** in the crankshaft and **ASM_FRONT** in the assembly. The crankshaft displays as shown in Figure 2–62. Click **Flip**, if required.

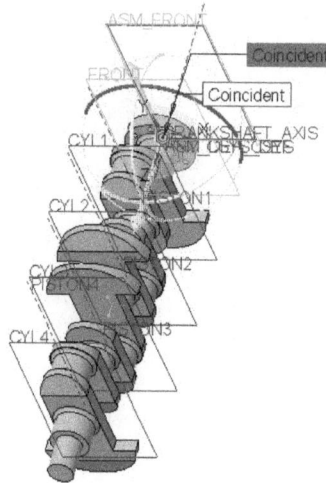

Figure 2–62

7. Click ✔ (OK).

Task 3 - Assemble conn_rod.prt using connections.

Design Considerations

In this task, you will assemble the connecting rod component to the crankshaft using a pin connection. Pin connections enable you to assemble a component so that it can rotate about an axis. Two constraints are required for this type of connection: the axis alignment and the translation constraint. This constraint alone is not going to limit the rotation of the connection rod around the crankshaft. However, once you assemble additional components this rotation ability will be further controlled.

1. Assemble **conn_rod.prt**.

2. Select **Pin** in the Connection Type drop-down list.

3. Use the 3D Dragger to move and rotate the connecting rod approximately to the location shown in Figure 2–63. Select the surfaces shown for the axis alignment.

3D Dragger toggled off for clarity.

Select these surfaces

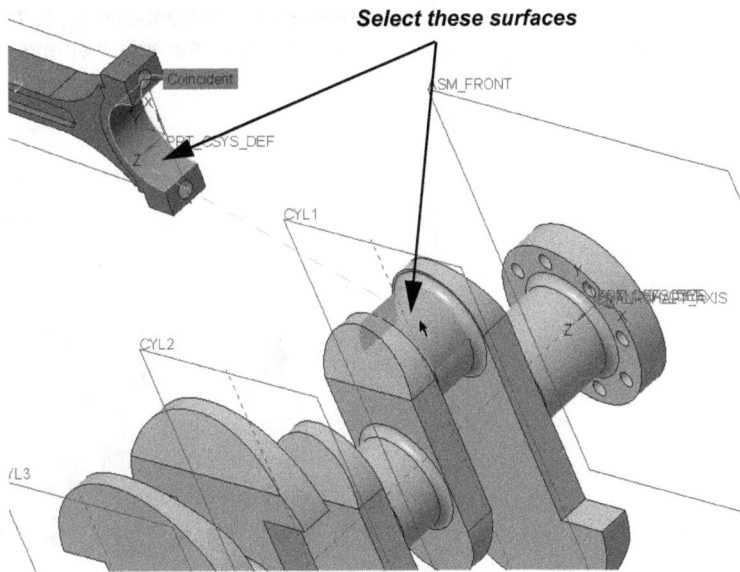

Figure 2–63

4. For the translation reference, select datum plane **CYL** in the **conn_rod** and datum plane **CYL1** in the **crankshaft**.

5. Use the 3D Dragger to rotate the connecting rod to sit vertically, and click ✓ (OK). The model displays as shown in Figure 2–64.

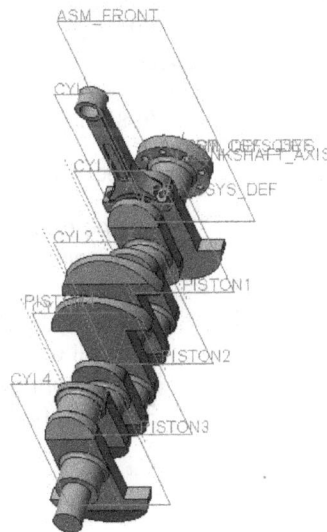

Figure 2–64

6. Repeat the steps in this task for the other cylinders. Select references corresponding to the other cylinders. The completed assembly displays as shown in Figure 2–65.

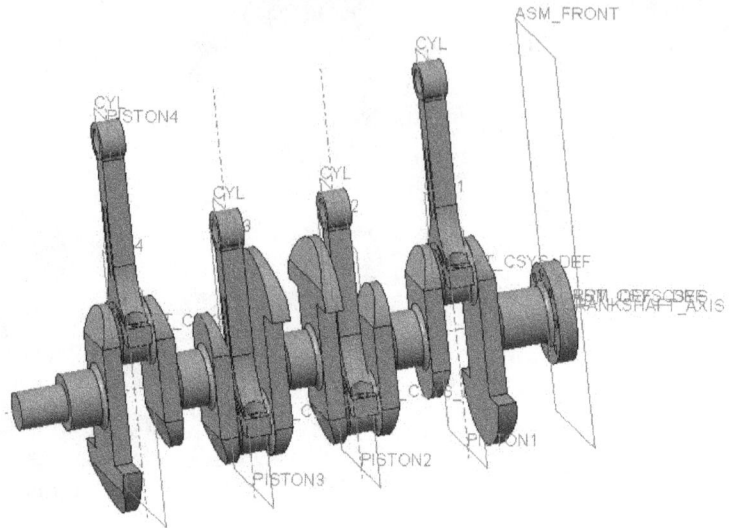

Figure 2–65

Task 4 - Assemble the conn_rod_cap.prt.

In this task, you will assemble the connection rod cap component to the connection rod using a rigid connection so that it is fully constrained to the connecting rod. A rigid connection is used to assemble a component using standard assembly constraints.

The cap does not move relative to the connecting rod because it is fixed to the rod.

1. Assemble **conn_rod_cap.prt**.

2. Select **Rigid** in the Connection Type drop-down list.

3. Fix the cap to the first connecting rod using three **Coincident** constraints. Add a **Coincident** constraint for the two planar surfaces that touch, and a **Coincident** constraint for each pair of bolt holes. There are other combinations of constraints that will work, but it is critical that you only select references on the connecting rod. The assembly displays as shown in Figure 2–66.

*Datum entities toggled
off for clarity.*

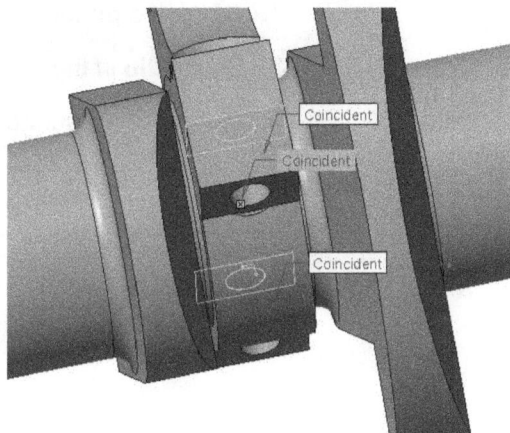

Figure 2–66

4. Click ✔ (OK).

5. Repeat this procedure for the other connecting rods as
   shown in Figure 2–67.

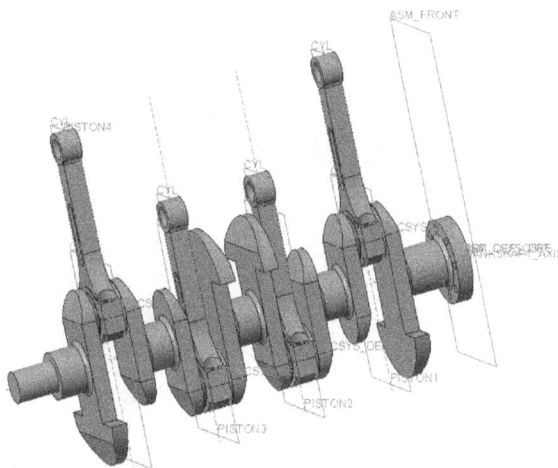

Figure 2–67

Task 5 - Assemble the piston_head.prt.

**Design
Considerations**

In this task, you will assemble the piston head component to the
connection rod using a pin and cylinder connection. Once these
two connections have been assigned, the connecting rod will
only be able to translate up and down relative to the piston head.
The rotation of the connecting rod will be limited by the up and
down translation of the piston head.

1. Assemble **piston_head.prt**.

2. Select **Pin** in the Connection Type drop-down list.

3. Select the pin surfaces shown in Figure 2–68.

Datum entities toggled off for clarity.

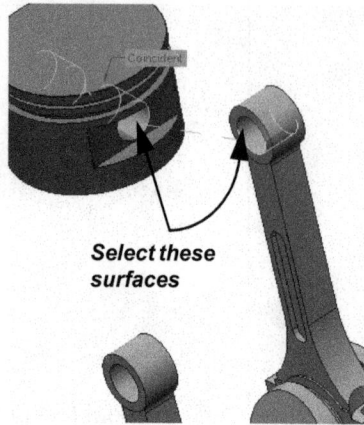

Figure 2–68

4. Select datum plane **CYL** from the piston and datum plane **CYL** from the rod as the translation references.

5. Click **Flip**, if required, to ensure that the piston is not interfering with the rod. The assembly displays as shown in Figure 2–69.

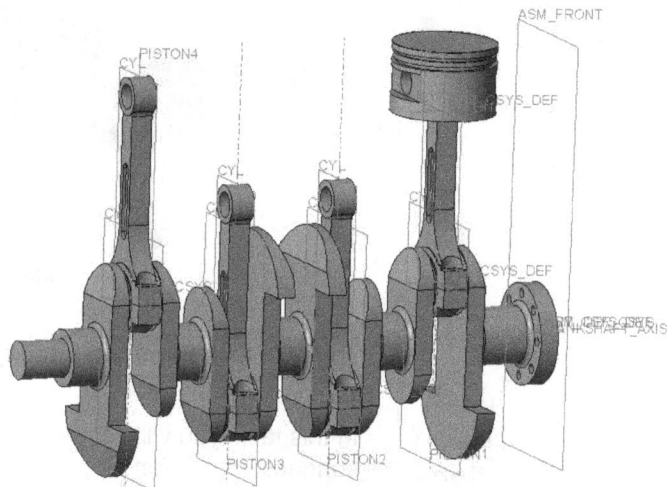

Figure 2–69

6. Click **New Set** to add a new connection.

7. Select **Cylinder** in the Connection Type drop-down list.

8. Select axis **PISTON** on the **piston_head** part and axis **PISTON1** in the assembly.

9. Click ✓ (OK).

10. Toggle off the display of datum entities.

11. Repeat Steps 1 to 9 for the remaining cylinders. The completed assembly should display as shown in Figure 2–70.

If the first piston and connecting rod are oriented differently on your model, redefine the connecting rod. You might need to flip the cylinder connection of the piston. Regenerate the assembly.

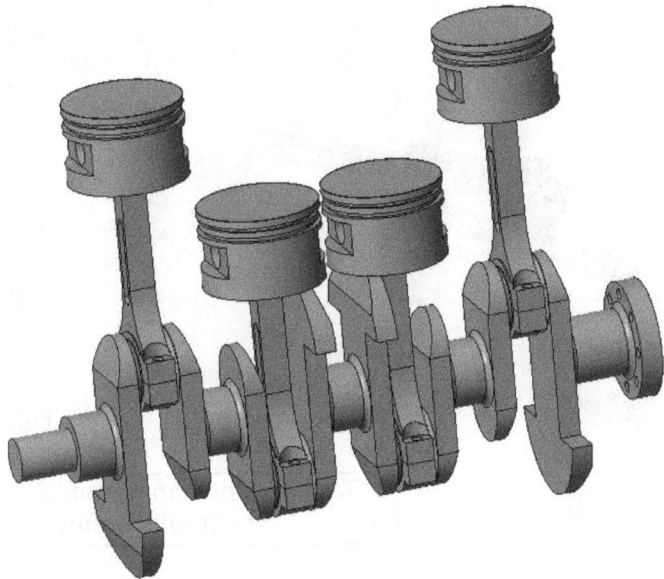

Figure 2–70

12. Save the assembly. You will save the assembly before moving the components so that they are in the original locations next time the assembly is retrieved.

13. Press and hold <Ctrl>+<Alt>, and drag the components using the left mouse button to show their range of motion. Erase the assembly from memory.

Practice 2e

Project - Hydraulic Boom

Practice Objective

- Assemble a complex assembly using mechanism connections that permit the required range of motion.

In this practice, you will begin work on a hydraulic boom assembly, similar to that of a backhoe. The model units for this practice are millimeter Newton's seconds (mmNs). Initially, the practice will tell you which connection type to assign. However, as the lab progresses you will be required to select the connection types yourself. Use <Ctrl> and <Alt> to drag the components through their range of motion. The final assembly displays as shown in Figure 2–71.

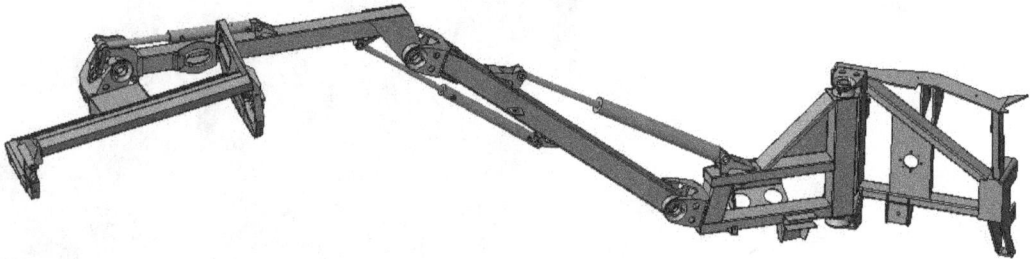

Figure 2–71

Task 1 - Open an assembly and add component to create a hydraulic boom assembly.

1. Set the working directory to the *MDX_Boom_I* folder.

2. Open **hydraulic_boom**.asm

3. Set the model display as follows:

   - *(Datum Display Filters)*: All Off

   - *(Spin Center)*: Off

   - *(Display Style)*: (Shading With Edges)

4. To display model colors during the assembly process we will temporarily set a configuration option. Select **File, Options** to open the Creo Parametric Options dialog box.

5. Select **Configuration Editor** and click **Find**.

6. Enter **preserve** as the keyword as shown in Figure 2–72 and click **Find Now**.

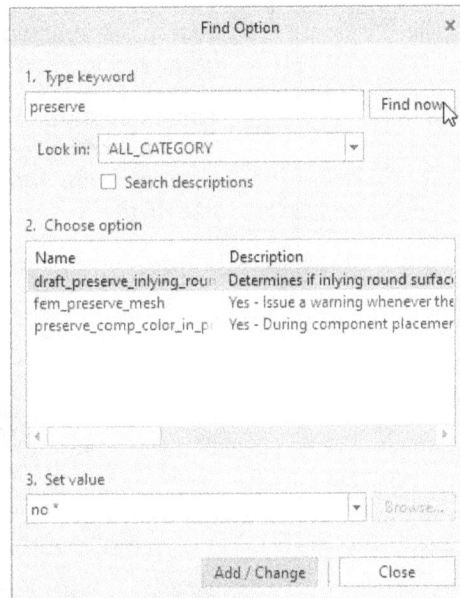

Figure 2–72

7. Click on **preserve_comp_color_in_preview** and select **yes**, as shown in Figure 2–73.

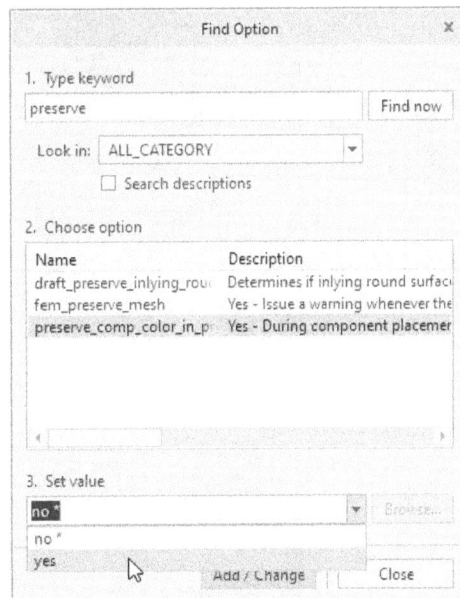

Figure 2–73

8. Select **Add/Change** and **Close**.

9. Select **OK**.

10. To set this option only for this Creo session, select **No** when prompted to save.

11. Assemble **pivot-arm.prt** using a pin connection. Use the black cylindrical surfaces for the axis alignment and the orange planar surfaces for the translation. Once connected, use <Ctrl> and <Alt> to drag the component, as shown in Figure 2–74.

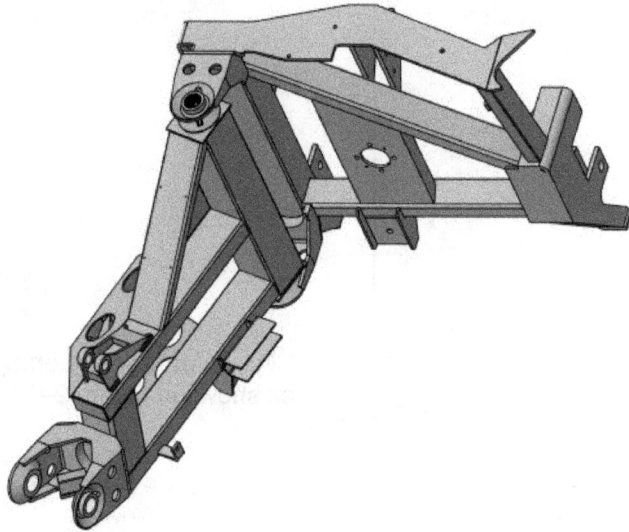

Figure 2–74

12. Assemble **boom1.prt** using a pin connection. Use the yellow cylindrical surfaces for the axis alignment and the red planar surfaces for the translation. Once connected, use <Ctrl>+<Alt> to drag the components, as shown in Figure 2–75.

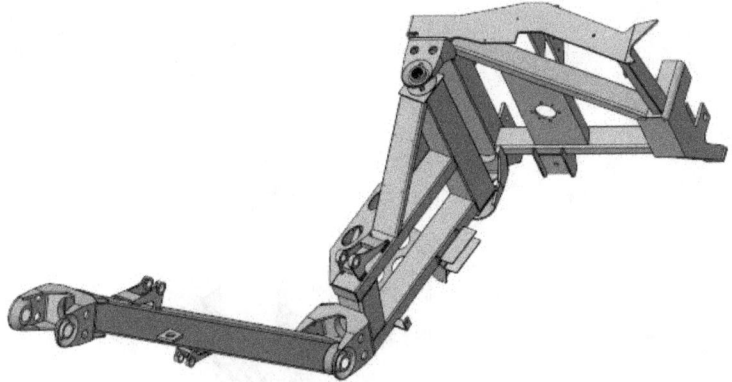

Figure 2–75

13. Save the assembly.

14. Assemble **boom2.prt** using a pin connection. Use the green cylindrical surfaces for the axis alignment and the blue planar surfaces for the translation. Drag the components as shown in Figure 2–76.

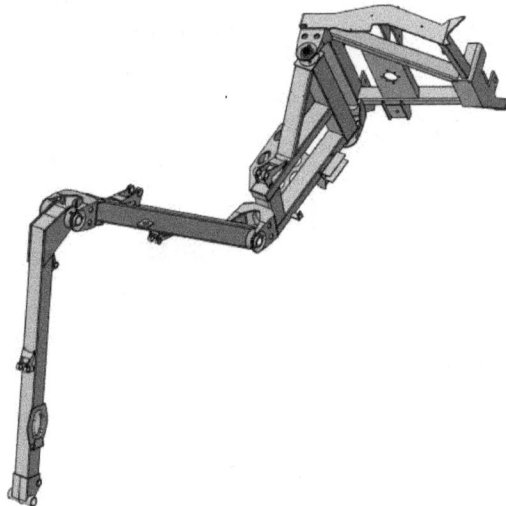

Figure 2–76

15. Assemble **bucket-1.prt** using a pin connection. Use the purple cylindrical surfaces for the axis alignment and brown planar surfaces for the translation. Drag the components as shown in Figure 2–77.

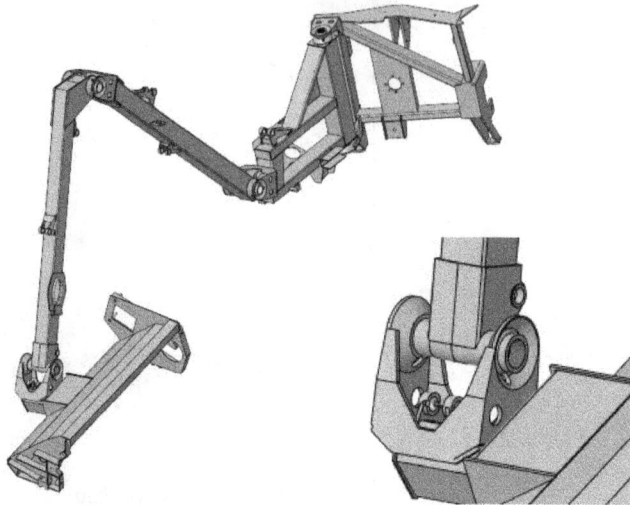

Figure 2–77

16. Save the assembly.

17. Assemble **y-prt.prt** using a pin connection. Us the yellow cylindrical surfaces for the axis alignment and the red planar surfaces for the translation.The assembly displays as shown in Figure 2–78.

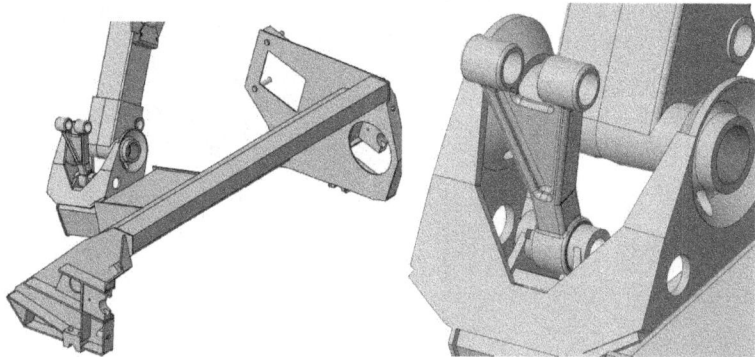

Figure 2–78

18. Save the assembly.

19. Assemble **link1.prt**. Start with a pin connection using the black cylindrical surfaces for the axis alignment and the green planar surfaces for the translation (you may need to flip the translation direction), as shown in Figure 2–79.

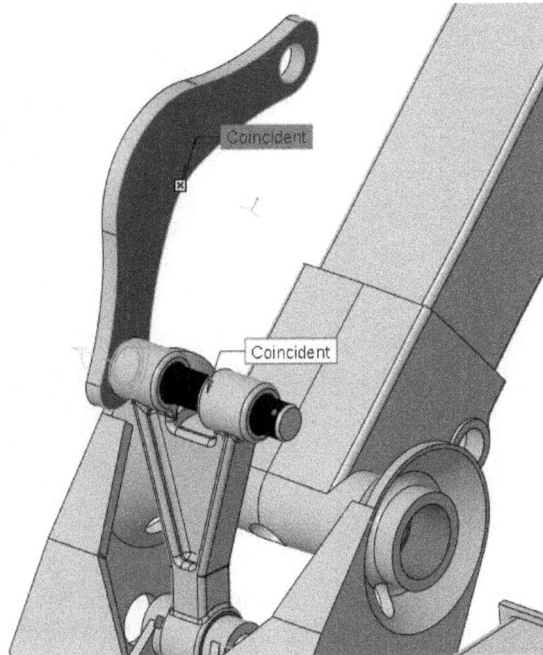

Figure 2–79

20. Now add a cylinder connection using the orange cylindrical surfaces. The assembly displays as shown in Figure 2–80.

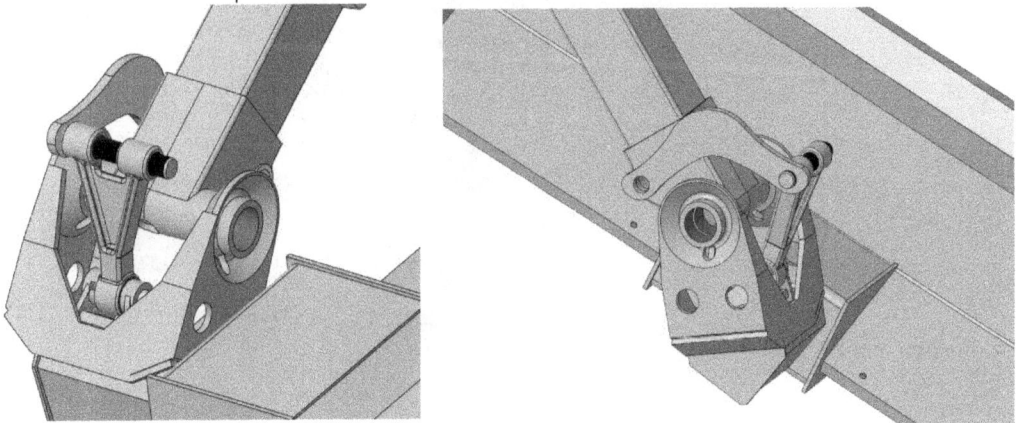

Figure 2–80

21. Save the assembly.

22. Assembly **link2.prt**. Start with a pin connection using the orange cylindrical surfaces for the axis alignment and the yellow planar surfaces for the translation. Drag **link2** to the position shown in Figure 2–81.

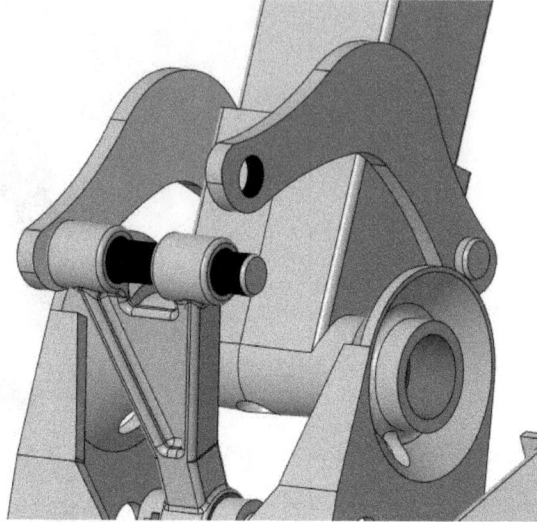

Figure 2–81

23. Now add a cylinder connection using the black cylindrical surfaces. The assembly displays as shown in Figure 2–82.

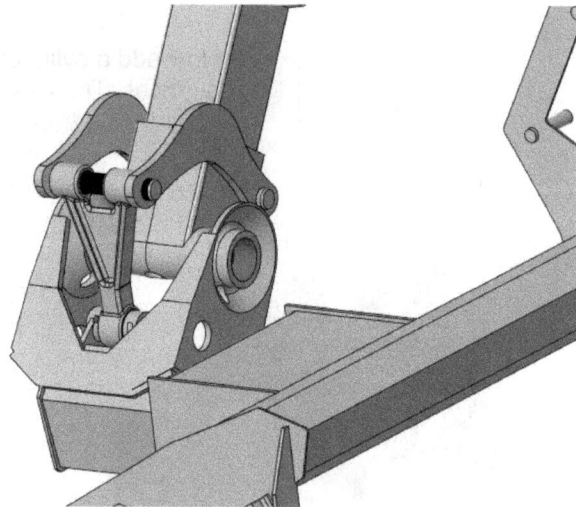

Figure 2–82

24. Assemble **cyl1.prt**.using a pin connection. Use the purple cylindrical surfaces for the axis alignment and the green planar surfaces for the translation. The assembly displays as shown in Figure 2–83.

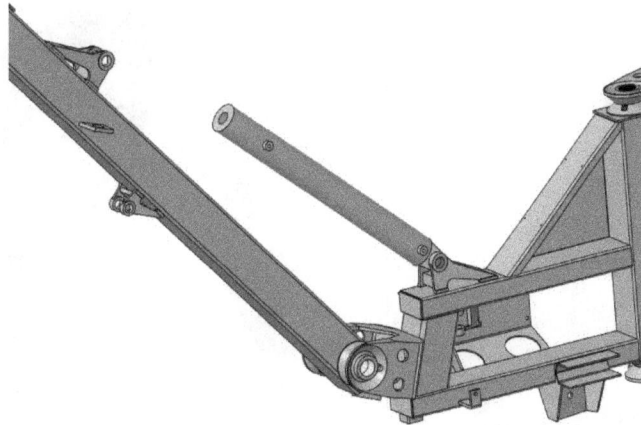

Figure 2–83

25. Assemble **piston1.prt** using two cylinder connections. Use the red cylindrical surfaces for one cylinder connection and the blue for the other. (You might need to flip a connection). The assembly displays as shown in Figure 2–84.

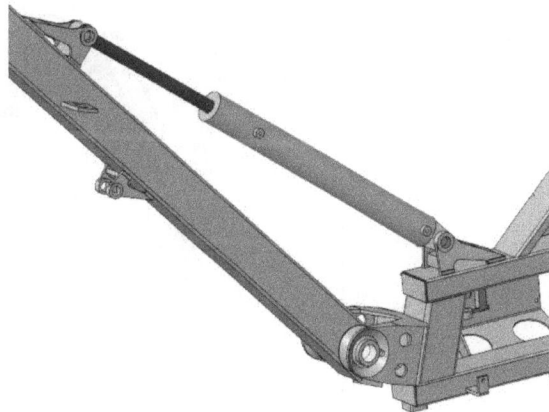

Figure 2–84

26. Save the assembly.

27. Assemble **cyl2.prt** with a pin connection. Use the black cylindrical surfaces for the axis alignment and the orange planar surfaces for the translation. The assembly displays as shown in Figure 2–85.

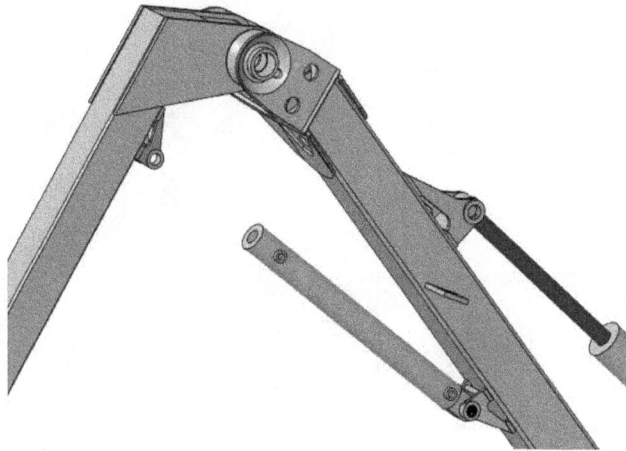

Figure 2–85

28. Assemble **piston2.prt** with two cylinder connections. Use the yellow cylindrical surfaces for one connection and the purple for the other. The assembly displays as shown in Figure 2–86.

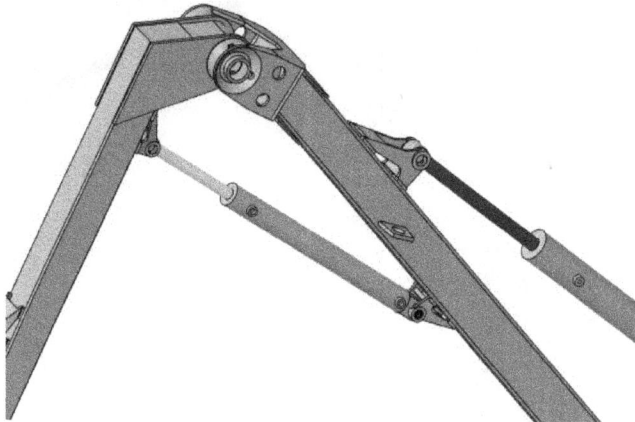

Figure 2–86

29. Save the assembly.

30. Assemble **cyl3.prt** using a pin connection. Use the green cylindrical surfaces for the axis alignment and the blue planar surfaces for the translation. The assembly displays as shown in Figure 2–87.

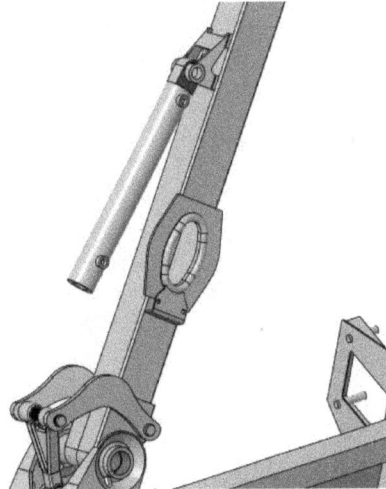

Figure 2–87

31. Assemble **piston3.prt** using two cylinder connections. Use the red cylindrical surface for one connection and the black for the other. The assembly displays as shown in Figure 2–88.

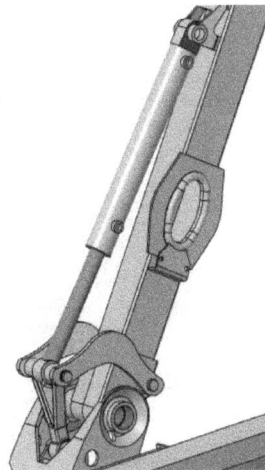

Figure 2–88

32. Save the assembly.

33. In the *Model* tab, select **Appearances**, as shown in Figure 2–89.

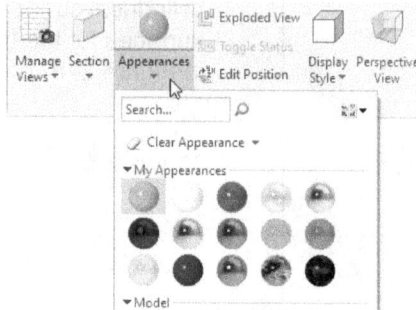
Figure 2–89

34. Select **Clear Appearance> Clear All Appearances**, as shown in Figure 2–90.

Figure 2–90

35. Select **Yes** to confirm the removal of all appearances. The assembly updates as shown in Figure 2–91.

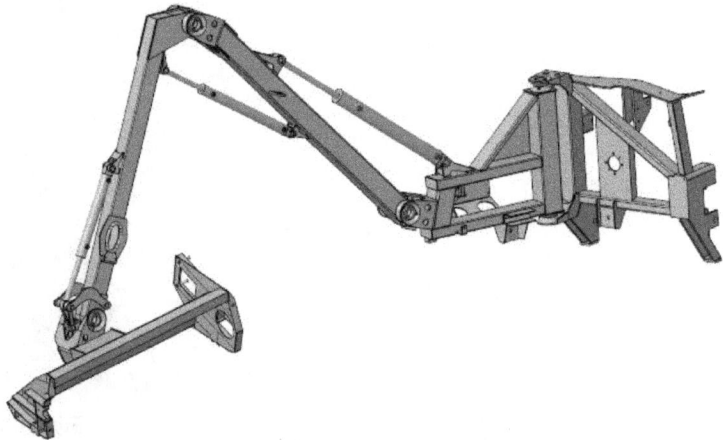
Figure 2–91

36. Select **File, Options, Configuration Editor**.

37. In the list of options locate and set
    preserve_comp_color_in_preview to **no** as shown in
    Figure 2–92.

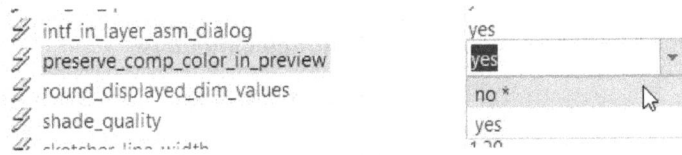

intf_in_layer_asm_dialog	yes
preserve_comp_color_in_preview	yes
round_displayed_dim_values	no *
shade_quality	yes

Figure 2–92

38. Select **OK** and **No**.

39. Save the assembly and erase it from memory.

Practice 2f	# (Optional) Project - Geneva Mechanism

Practice Objective

• Create an assembly of a Geneva mechansim

In this practice, you will assemble a driving rotor and a 6 slot Geneva wheel. Both the driver and wheel will be assembled using a single Pin connection to a mounting bracket. The final assembly displays as shown in Figure 2–93.

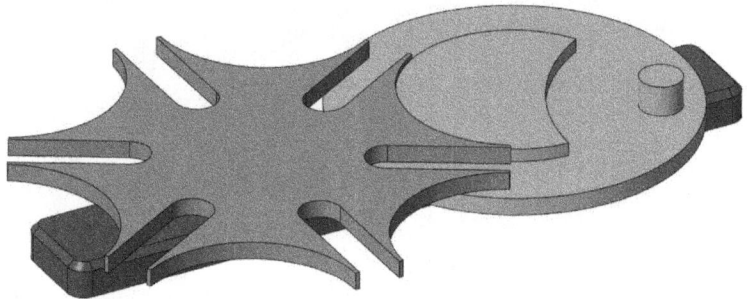

Figure 2–93

Task 1 - Open an existing assembly and assemble components.

1. Set the working directory to the Geneva_I folder.

2. Open **geneva_mechanism.asm**.

3. Set the model display as follows:

  • *(Datum Display Filters)*: (Axis Display)

  • *Datum Tag Display:* (Plane Tag Display), (Axis Tag Display), (Csys Tag Display)

  • *(Spin Center)*: Off

  • *(Display Style)*: (No Hidden)

4. In the *Model* tab, click (Assemble).

5. Double click on **gm-driver.prt**.

6. Select **Pin** as the connection type as shown in Figure 2–94.

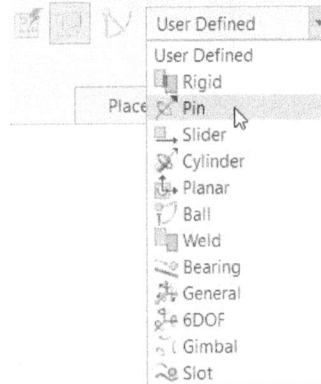

Figure 2–94

7. Select the two cylindrical surfaces (the mounting shaft and the hole) shown in Figure 2–95.

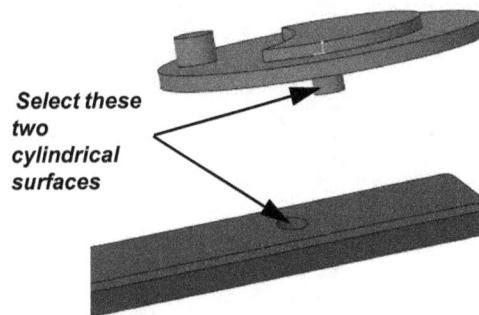

Select these two cylindrical surfaces

Figure 2–95

8. Select the two planar surfaces (the bottom of the mounting shaft and bottom face of the bracket) as shown in Figure 2–96.

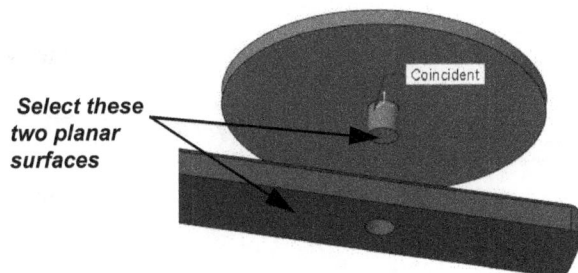

Select these two planar surfaces

Figure 2–96

9. Drag the gm-driver part to the position shown in Figure 2–97.

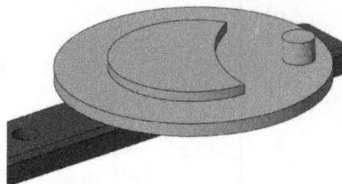

Figure 2–97

10. Click ✔ (OK).

11. In the *Model* tab, click 🖰 (Assemble).

12. Double click on **gm-slot-wheel.prt**.

13. Select **Pin** as the connection type as shown in Figure 2–98.

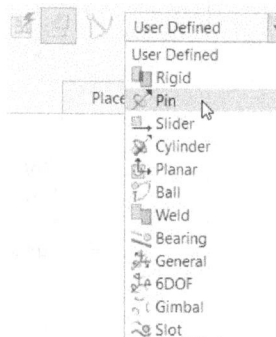

Figure 2–98

14. Select the two cylindrical surfaces (the mounting shaft and the hole) shown in Figure 2–99.

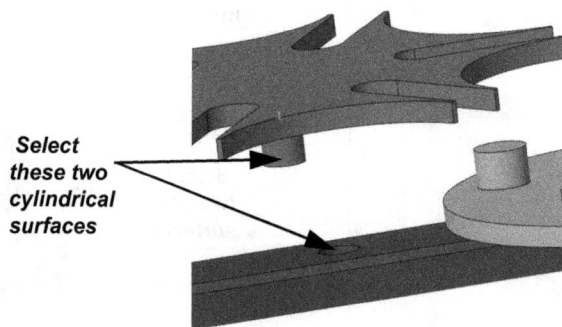

Select these two cylindrical surfaces

Figure 2–99

15. Select the two planar surfaces (the bottom of the mounting shaft and bottom face of the bracket), as shown in Figure 2–100.

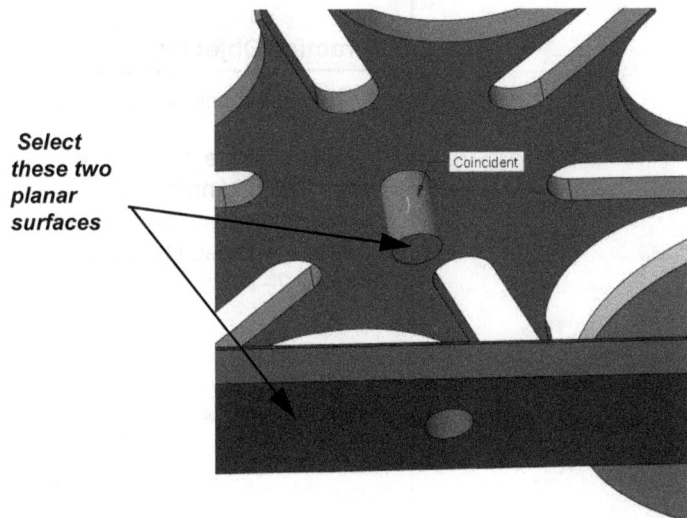

Select these two planar surfaces

Coincident

Figure 2–100

16. Drag the gm-slot-wheel part to the position shown in Figure 2–101.

Do not be concerned with any interference you may have between the gm-driver part and the gm-wheel part. The models will be rotated to the correct angles to avoid interference with settings applied in the next chapter.

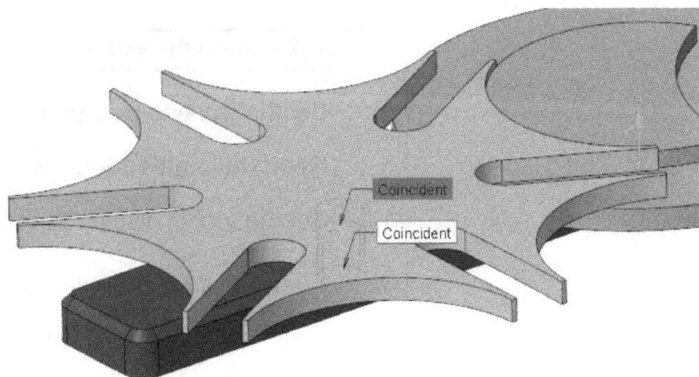

Coincident
Coincident

Figure 2–101

17. Click ✓ (OK).

18. Save the assembly and erase it from memory.

Practice 2g

(Optional) Project - Double Slider Project

Practice Objective

- Create a double slider mechanism.

In this practice, you will assembly two sliding blocks and a crank arm. The sliding blocks are assembled with one slider connection each and the arm is assembled with one pin and one cylinder connection. The final assembly displays as shown in Figure 2–102

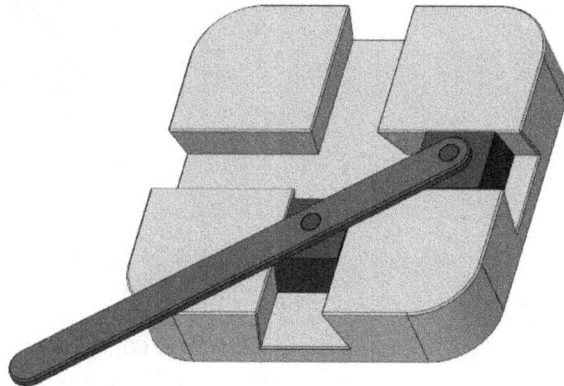

Figure 2–102

Task 1 - Open an existing assembly and add components.

1. Set the working directory to the *Double_Slider_I* folder.

2. Open **dovetail-slider.asm**.

3. Set the model display as follows:

   - *(Datum Display Filters)*: (Axis Display)

   - *(Spin Center)*: Off

   - *(Display Style)*: (Shading With Edges)

4. In the *Model* tab, click (Assemble).

5. Double click on **slider-dovetail.prt**.

6. Select **Slider** as the connection type as shown in Figure 2–103.

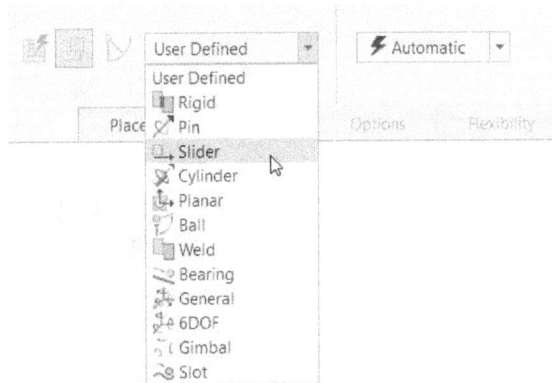

Figure 2–103

7. Select axis **A_2** in slider-dovetail and axis **A_2** in block-dovetail as shown in Figure 2–104 as the Axis Alignment.

Shading toggled off for clarity.

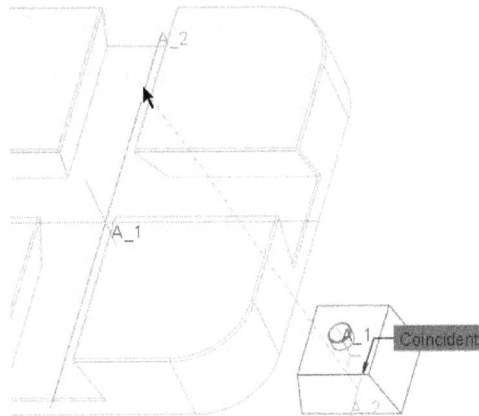

Figure 2–104

8. For the Rotation references select the top planar faces of the slider-dovetail and block-dovetail parts as shown in Figure 2–105.

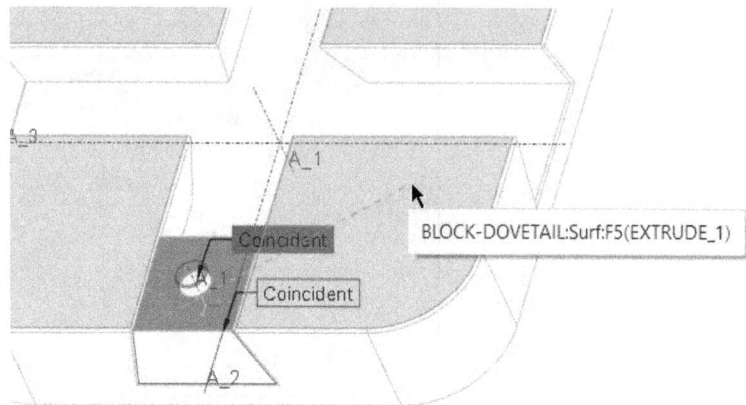

Figure 2–105

9. Click ✔ (OK).

10. In the *Model* tab, click 🖉 (Assemble).

11. Double click on **slider-dovetail.prt**.

12. Select **Slider** as the connection type.

13. Select axis **A_2** in slider-dovetail and axis **A_3** in block-dovetail as shown in Figure 2–106.

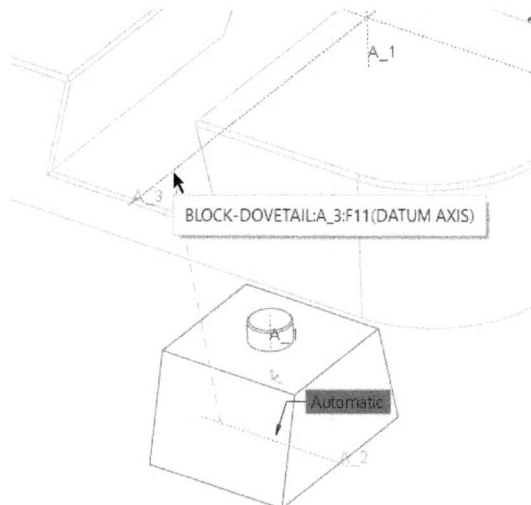

Figure 2–106

14. For the Rotation references, select the top planar faces of the slider-dovetail and block-dovetail parts as you did for the first slider-dovetail part.

15. In the *Model* tab, click 🗗 (Assemble).

16. Double click on **crank-arm.prt**.

17. Select **Pin** as the connection type.

18. Select the cylindrical surface of the post on the second slider-dovetail part and the surface of the hole nearest the end of the crank-arm as shown in Figure 2–107.

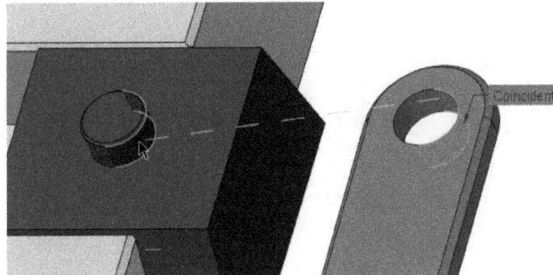

Figure 2–107

19. Select the planar top surface of the post in the slider-dovetail part and the planar top surface of the crank-arm part as the Translation references as shown in Figure 2–108.

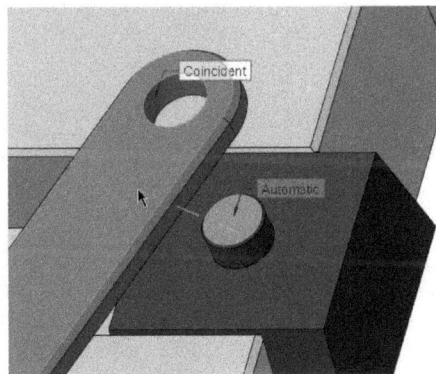

Figure 2–108

20. In the *Placement* tab, select **New Set** to add a second connection. Click on the second connection in the list and change the second connection type to **Cylinder** as shown in Figure 2–109.

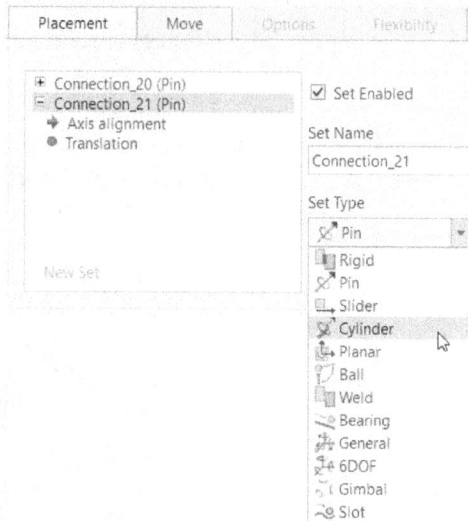

Figure 2–109

21. Select the cylindrical surface of the post on the slider-dovetail part the cylindrical surface of the other hole on the crank-arm part as shown in Figure 2–110.

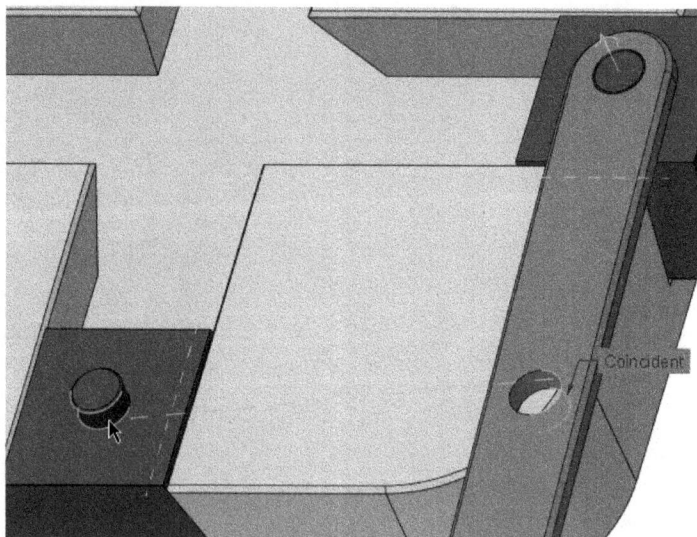

Figure 2–110

22. Click ✔ (OK). The assembly updates as shown in Figure 2–111.

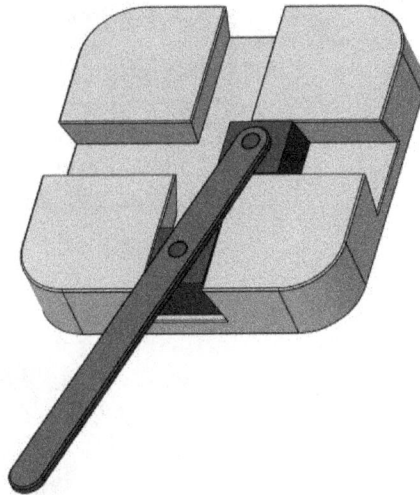

Figure 2–111

23. Save the Assembly and erase it from memory.

Practice 2h

(Optional) Project - Scotch Yoke

Practice Objective

- Create a Scotch yoke mechanism.

In this practice, you will build a Scotch yoke assembly, as shown in Figure 2–112. The yoke will be assembled with slider connection and the rotating wheel driving the mechanism is assembled with a pin connection. The wheel and yoke will be connected with 3D contact connection.

Figure 2–112

Task 1 - Open an existing assembly and add components.

1. Set the working directory to the *Scotch_Yoke_I* folder.

2. Open **scotch-yoke.asm**.

3. Set the model display as follows:

   - ⁺⸚⸜ *(Datum Display Filters)*: All Off

   - ⸝ *(Spin Center)*: Off

   - ⬚ *(Display Style)*: ⬚ (Shading With Edges)

4. In the *Model* tab, click ⬚ (Assemble).

5. Double click on **yoke.prt**.

6. Select **Slider** as the connection type as shown in Figure 2–103.

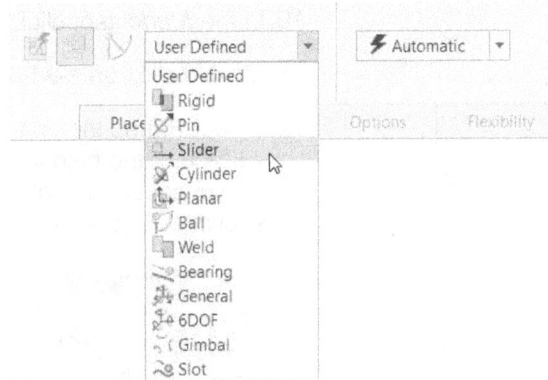

Figure 2–113

7. Select the cylindrical surface of the long cylinder in the yoke and the cylindrical surface of the hole in the pillow-block as shown in Figure 2–114.

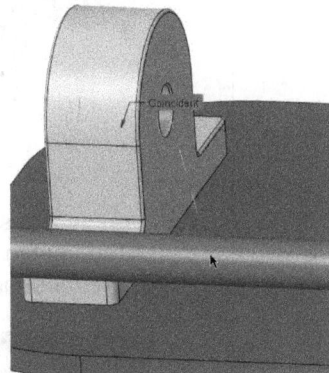

Figure 2–114

8. For the Rotation reference select the datum plane **TOP** in the yoke part and the datum plane **TOP** in the pillow-block.

9. Click ✓ (OK). The assembly updates as shown in Figure 2–115.

Figure 2–115

10. In the *Model* tab, click 🖳 (Assemble).

11. Double click on **s-wheel.prt**.

12. Select **Pin** as the connection type and select the cylindrical surface of the hole in the mounting-plate part and the cylindrical surface of the lower post in the s-wheel part as shown in Figure 2–116.

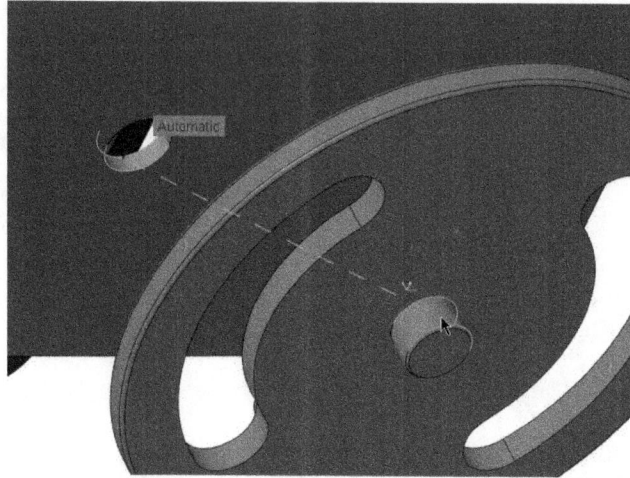

Figure 2–116

13. For the Translation references, select bottom planar surface of the post in the s-wheel part and the planar bottom surface of the mounting-plate part as shown in Figure 2–117.

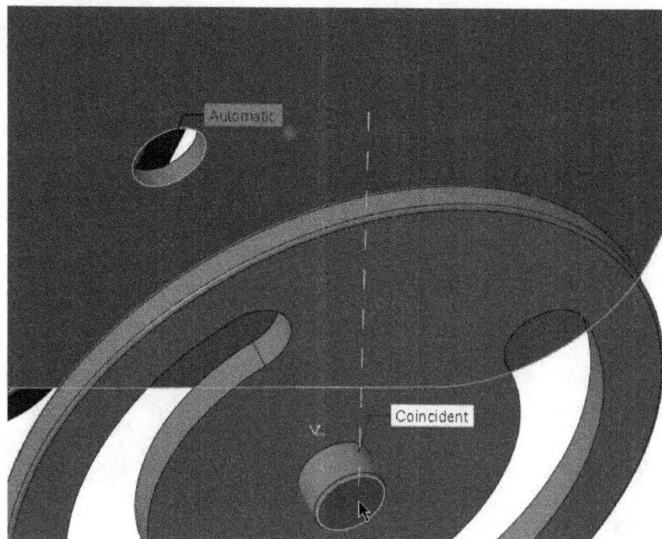

Figure 2–117

14. Click ✓ (OK). The assembly updates as shown in Figure 2–118.

Figure 2–118

15. Save the assembly and erase it from memory.

Practice 2i

(Optional) Project - Quick Return Mechanism

Practice Objective

- Create a quick return mechanism.

In this practice, you will build a Whitworth style quick return mechanism. The wheel and linkage arm will be assembled with single pin connections and the bar will be assembled with a slider connection. The sliding washers are constrained with a slider and cylinder connection. The final assembly displays as shown in Figure 2–119.

Figure 2–119

Task 1 - Open an existing assembly and add components.

1. Set the working directory to the Quick_Return_I folder.

2. Open **whitworth.asm**.

3. Set the model display as follows:

- ⚓ *(Datum Display Filters)*: All Off

- ✣ *(Spin Center)*: Off

- ▱ *(Display Style)*: ▱ (Shading With Edges)

4. In the *Model* tab, click ⬚ (Assemble).

5. Double click on **quick-return.prt**.

6. Select **Slider** as the connection type as shown in Figure 2–120.

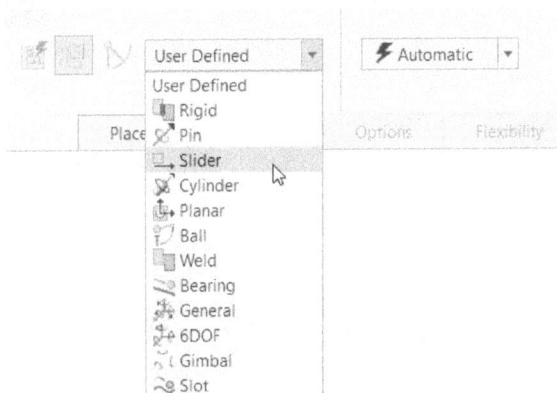

Figure 2–120

7. Select the axis **BAR-SLIDE** in both the assembly and quick-return part, as shown in Figure 2–121.

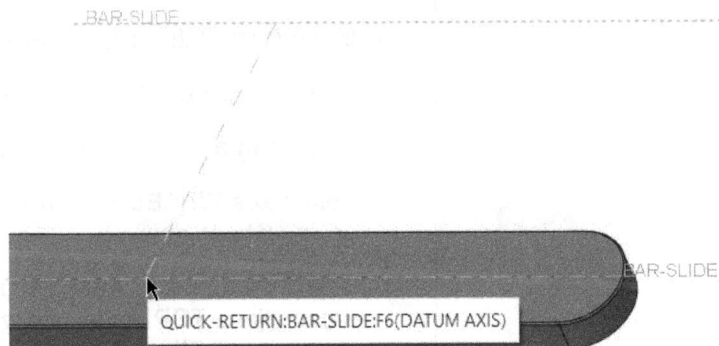

QUICK-RETURN:BAR-SLIDE:F6(DATUM AXIS)

Figure 2–121

8. Select datum plane **ASM_FRONT** in the assembly and the planar top surface of the quick-return part, as shown in Figure 2–122.

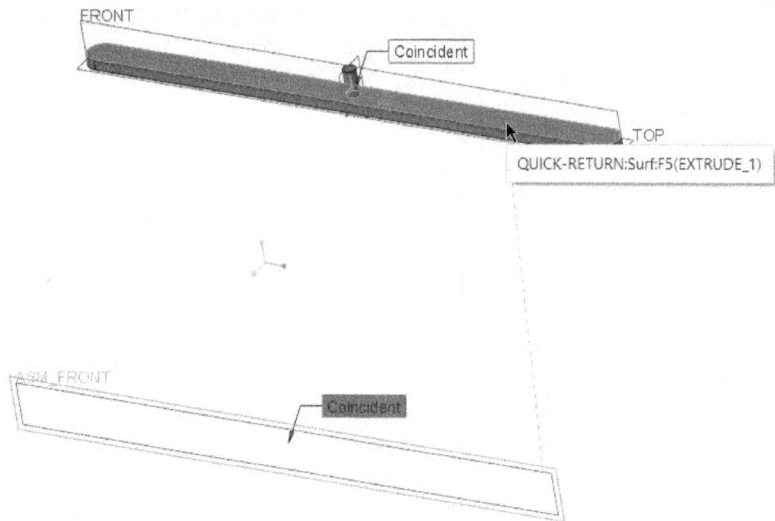

FRONT

Coincident

TOP

QUICK-RETURN:Surf:F5(EXTRUDE_1)

ASM_FRONT

Coincident

Figure 2–122

9. Click ✔ (OK).

10. In the *Model* tab, click 🗗 (Assemble).

11. Double click on **driving-wheel.prt**.

12. Select **Pin** as the connection type.

13. Select axis **WHEEL-ROTATION** in both the assembly and driving-wheel parts.

14. Select datum plane **ASM_FRONT** in the assembly and datum plane **TOP** in the driving-wheel part. In the Placement panel, select **Flip**, as shown in Figure 2–123.

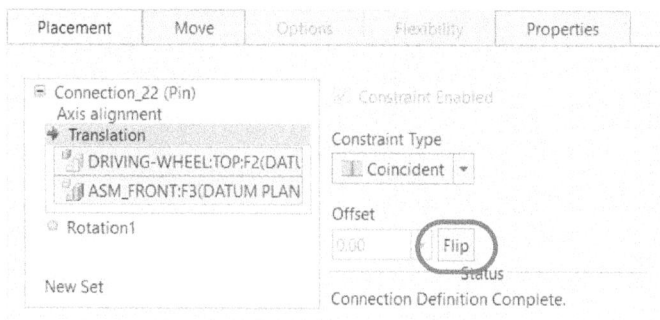

| Placement | Move | Options | Flexibility | Properties |

⊟ Connection_22 (Pin)
   Axis alignment
   ⬦ Translation
      DRIVING-WHEEL:TOP:F2(DATU
      ASM_FRONT:F3(DATUM PLAN
   ⟳ Rotation1

New Set

☑ Constraint Enabled

Constraint Type
   Coincident ▼

Offset
   0.00   Flip

Status
Connection Definition Complete.

Figure 2–123

15. Ensure that the pins are facing in the same direction as shown in Figure 2–124 (if not, select **Flip**) and, click ✓ (OK).

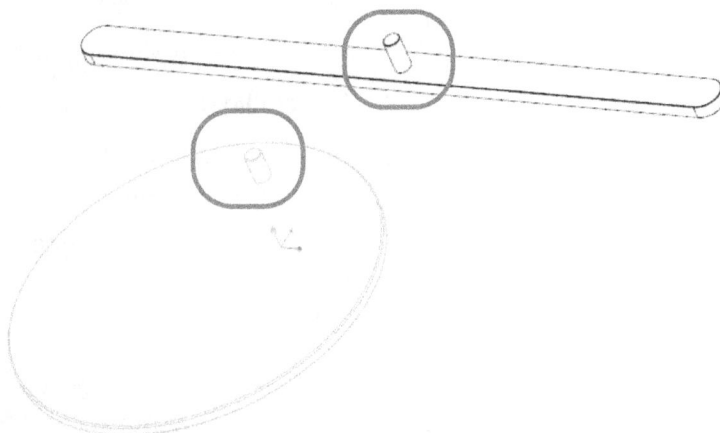

Figure 2–124

16. In the *Model* tab, click 🖳 (Assemble).

17. Double click on **link-arm.prt**.

18. Select **Pin** as the connection type.

19. Select axis **ARM-ROTATION** in both the assembly and driving-wheel parts.

20. For the Translation references select datum plane **WHEEL** in the driving-wheel part and datum plane **ASM_FRONT** in the assembly. Verify the arm sits above the wheel and drag the arm to the position shown in Figure 2–125.

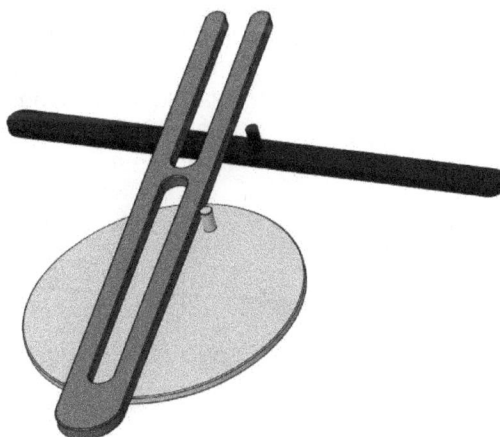

Figure 2–125

21. Click ✓ (OK).

22. In the *Model* tab, click ⬚ (Assemble).

23. Double click on **sliding-washer.prt**.

24. Select **Slider** as the connection type.

25. Select axis **WASHER** in the link-arm part and axis **A_2** in the sliding-washer part.

26. Select the top planar surface of the link-arm part and the top planar surface of the sliding-washer part, as shown in Figure 2–126.

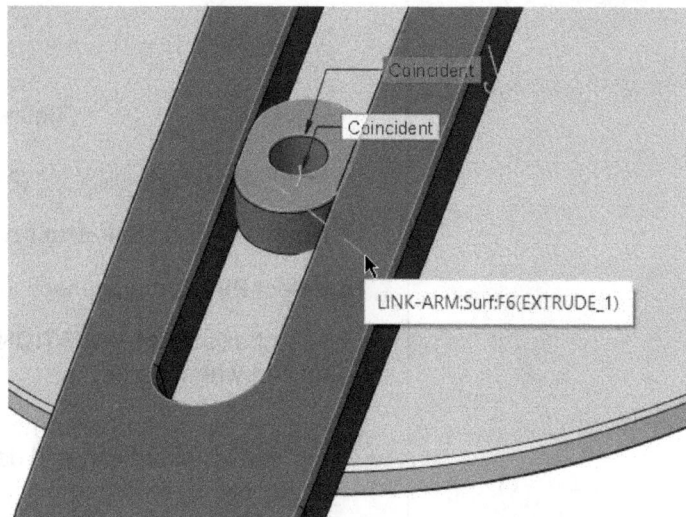

Figure 2–126

27. In the *Placement* tab, select **New Set** to add a second connection. Click on the second connection in the list and change the second connection type to **Cylinder**, as shown in Figure 2–127.

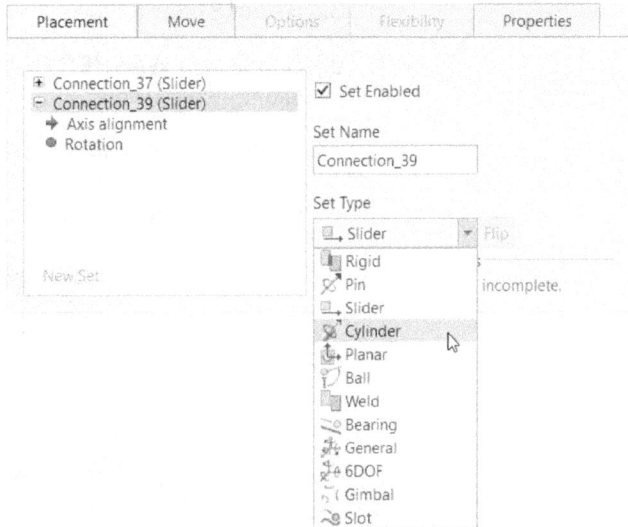

Figure 2–127

28. Select the cylindrical surface of the hole in sliding-washer part and the cylindrical surface of the pin in the driving wheel part, as shown in Figure 2–128.

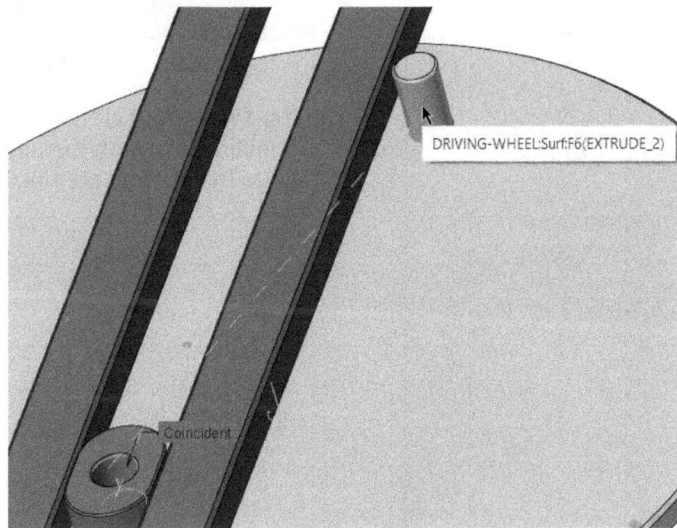

Figure 2–128

29. Click ✔ (OK).

30. In the *Model* tab, click 🖫 (Assemble).

31. Double click on **sliding-washer.prt**.

32. Select **Slider** as the connection type.

33. Select axis **WASHER** in the link-arm part and axis **A_2** in the sliding-washer part.

34. Select the top planar surface of the link-arm part and the top planar surface of the sliding-washer part, as shown in Figure 2–129.

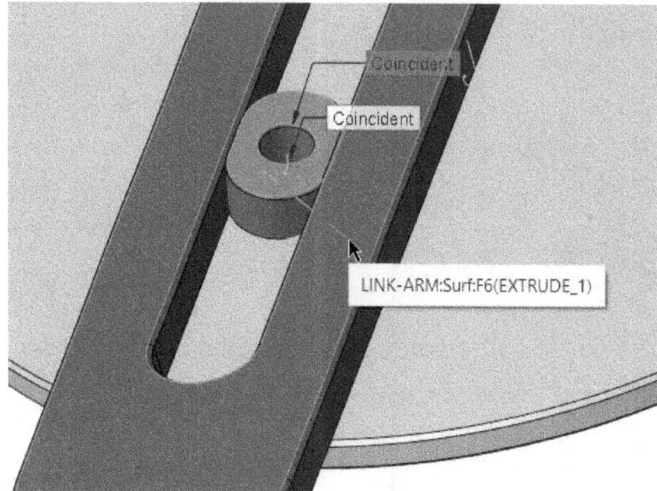

Figure 2–129

35. In the *Placement* tab, select **New Set** to add a second connection. Click on the second connection in the list and change the second connection type to **Cylinder**, as shown in Figure 2–130.

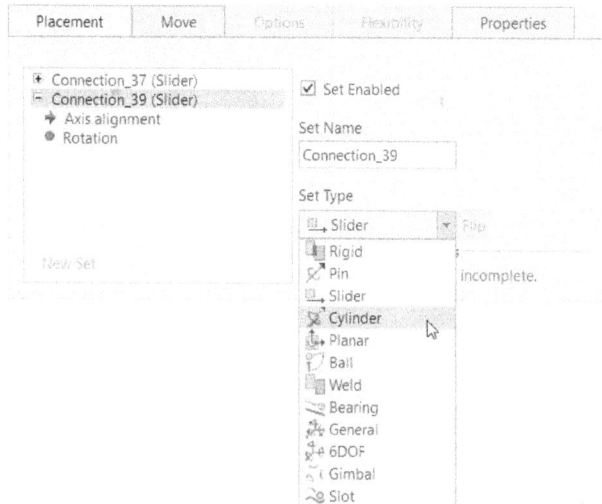

Figure 2–130

36. Select the cylindrical surface of the hole in sliding-washer part and the cylindrical surface of the pin in the quick-return part, as shown in Figure 2–131.

Figure 2–131

37. Click ✔ (OK). The assembly updates as shown in Figure 2–132.

Figure 2–132

38. Save the assembly and erase it from memory.

Chapter Review Questions

1. Components that have at least one degree of freedom open are listed as packaged in the model tree.

   a. True

   b. False

2. Which mechanism connection allows a point or vertex on one component to be constrained to an axis or linear edge on another component?

   a. Rigid

   b. Pin

   c. Cylinder

   d. Slider

   e. Ball

   f. Bearing

   g. Weld

3. Which of the following connection types is used to assemble a component using standard assembly constraints to fully constrain the component in all degrees of freedom?

   a. Rigid

   b. Pin

   c. Cylinder

   d. Slider

   e. Ball

   f. Bearing

   g. Weld

4. Which mechanism connection only permits rotation about one axis?

   a. Rigid

   b. Pin

   c. Cylinder

   d. Slider

   e. Ball

   f. Bearing

   g. Weld

5. Which of the following connection types only permits translation along a single axis?

    a. Rigid

    b. Pin

    c. Cylinder

    d. Slider

    e. Ball

    f. Bearing

    g. Weld

6. Which of the following connection types permits translation along and rotation about a single axis.

    a. Rigid

    b. Pin

    c. Cylinder

    d. Slider

    e. Ball

    f. Bearing

    g. Weld

7. A 6DOF connection enables you to assemble a component so that it has three rotational and three translational degrees of freedom.

    a. True

    b. False

Answers: 1a, 2f, 3a, 4b, 5d, 6c, 7a

Simulating Motion

Once components have been assembled using the required connections, the assembly can be opened in Mechanism mode to further manipulate and study the motion of the components.

Learning Objectives in this Chapter

- Learn how to activate Mechanism mode in the *Application* tab, and how to move the assembly interactively using the Drag function.
- Use the Drag function to move components, create snapshots, and specify a new ground coordinate system.
- Learn to move the components in the assembly and save a snapshot of the mechanism that can be retrieved for a reference.
- Use the icons in the *Constraints* tab to define constraints, fix joint connections, lock components, unlock components, and disable connections.
- Learn to use the joint axis settings to specify a zero reference, a regeneration value, and a total range of motion to limit the movement for the component.

3.1 Dynamic Drag

Once all of the connections have been assigned, select the *Applications* tab and click 🌀 (Mechanism) to enable the Mechanism mode. Once activated, the assembly can be moved interactively using the Drag functionality. This enables you to view how the mechanism behaves. It also enables you to position the mechanism in specific orientations and save them (snapshots). In addition, the entire mechanism or a portion of it can be investigated using body lock and joint capabilities. Body locks restrict movement and joints limit the range of motion.

To activate the Drag function, click 🖐️ (Drag). The Drag dialog box opens as shown in Figure 3–1.

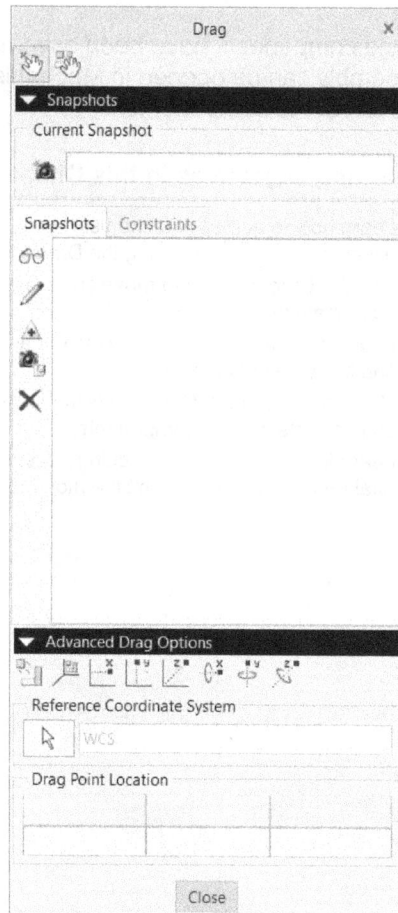

Figure 3–1

The icons at the top of the dialog box enable you to define the movement, take snapshots of moved components, and undo/redo actions as required. The icons are described as follows:

Icon	Description
	Enables you to take a snapshot of the current drag configuration for future retrieval. Saved snapshots are listed in the *Snapshots* tab in the Drag dialog box.
	Enables you to drag a component by selecting a point and moving it to a new X,Y,Z location in the model. All components update according to how the joints have been defined.
	Enables you to drag a body according to the current orientation of the model. The drag extent is as permitted by the connections that are defined in the model. This drag option is recommended for obtaining the required snapshots for a defined model orientation.

All movement occurs around the ground coordinate system. A ground coordinate system is automatically selected by Creo Parametric. If the default ground coordinate system is unsuitable, the coordinate system of another component can be selected. The coordinate systems located at the intersection of default datum planes or at existing datum coordinate systems can be selected as alternatives. To select a new coordinate system, click (Select Coordinate System) in the *Advanced Drag Options* area in the dialog box. The remaining coordinate system icons available in the *Advanced Drag Option* area enable you to customize translation and rotation about the X-, Y-, or Z-axis.

To use an additional advanced move options, select an object, and use the package functionality. Click ⬛ (Package Move) to open the Move dialog box as shown in Figure 3–2.

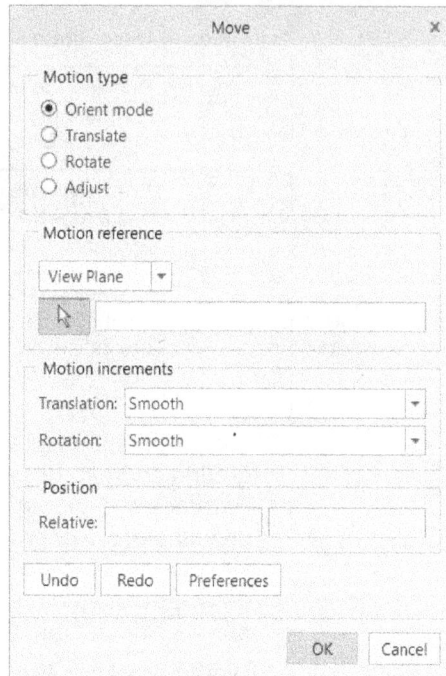

Figure 3–2

3.2 Saved Views

When a required model orientation is obtained, a saved view (snapshot) can be taken of the mechanism. This snapshot provides a configuration that can be retrieved for reference at any time. To create a snapshot, orient the model as required and click 🖼 (Take Snapshot). By default, snapshots are saved with system-defined names. To rename a snapshot, select it and enter a name in the *Current Snapshot* field.

All saved snapshots are listed in the *Snapshot* tab in the Drag dialog box. The additional icons that are available on this tab are described as follows.

Icon	Description
👓	Enables you to retrieve a selected snapshot configuration. To restore a configuration, select the snapshot name in the list and click the icon.
🖊	Enables you to use other snapshot configurations to create new ones.
⊕	Enables you to redefine the snapshot configuration. To do so, drag the components to their new positions, select the snapshot in the list, and click the icon.
📷	Enables the snapshot to be used in a drawing. If enabled, 🖼 displays next to the snapshot name.
✕	Enables you to delete a snapshot. To do so, select the snapshot name in the list, and click the icon.

3.3 Control the Drag Function

You can further control the Drag function using the icons in the *Constraints* tab in the Drag dialog box. The options enable you to do the following:

- Define geometric constraints (i.e., Align, Mate, or Orient) to position components in the assembly.

- Fix joint connections to prevent movement in its DOF.

- Lock or unlock components in their current assembly position.

- Enable or disable connections that were assigned in the assembly.

The *Constraints* tab in the Drag dialog box is shown in Figure 3–3.

Figure 3–3

The *Constraint* tab icons are described as follows:

Icon	Description
	Enables you to constrain components by aligning two surfaces.
	Enables you to constrain components by mating two surfaces.
	Enables you to constrain components by orienting two surfaces.
	Enables you to fix a specific joint axis in its current position. You must select the connection icon for the item to prevent movement in that DOF.
	Enables you to specify whether the two bodies in your cam-follower connection remain in contact while dragging or during a motion run.
	Enables you to temporarily lock a component in its current position relative to the ground or another component. It is possible for the mechanism to remain fixed if this option is used.
	Enables you to temporarily disable connections. Shows how components would move relative to each other if they were one body.
	Enables you to force the mechanism to assemble using the previous options.
✗	Enables you to delete any of the constraints that have been applied in the Drag dialog box.

3.4 Joint Axis Settings

After components are assembled and connections have been defined, the components in a mechanism can be moved within the available degrees of freedom (DOF). In the DOF, the mechanism has an unlimited range of motion. For example, a component assembled with a pin connection can rotate a full 360°. Depending on the component, intersection can occur with other components while it moves through its full range of motion. To limit this range of motion, joint axis settings can be used to create realistic results.

You can also access the Joint Axis Settings in Assembly mode by selecting a component,

selecting 🖑 *(Edit Definition), and selecting the Rotation Axis or Translation Axis in the Placement tab.*

Joint axis settings enable you to specify a zero reference and a total range of motion. You can also specify which position the mechanism must display in after regeneration. To open the Joint Axis Settings dialog box, select the connection icon on the model, and select 🖑 (Edit Definition) in the mini toolbar. The MOTION AXIS dialog box opens as shown in Figure 3–4.

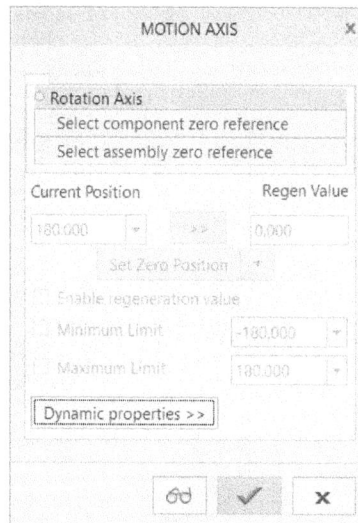

Figure 3–4

Defining the References

The position of a body in the joint axis direction is controlled by the zero position. The zero position must be set by selecting references on the component and the assembly.

To designate the joint axis zero, select references on the component and in the assembly. The joint axis is set to zero where these references are aligned or are parallel. The MOTION AXIS dialog box opens as shown in Figure 3–5.

Figure 3–5

The **Set Zero Position** option, located in the Motion Axis dialog box, enables you to change the zero position. Note that the assembly shown Figure 3–6 has the initial zero position set where the two highlighted planes are parallel (e.g. the angle is zero degrees).

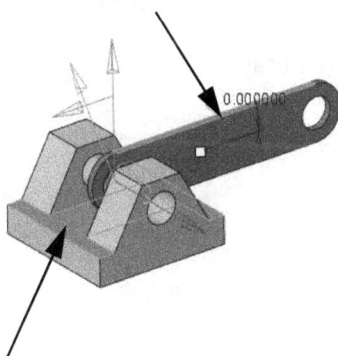

Zero position is when the two planes are parallel.

Figure 3–6

Setting the Current Position to 45 degrees and clicking **Set Zero Position** changes the zero position to where the two planes are 45 degrees from one another, as shown in Figure 3–7. This option is located in the *Component Placement* dashboard in the standard application, and in the Joint Axis Setting dialog box in the mechanism application.

Component set to 45 degrees, then zero position set

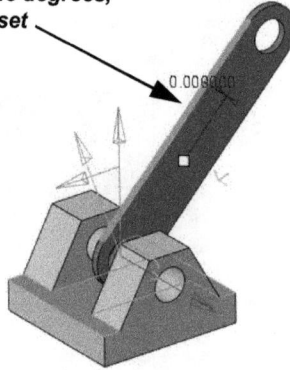

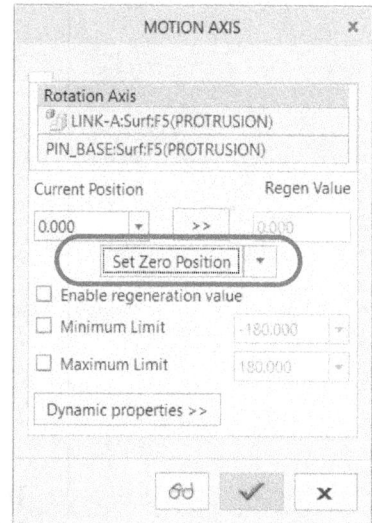

Figure 3–7

To reset the zero position, click ˅ and select **Default Zero Position**.

Setting a Regeneration Value

Regeneration occurs after modifications have been made to an assembly. Joint axis settings enable you to specify where, within the specified limits, a component can be positioned after regeneration.

How To: Specify the Regeneration Position

1. Enter the required value as the current position, as shown in Figure 3–8.

It is important to observe the direction of the arrow on the joint axis when specifying numerical values. The arrow controls the positive direction.

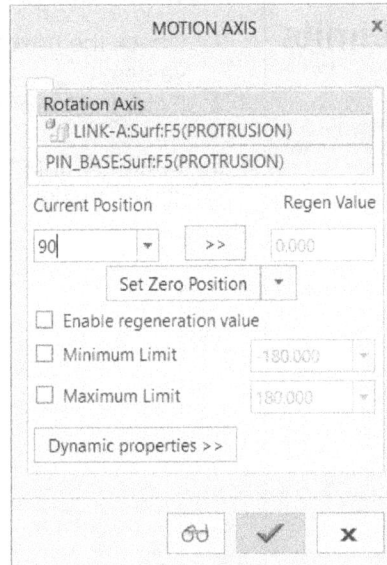

Figure 3–8

2. Click ▸▸ (Set Regeneration Value) to set the current position as the regeneration value. Then check the box next to Enable regeneration value as shown in Figure 3–9.

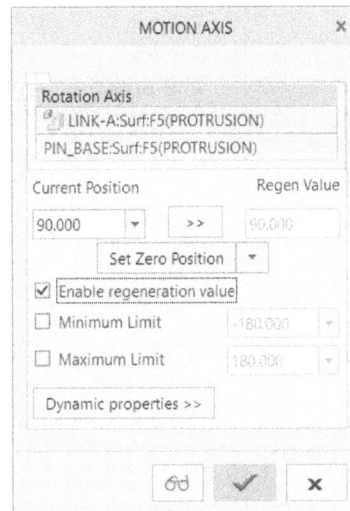

Figure 3–9

Setting the Minimum and Maximum Limits

You can specify the range of motion for the created or redefined joint. Limits can be applied to a translational or rotational joint axis.

How To: Set the Limits

1. Check the boxes to enable the minimum and maximum values.
2. Enter the lower limit value in the *Minimum Limit* field.

3. Enter the upper limit value in the *Maximum Limit* field as shown in Figure 3–10.

Figure 3–10

The specified limits should be examined using the Drag function to ensure that they do not produce interference.

Practice 3a	**Joint Axis Settings**

Practice Objective

- Define joint axis settings to limit motion.

Once the components have been constrained using mechanism connections, the available degrees of freedom might still permit movement that interferes or separates the components from other components. Joint axis settings enable you to create a mechanism assembly that is limited in its available motion to more accurately simulate a real manufactured product.

In this practice, you will investigate the motion that is permitted by each connection type. For each assembly you will apply joint axis settings to limit the range of motion of the components.

Task 1 - Open the slider assembly and drag the component.

1. Set the working directory to the *Joint_Axis_Settings* folder.

2. Open **slider_3.asm**.

3. Set the model display as follows:

    - ⅍ *(Datum Display Filters)*: All Off

    - ⅓ *(Spin Center)*: Off

    - ▢ *(Display Style)*: ▢ (Shading With Edges)

4. Select the *Applications* tab and click ⚙ (Mechanism) to enable Mechanism mode. A slider icon displays on the model, indicating the type of component connection.

5. Click 👆 (Drag Components) to activate the Drag function. The Drag dialog box opens and a green coordinate system displays at the default coordinate system. By default, ✋ (Point Drag) is set as the drag selection.

6. Select **shock2.prt** (the smaller diameter part) and drag the cursor around the display area. The components maintain their axis alignment with each other. Note that the components can intersect or separate in certain positions.

7. Press the middle mouse button to abort the drag action. The system restores the assembly to its original position.

8. Expand the *Shapshots* area and *Advanced Drag Options* area in the Drag dialog box and click ⌐⋮ᵡ (Translation In X).

9. Select **shock-2.prt** and drag the cursor around the display area. The component does not translate in the X-direction because the slider constraint removes this DOF with the axis alignment.

10. Press the middle mouse button to abort the drag action.

11. Click ⟲ᶻ (Rotation About Z). Select **shock-2.prt** and drag the cursor around the display area. The component does not rotate about the Z-axis because the slider constraint removes this DOF with the rotation constraint.

12. Press the middle mouse button to abort the drag action.

13. Click **Close** to close the Drag dialog box.

Task 2 - Specify the joint axis settings to prohibit separation and interference.

Design Considerations

In Task 1, the **shock-2** component was moved in the assembly based on the joint connection constraints. In some positions, it separated from the assembly and in others it interfered. In this task, you will use **Motion Axis** settings to confine the extent of movement to prevent separation and interference from occurring.

1. Click the motion axis of the slider connection on the model and select 🖌 (Edit Definition) in the mini toolbar, as shown in Figure 3–11.

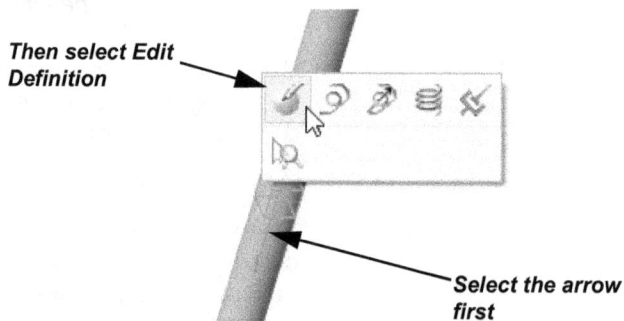

Then select Edit Definition

Select the arrow first

Figure 3–11

The MOTION AXIS dialog box opens as shown in Figure 3–12.

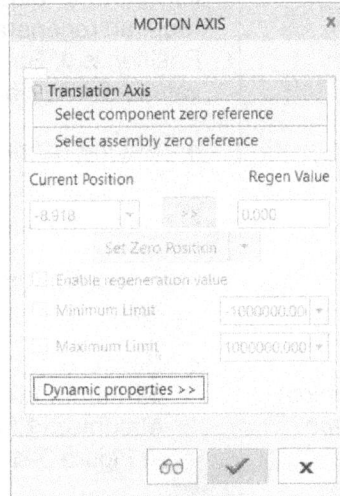

Figure 3–12

2. References must be selected to specify a zero position or a point of known value. In the Model Tree, select datum plane **FRONT** on **shock-2** and datum plane **FRONT** on **shock-1**. When these two planes are aligned, the model is at its zero position.

3. Enter **0** in the *Current Position* field and press <Enter>. The model moves to the zero position. The model should display as shown in Figure 3–13.

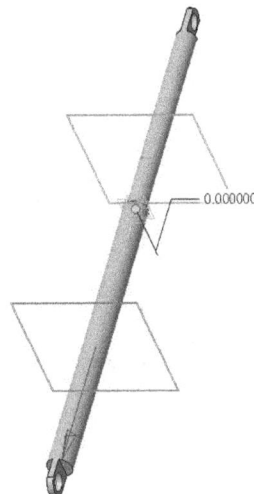

Figure 3–13

Design Considerations

If the Regeneration Value and Limits are to be defined for the Motion Axis, that may require the Current Position to be changed if its current value is outside the required limits or not the required regeneration value. In this case, the original Current Position is **0**. Before assigning the limits and regeneration values, this will be changed to **1**.

4. Set the *Current Position* to **1**, press <Enter>, and click

    >> (Set Regeneration Value) to specify a position that should be assigned after regeneration.

5. Select **Enable regeneration value** in the Motion Axis dialog box.

Before you enter the minimum and maximum values, verify that the current component position lies between these two values.

6. Because the travel of **shock-2.prt** should be limited, select **Minimum Limit** and set the *Minimum Value* to **1**. Select **Maximum Limit** and set the *Maximum Value* to **9**, as shown in Figure 3–14.

Figure 3–14

7. Click ✓ (OK).

Task 3 - Test the joint axis settings.

1. Click 👆 (Drag Components).

2. Select **shock-2.prt** and drag it to a new position. The component no longer disconnects from the cylinder and does not intersect.

3. While dragging, select a new position for the part by selecting an area about halfway through the range of motion with the left mouse button. The component is now positioned in this location, as shown in Figure 3–15.

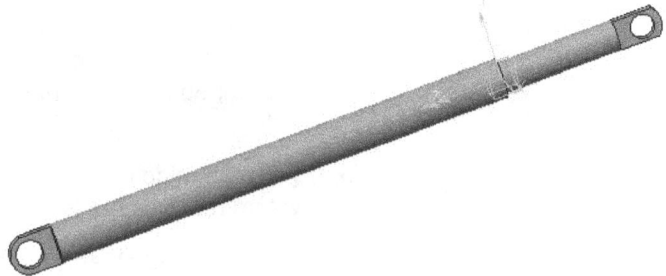

Figure 3–15

4. Click **Close** in the Drag dialog box. The component's selected drag position is maintained.

5. Regenerate the model. The component returns to its lower translation limit (fully extended) after regeneration, as shown in Figure 3–16. This is because you set the Regeneration value to 1 ensuring that the model always returns to this location, regardless of the drag location after it is regenerated.

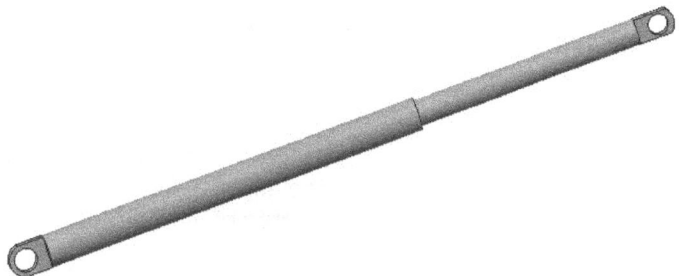

Figure 3–16

6. Save the model and erase it from memory.

Task 4 - Open the Cylinder assembly and drag the component.

1. Open **cylinder_3.asm**.

2. Select the *Applications* tab and click (Mechanism) to enable Mechanism mode. The **Cylinder Connection** icon is now displayed on the model.

3. Click (Drag Components) to activate the drag function. An orange coordinate system displays where the default coordinate system is located. **Point Drag** is the default selection.

4. Select **handle.prt**. Drag the cursor around the display area. The handle component can translate and rotate about the constrained axis. The handle can also be separate from the shaft.

5. Press the middle mouse button to abort the drag action. The system restores the assembly to its original position.

6. Investigate the other advanced icons to control both translational and rotational movement along the Z-axis independently.

7. When finished, click **Close**.

Task 5 - Specify joint axis settings to restrict translation.

Design Considerations

Alternatively, you can click the TRANSLATION AXIS in the Model Tree and select (Edit Definition).

A cylinder connection constraint has two degrees of freedom. For each degree of freedom, a motion axis setting can be specified to further constrain its extent of motion.

1. Hover the cursor over the arrow icon on the model in the main window. Right-click and select (Pick From List). In the Pick From List dialog box, select the translation axis (**connection_1.first_ trans_axis**) and select **OK**.

2. Once selected, right-click and select (Edit Definition) in the mini toolbar. The MOTION AXIS dialog box opens for this degree of freedom.

3. To specify the references to use for the initial known position, select the end surface of the shaft and the end surface of the handle, as shown in Figure 3–17.

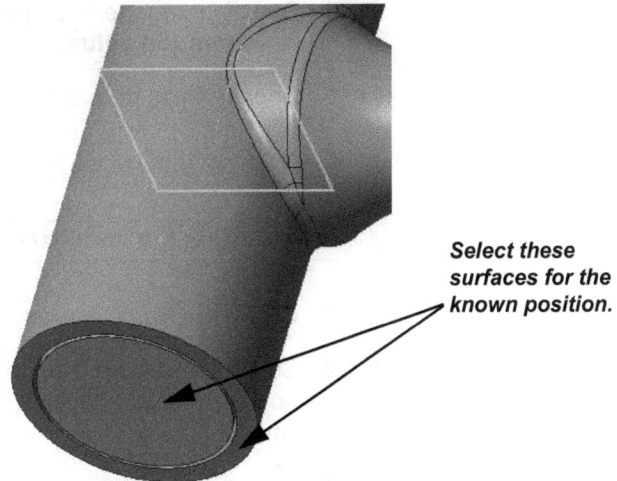

Select these surfaces for the known position.

Figure 3–17

4. Enter **0** in the *Current Position* field and press <Enter>. The model moves to the zero position.

5. Click ▸▸ (Set Regeneration Value) to specify a position that should be assigned after regeneration.

6. Select **Enable regeneration value** in the Motion Axis dialog box.

Before you enter minimum and maximum values, verify that the current component position lies between these two values.

7. The arrow on the **Cylinder** icon indicates the positive direction. Select **Minimum Limit** and set the *Minimum Value* to **-6**. Select **Maximum Limit** and set the *Maximum Value* to **0**.

8. Click ✔ (OK) to finish this joint for the first degree of freedom.

Task 6 - Specify joint axis settings to restrict rotation.

1. Hover the cursor over the cylinder icon on the model in the main window. Right-click and select 🔲 (Pick From List) to select the axis (**connection_1.first_rot_axis**).

2. Once selected, right-click and select 🖌 (Edit Definition). The MOTION AXIS dialog box opens for this degree of freedom.

3. Select datum plane **TOP** in both components as the references for constraining the rotational degree of freedom.

4. Specify a regeneration position of **45** and select **Enable regeneration value**.

5. Specify limits from **0** to **180**.

6. Click ✔ (OK) to complete the joint axis setting.

Task 7 - Test the joint axis settings.

1. Click ✍ (Drag Components).

2. Select **handle.prt** and drag it in its defined settings. The part no longer disconnects from the shaft and its rotation is limited.

3. Select a new position for the part by selecting an area about halfway in the range of motion with the left mouse button, as shown in Figure 3–18.

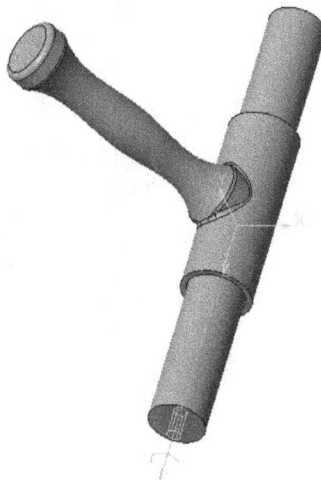

Figure 3–18

4. Click **Close**. The part position is maintained as specified in the Drag dialog box.Regenerate the model. The part returns to the positions you specified in the *Regen Value* tabs for both joint axis constraints.

5. Save the model and erase it from memory.

Task 8 - Open the Planar assembly and drag the component.

1. Open **planar_3.asm**.

2. Select the *Applications* tab and click 🛠 (Mechanism) to enable Mechanism mode. The planar icon displays on the model.

3. Click 👋 (Drag Components). A coordinate system displays at the center of the ice surface.

4. Drag the puck to a new position on the ice surface and press the left mouse button to accept the position.

5. Click ⬨ (Rotation About Y) in the *Advanced Drag Options* area in the dialog box.

6. Note that the coordinate system the puck rotates about displays in orange. Select the puck and drag it to a new position to investigate the motion. Press the middle mouse button to cancel the movement.

7. Click 🗺 (Select Coordinate System). Select the puck. This enables you to change the coordinate system that will be used to rotate about.

8. Click ⬨ (Rotation About Y) and select the puck. The puck rotates about the newly selected coordinate system.

9. Click **Close**.

10. Save the model and erase it from memory.

Design Considerations

Motion axis settings can also be placed on planar connections. Note that three degrees of freedom might mean three separate joint axis settings.

Task 9 - Open the Ball assembly and drag the component.

1. Open **ball_3.asm**.

2. Select the *Applications* tab and click 🛠 (Mechanism) to enable Mechanism mode. The ball icon displays on the model.

3. Click 👋 (Drag Components). A coordinate system displays on the model.

4. Select **ball1.prt** and drag it through the degrees of freedom.

5. Experiment with ⊕ (Rotation About X), ⊕ (Rotation About Y), and ⊗ (Rotation About Z) in the *Advanced Drag Options* area.

6. Click **Close**.

7. Save the assembly and erase it from memory.

Task 10 - Open the Bearing assembly and drag the component.

---

1. Open **bearing_3.asm**.

2. Select the *Applications* tab and click ⚙ (Mechanism) to enable Mechanism mode. The **Bearing** icon displays on the model.

3. Click ✋ (Drag Components).

4. Select **ball1.prt** and drag it through the degrees of freedom.

5. Experiment with ⌐ (Translation In Z), ⊕ (Rotation About X), ⊕ (Rotation About Y), and ⊗ (Rotation About Z) in the *Advanced Drag Options* area.

6. Click **Close**.

7. Assign a motion axis setting for the translational degree of freedom in the bearing connection. Use datum plane **ASM_FRONT** as the reference (only one reference is required) and set the *Minimum Limit* to **-2.5** and *Maximum Limit* to **2.5**.

8. Save the assembly and erase it from memory.

Practice 3b

Snapshots

Practice Objective

- Define snapshots for a mechanism.

Snapshots enable you to save specific mechanism positions for future use. You can use them to set your mechanisms into required positions quickly and easily. In this practice, you will investigate the range of motion for the four-bar linkage and create snapshots of the mechanism throughout this range.

Task 1 - Open the pin assembly and position the components using the Drag option.

1. Set the working directory to the *Snapshots* folder.

2. Open **pin_3.asm**.

3. Set the model display as follows:

   - ⋆⁄⋏ *(Datum Display Filters)*: All Off

   - ⊱ *(Spin Center)*: Off

   - ⬚ *(Display Style)*: ⬚ (Shading With Edges)

4. Activate the Mechanism mode.

5. Click ✋ (Drag Components).

6. In the Drag dialog box, click 📷 (Take Snapshot). A snapshot of the current configuration is created and saved. You can modify the snapshot name in the *Current Snapshot* field and press <Enter> to save this change.

7. Select **LINK-A**. Drag the link throughout the range of motion. The other links move while maintaining the connections.

8. Select **LINK-B**. Drag the link throughout the range of motion. The drag motion is not as smooth as it is with the input link.

9. Select **LINK-C**. Drag it in one direction to get the position shown in Figure 3–19. The mechanism stops. Based on the current constraints, **LINK-C** cannot rotate 360° while keeping the assembly connected.

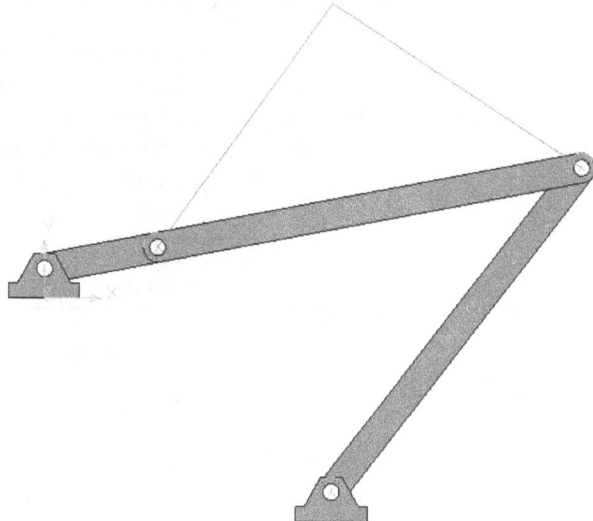

Figure 3–19

10. Select the previously saved snapshot and click 𝒪𝒅 (Display Snapshot) to retrieve it. The assembly reverts back to its saved snapshot state.

11. Drag the model to other positions of interest and create additional snapshots. Note that you can modify a snapshot's name.

12. Close the drag dialog box.

Task 2 - (Optional) Assign the motion axis settings for the link A.

---

1. If time permits, configure the motion axis settings for the rotation axis of the pin connection on LINKA.

2. Save the assembly and erase it from memory.

Practice 3c | Project - Engine Assembly

Practice Objectives

- Drag components.
- Set motion axis settings.
- Create Snapshots.

In this practice, you will apply your knowledge of dragging to the more complex engine mechanism. You will drag the components to mimic the function of the engine. In addition, you will set the motion axis settings and take snapshots of a specified drag configuration.

Task 1 - Open the engine assembly and move the components using the Drag option.

1. Set the working directory to the *MDX_Engine_II* folder.

2. Open **engine_3.asm**.

3. Set the model display as follows:

    - ✗ (Datum Display Filters): All Off

    - ⤳ (Spin Center): Off

    - ◻ (Display Style): ▱ (Shading With Edges)

4. Activate Mechanism mode.

5. Click ✌ (Drag Components).

6. Select a point on the crankshaft and drag it to simulate the engine turning, as shown in Figure 3–20. Press the middle mouse button to cancel the drag operation and return the model to its previous position.

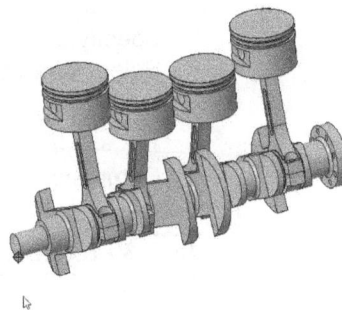

Figure 3–20

7. Select a point on any of the **piston_head** components and try and drag it. It cannot be dragged using the cursor.

8. Click **Close** to close the Drag dialog box.

Task 2 - Apply a motion axis setting.

1. Select the **Pin Connection** icon used to assemble the crankshaft and select (Edit Definition) in the mini toolbar, as shown in Figure 3–21.

Figure 3–21

2. Specify the Zero References by selecting datum plane **TOP** in the crankshaft and datum plane **ASM_TOP** in the assembly. Use the Model Tree to select the references.

3. Specify a regeneration position and enter **0** as the value. Select **Enable regeneration value**.

4. Do not specify any limits.

5. Complete the motion axis settings.

Task 3 - Explore additional Drag options.

1. Click (Drag Components).

2. Select the *Constraints* tab in the Drag dialog box.

3. Click ⬚ (Enable/Disable Connections).

4. Select the pin connection icon for the first piston head to the first connecting rod, as shown in Figure 3–22.

Figure 3–22

5. Press <Ctrl> and select the first connecting rod connection to the crankshaft as shown in Figure 3–23.

Figure 3–23

6. Press the middle mouse button to accept the selection.

7. Both of these constraints are now disabled in the *Constraints* area in the dialog box. Select the *Snapshots* tab and click ⬚ (Select Coordinate System). This enables you to assign a new coordinate system.

8. Select the first **piston_head** component. This component's connection was disabled in the Step 5.

9. Click ⌊ᵧ (Translation In Y) and select the piston. Drag the piston away from the connecting rod as shown in Figure 3–24.

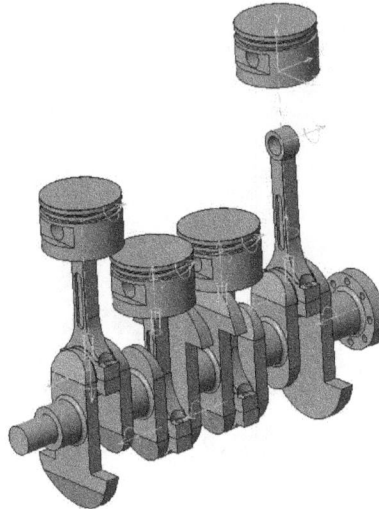

Figure 3–24

10. Select the connecting rod and drag it to the position shown in Figure 3–25.

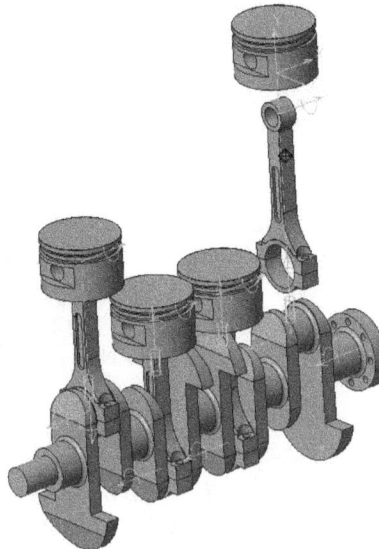

Figure 3–25

11. Click 📷 (Take Snapshot) to take a snapshot of the current configuration. Enter **disabled1** in the *Current Snapshot* field as its name and press <Enter>.

12. Click 👆 (Point Drag) and rotate the crankshaft.

13. Press the middle mouse button to stop dragging. With these connections temporarily disabled, the two parts become disconnected from the assembly and they move freely.

14. Select **Close** and click ⮀ (Regenerate) from the Quick Access toolbar. The connections are now restored.

15. Click 👆 (Drag Components) and double-click on the **disabled1** snapshot that was taken earlier. The connections are disabled again.

16. Select **Close** and regenerate the model.

17. Save the model and erase it from memory.

Practice 3d

Project - Hydraulic Boom Assembly

Practice Objective

- Create settings for joint axes.

The Hydraulic Boom assembly gives you an opportunity to practice specifying joint axes settings in a complex assembly. In this practice, you will create settings for the four joint axes of interest. Snapshots of important positions are also created.

Task 1 - Open the hydraulic boom assembly and move the components using the Drag option.

1. Set the working directory to *MDX_Boom_II* folder.

2. Open **hydraulic_boom_3.asm**.

3. Set the model display as follows:

   - ⅍ *(Datum Display Filters)*: All Off

   - ⤸ *(Spin Center)*: Off

   - ▱ *(Display Style)*: ▱ (Shading With Edges)

4. Activate Mechanism mode.

5. Open the Drag dialog box.

6. Select a point on the **pivot-arm** part and drag it throughout its range of motion, as shown in Figure 3–26. Note that it can intersect the base part. Cancel the movement.

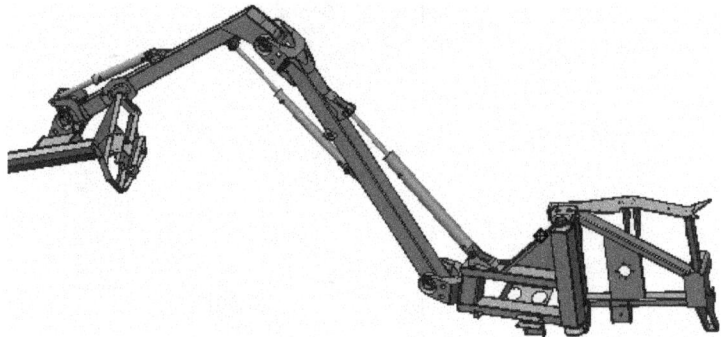

Figure 3–26

7. Select a point on the **boom2** part and drag it throughout its range of motion, as shown in Figure 3–27. The movement of the **boom2** part can force other components to interfere with each other. Cancel the movement.

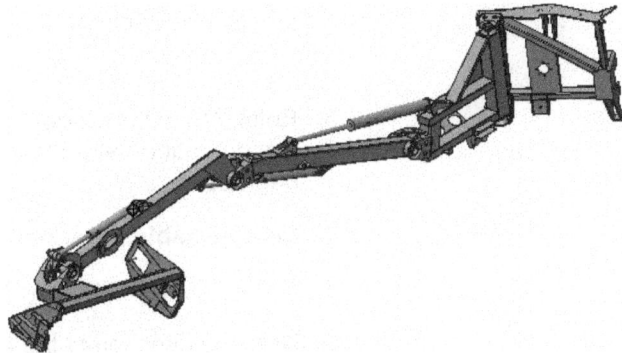

Figure 3–27

8. Select **Close**.

Task 2 - Apply motion axis settings to the pivot-arm part.

1. Select the pin axis for the pivot-arm and select 🥄 (Edit Definition) in the mini toolbar to configure the motion axis settings, as shown in Figure 3–28.

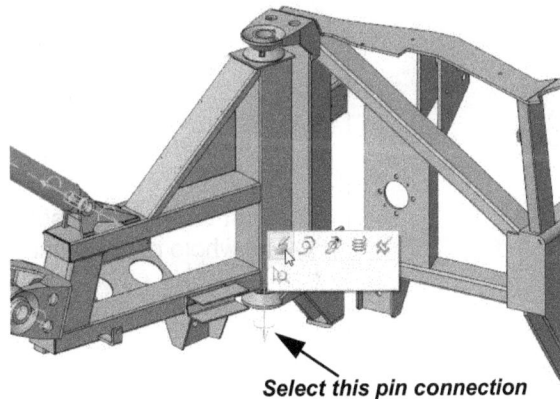

Select this pin connection

Figure 3–28

2. Select datum plane **ZERO_REF** in the **pivot-arm** part and datum plane **ZERO_REF_ROT** in the **base** part as the zero references. (To select those references in the Model Tree, the pivot-arm part will be at the bottom of the tree and the base part will be the first component at the top of the tree. In both models the datum to be selected is the last feature in the part.)

3. Enter **175** in the *Current Position* field and select ≫ (Set Regeneration Value) to set the regeneration position to **175** degrees.

4. Select **Enable regeneration value**.

5. Set the *Current Position* angle to **135**. Press <Enter>.

6. Note the direction of the arrow for the **Pin** icon and the current position of your pivot-arm. Specify limits from **0** to **175**.

7. Click ✔ (OK). The model displays as shown in Figure 3–29.

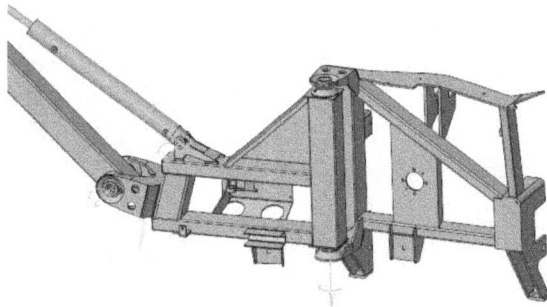

Figure 3–29

8. Test the joint axis settings by dragging the pivot-arm through its whole range of motion.

Task 3 - Apply joint axis settings to the piston1 part.

1. Use Pick From List to select the cylinder translation axis for **piston1** and select Edit Definition to activate the motion axis settings as shown in Figure 3–30.

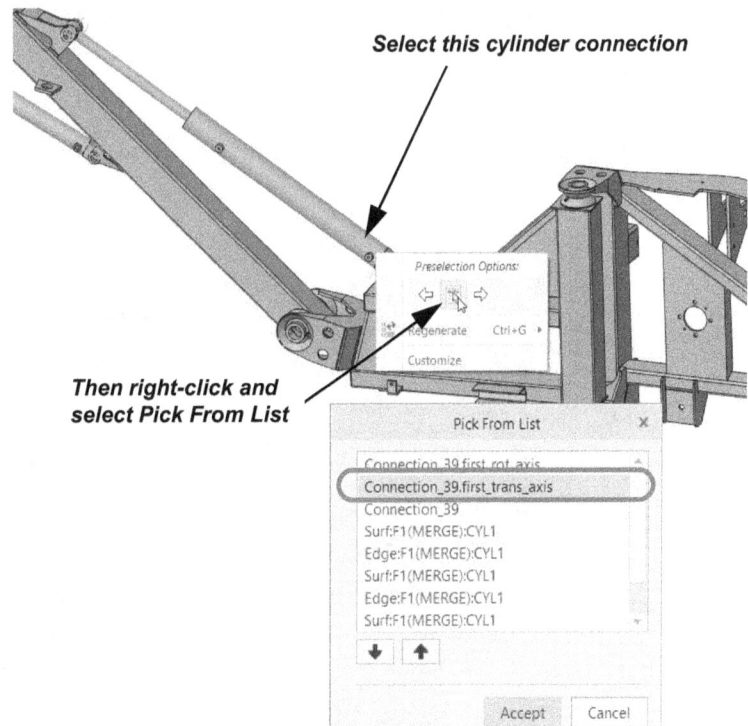

Select this cylinder connection

Then right-click and select Pick From List

Figure 3–30

2. Specify the references as the datum plane **ZERO_REF** in both the **piston1** and the **cyl1** parts. The current position of the piston is in the negative direction.

3. Set the regeneration position to **-699**. Note that you might encounter difficulties if you set regeneration position to the value specified in minimum or maximum limit. Enable the Regeneration Value.

4. Enable and set the Minimum Limit to **-700** and the Maximum Limit to **-75**, as shown in Figure 3–31.

Figure 3–31

5. Click ✓ (OK). The model should display as shown in Figure 3–32.

Figure 3–32

6. Test the joint axis settings by dragging the **piston1** component through its entire range of motion.

Task 4 - Apply joint axis settings to the piston2 part.

1. Select the cylinder translation axis for **piston2** and activate the motion axis settings. The translation arrow (not the curved rotation arrow) must be selected. You will either need to use Pick From List or right-click until just the straight translation arrow highlights.

2. Specify the references as the datum plane **ZERO_REF** in both the **piston2** and the **cycl2** parts.

3. Set the regeneration position to **-574**. Note that you might encounter difficulties if you set the regeneration position to the value specified in minimum or maximum limit.

4. The current position of the piston is in the negative direction. Set the limits of translation from **-575** to **-50**.

5. Click ✔ (OK). The model should display as shown in Figure 3–33.

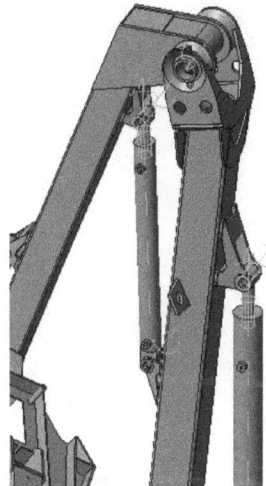

Figure 3–33

6. Test the joint axis settings by dragging the **piston2** component through its entire range of motion.

Task 5 - Apply joint axis settings to the piston3 part.

1. Select the cylinder translation axis for piston3 and activate the motion axis settings. The translation arrow (not the rotation arrow) must be selected.

2. Specify the references as the datum plane **ZERO_REF** in the **piston3** part and the **cycl3** part.

3. Set the regeneration position to **-449**. Note that you might encounter difficulties if you set the regeneration position to the value specified in minimum or maximum limit.

4. The current position of the piston is in the negative direction. Set the limits of translation from **-450** to **-125**.

5. Click ✔ (OK). The model should display as shown in Figure 3–34.

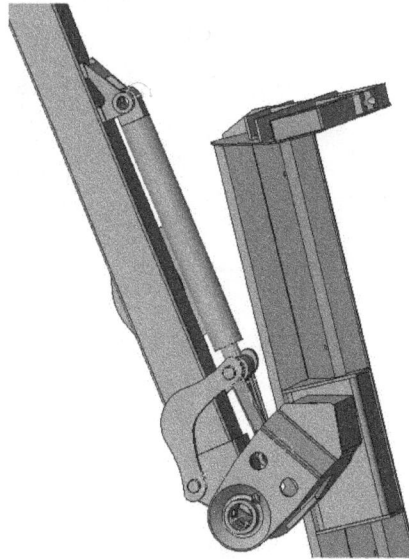

Figure 3–34

6. Test the joint axis settings by dragging the **piston3** component through its entire range of motion.

Task 6 - Create a snapshot of a component position.

1. Switch to the saved **FRONT** view.

2. Click 👆 (Drag Components) and create a snapshot. Set the snapshot Name in the *Current Snapshot* field to **3_1**.

3. Select the *Constraints* tab and click 🔒 (Body-Body Lock).

4. Select **base.prt** in the Model Tree as the reference part to lock bodies to.

5. Press and hold <Ctrl> and select **pivot-arm**, **boom1**, **cyl1**, and **piston1** in the Model Tree. These define the parts that will be locked.

6. Press the middle mouse button to accept the selections. Once locked, these parts will not move during the drag operation.

7. Select the *Snapshots* tab and click 🖐 (Point Drag).

8. Select a point on **boom2** and drag it to the upper limit in the range of motion. Finalize the position with the left mouse button.

9. Create a snapshot of this configuration. Set the Name of the snapshot to **3_2**. The model should display similar to that shown in Figure 3–35.

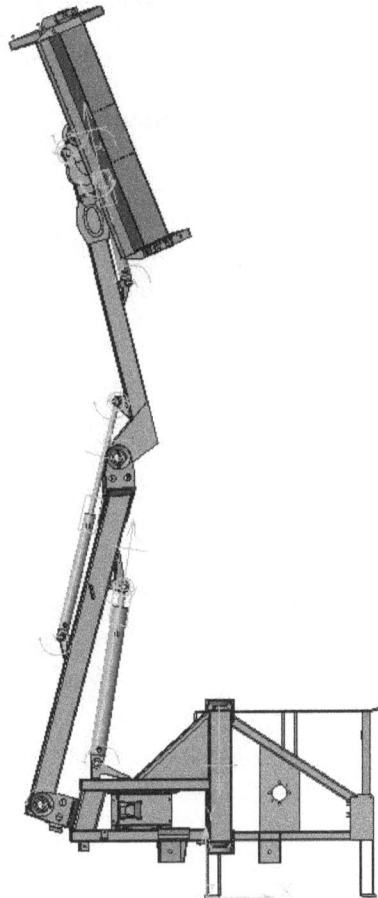

Figure 3–35

Task 7 - Create additional snapshots.

1. Select the *Constraints* tab and delete the previous body lock by clicking ✕ (Delete Constraints).

2. Create a new body lock constraint between the base and the pivot-arm.

3. Select the *Snapshots* tab and select a point on **boom1**.

4. Drag **boom1** to fully extend the piston1-cyl1 hydraulic cylinder. Accept the position with the left mouse button.

5. Create a snapshot of this configuration. Set the snapshot *Name* to **3_3**.

6. Select the *Constraints* tab and delete the previous body lock by clicking ✕ (Delete Constraints).

7. Create a new body lock constraint between the base and **pivot-arm**, **boom1**, **boom2**, **cyl1**, **piston1**, **cyl2**, and **piston2**.

8. Select the *Snapshots* tab and select a point on **bucket-1**.

9. Drag the bucket to rotate approximately 180° to the upper limit of the joint axis set on **piston3**. Accept the position with the left mouse button.

10. Create a snapshot of this configuration. Set the snapshot *Name* to **3_4**.

11. Save the assembly and erase from memory.

All constraints are saved with snapshots and all constraints are removed when the Drag dialog box is not active.

Practice 3e

(Optional) Project - Geneva Mechanism

Practice Objective

- Apply motion axis setting to the geneva mechanism.

In this practice, you will set the initial rotation angle of both the gm-driver and gm-slot-wheel components using Motion Axis settings. It is important the two components do not interfere with each other at the initial position. The final assembly displays as shown in Figure 3–36.

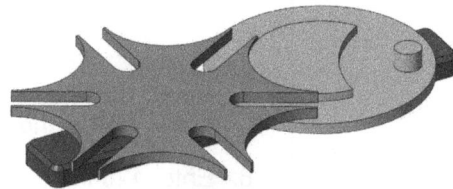

Figure 3–36

Task 1 - Open an existing assembly and assign Motion Axis settings.

1. Set the working directory to the *Geneva_II* folder.

2. Open **geneva_mechanism.asm**.

3. Set the model display as follows:

    - `⌖` *(Datum Display Filters)*: `⁄⊙` (Axis Display)

    - *Datum Tag Display:* `⊞` (Plane Tag Display), `⌁` (Axis Tag Display), `⊞` (Csys Tag Display)

    - `⤡` *(Spin Center)*: Off

    - `◫` *(Display Style)*: `⬚` (Shading With Edges)

    Motion Axis settings can be configured during the initial assembly of the components, or after the components have assembled using the Motion Axis settings in the Mechanism application. We'll look at appalling the Motion Axis settings during the assembly process first.

4. Select the **gm-driver** part and click `⬥` (Edit Definition) in the mini toolbar.

5. Display datum planes in the model.

6. In the Placement panel, select Rotation Axis as shown in Figure 3–37.

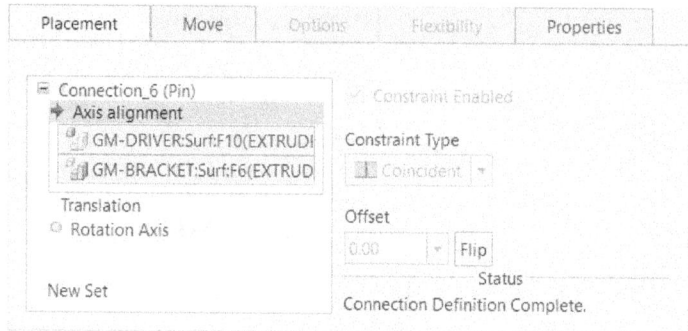

Figure 3–37

7. Select datum plane **RIGHT** in the gm-driver part and datum plane **TOP** in the gm-bracket part.

8. Enter **120** for the Current Position and confirm the position displays as shown in Figure 3–39.

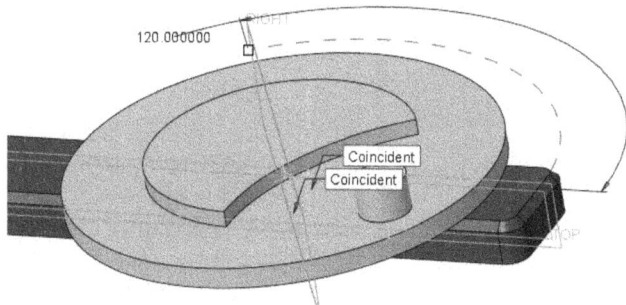

Figure 3–38

9. Select ⟫ (Set Regeneration Value) to set the regeneration position to 120 as shown in Figure 3–39.

Figure 3–39

10. Click **Enable regeneration value** as shown in Figure 3–40.

Figure 3–40

11. Click ✓ (OK).

Next you will configure similar settings for the gm-wheel component. However, instead of applying the settings from the Component Placement tab as we did in the previous steps, we will apply the settings in the Mechanism application.

12. Select the *Applications* tab and click ⚙ (Mechanism) to activate the Mechanism application.

13. Select the Pin joint icon for the connection between the gm-slot-wheel part and the gm-bracket part, as shown in Figure 3–41.

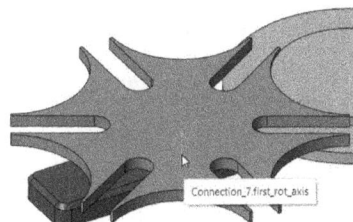

Figure 3–41

14. Click 🖌 (Edit Definition) in the mini toolbar.

15. If required, display datum planes in the model.

16. Select datum plane **RIGHT** in gm-wheel and datum plane **TOP** in gm-bracket.

17. Enter **60** as the Current Position as shown in Figure 3–42.

Figure 3–42

18. Select ➤➤ (Set Regeneration Value) to set the regeneration position to 60.

19. Enable the Regeneration Value.

20. Click ✔ (OK).

21. Save the assembly and erase it from memory.

Chapter Review Questions

1. Snapshots provide a configuration that can be retrieved for reference at any time.

   a. True

   b. False

2. Which of the following options are available in the Drag dialog box? (Select all that apply.)

   a. Define geometric constraints (i.e., Align, Mate, or Orient) to position components in the assembly.

   b. Lock a particular motion axis of a connection.

   c. Lock or unlock components in their current assembly position.

   d. Enable or disable connections that were assigned in the assembly.

3. Which statement below is correct, when a connection is disabled using the Drag dialog box?

   a. You cannot disable a joint.

   b. The setting is saved until the assembly is closed.

   c. The setting is saved with the snapshot.

4. Which option must be set to limit a component's range of motion and obtain realistic results?

   a. Lock Components

   b. Joint Axis Settings

   c. Connections

   d. Arrow Direction

5. The regeneration position and the *Set Zero Position* must be the same value in the Motion Axis dialog box.

   a. True

   b. False

6. A snapshot can be used to define component positions in a drawing.

   a. True

   b. False

7. Snapshots cannot be updated to change the component positions.

   a. True

   b. False

Advanced Connections

Complex motion, such as helical movement and cam motion, can be difficult to simulate using standard connections. MDX provides additional advanced connection types such as: slot, cam, belt, 3D contact, and gear. These connections can be used to simulate complex motion.

Learning Objectives in this Chapter

- Learn to create a slot connection between two components using a point and a curve as references.
- Learn to create a cam connection between surfaces or curves of two components.
- Learn to control the velocity ratio between two joint axes using one of the five types of gear connections.
- Use the belt connection to simulate the rotating motion, connect pulleys together, set the Young's modulus, and set the value for the unstretched belt length.
- Use the tools available to create a new part and define a belt feature.

4.1 Slot Connection

The slot connection is a constraint set up between two components, where a point on one component follows a curve on another component in 3D space. This type of connection is useful for simulating the motion of a corkscrew or drill bit, as shown in Figure 4–1.

Slot connections cannot be transferred into Creo Simulate.

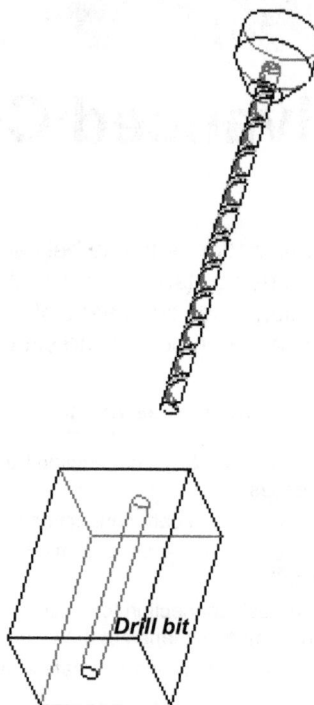

Drill bit

Figure 4–1

Creating a Slot Connection

How To: Create a Slot Connection

1. Select **Slot** in the **Connection Type** menu, in the *Component Placement* dashboard, as shown in Figure 4–2.

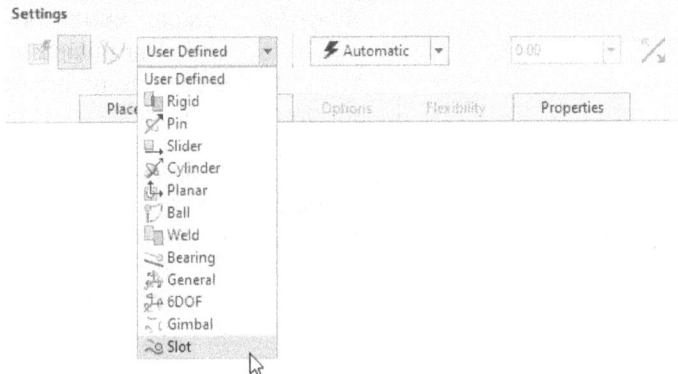

Figure 4–2

2. The Placement panel with the Slot Connection displays as shown in Figure 4–3.

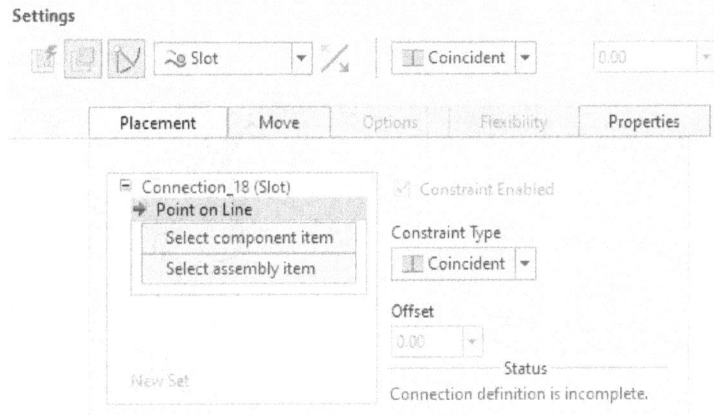

Figure 4–3

3. Enter a name for the new connection in the *Set Name* field.
4. Select a follower point on the assembly. A follower point can be any point or vertex in a component but cannot be an assembly-level point.
5. Select a slot curve in the assembly. A slot curve can be any continuous datum curve or edge on a component other than the follower point.
6. Click ✓ (OK) to complete the connection.

4.2 Cam Connection

The cam connection type is a constraint set up between the surfaces of two components that remain in contact. As an alternative, you can select curves instead of surfaces. If a curve is selected, Creo Parametric automatically forms a surface by extruding the curve to an arbitrary depth. If surfaces or curves are divided, all portions must be selected.

As the profile of one surface changes, the other component is forced to move in a direction normal to the surface. An example of this type of connection is the camshaft/rocker arm assembly of an engine, as shown in Figure 4–4. As the camshaft rotates, the valves move up and down with respect to the rocker's geometry.

Cam connections cannot be transferred into Creo Simulate.

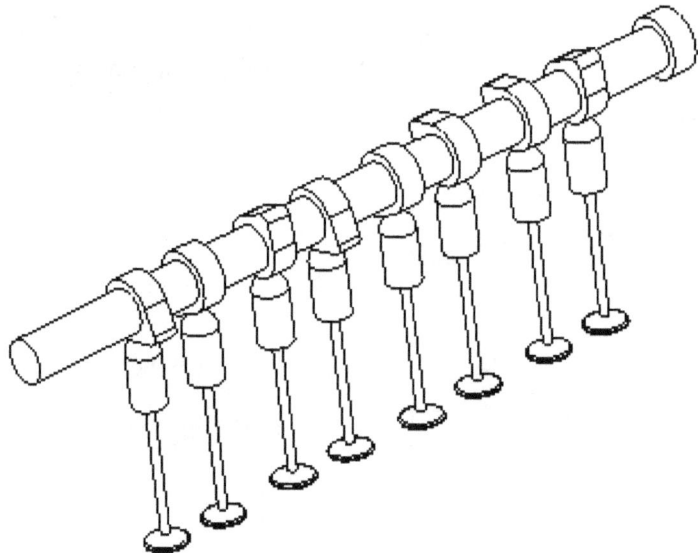

Figure 4–4

Creating a Cam-Follower Connection

How To: Create a Cam-follower Connection

1. In the Connections group of the *Mechanism* tab, click
   🐌 (Cams). The Cam-Follower Connection Definition dialog
   box opens as shown in Figure 4–5.

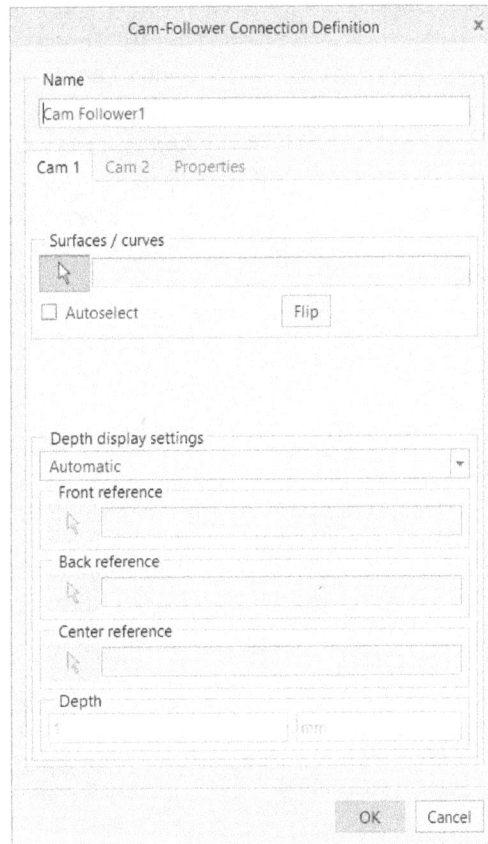

Figure 4–5

2. Enter a name for the new connection in the *Name* field.
3. Select the *Cam1* tab.
4. Click 🔍 (Select) in the *Surfaces/curves* area.
5. Select a curve or surface on one component and press the
   middle mouse button to complete the selection. The selected
   surfaces for the cam-follower connection can only curve in
   one direction. Creo Parametric displays its reference normal
   once selected. Select the **Autoselect** option in the
   Surfaces/curves area to automatically select tangent
   surfaces.
6. If an incorrect assumption is made about curves or surfaces
   that are not part of a volume, click **Flip**.

*Check the Gaussian
curvature of the surface
if you are not sure that
the surface is only
curved in one direction.*

7. Set **Depth Display Settings** to define how much of the surface the cam uses for contact. The contact area displays as a set of green lines.

   - If applicable, accept the default **Automatic** option.
   - Alternatively, you can use one of the following options: **Front & Back**, **Front, Back, & Depth**, or **Center & Depth**. These options enable you to manually specify the contact area. Based on the selected option, you must specify references using ▷ (Select) in the *Depth Display Settings* area and/or enter a Depth value.

8. Select the *Cam2* tab and define a second cam using the procedure described in Steps 5, 6, and 7.
9. Click **OK** to complete the connection.

4.3 Gear Connections

Gear pairs are used to control the velocity ratio between two joint axes. Gear pairs consist of two gear connections. Each gear connection requires two bodies (assembly components) that are connected by a joint connection. The first body (known as the carrier) remains stationary and the second body (known as the gear) moves. The gear pairs in MDX are velocity constraints and are not based on the geometry of the model. This means you can easily specify and change gear ratios without modifying or creating new geometry.

Mechanism Design gear pairs do not transfer to Creo Simulate.

You can create five types of gear pairs.

*   Create a **Generic** gear pair when you want two gears to rotate in the same or opposite directions. For example, you can use this type of gear pair to simulate a spur-spur or worm and wheel gear.

*   Create a **Spur** gear where there are two cylindrical gears with their rotation axis parallel to each other. The edges of the teeth are straight and aligned parallel to the axis of rotation.

*   Create a **Bevel** gear when you have two conical face gears to rotate and the axis are perpendicular.

*   Create a **Worm** gear when you have two cylindrical gears and the axes are perpendicular.

*   Create a **Rack and Pinion** gear pair when you want to convert rotational motion into translational motion.

Figure 4–6 shows an example of spur gears.

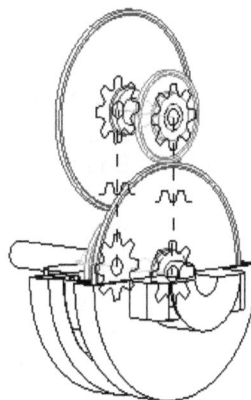

Figure 4–6

Standard Gear Connection

How To: Create a Generic Gear Connection

1. Click 🦷 (Gears). The Gear Connections dialog box opens as shown in Figure 4–7.

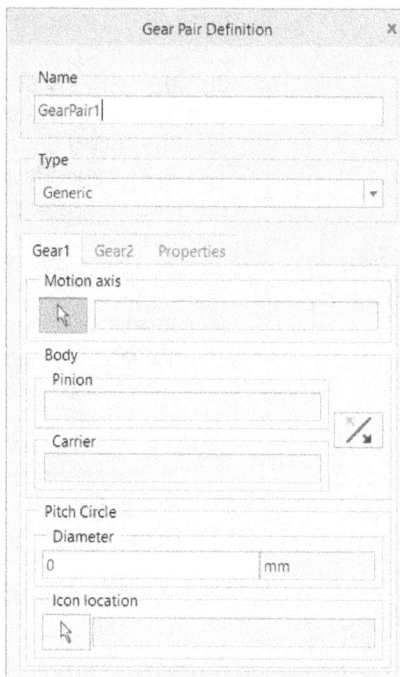

Figure 4–7

2. Enter a name for the new connection in the *Name* field.
3. Accept the **Generic** (default) gear type in the Type drop-down list.
4. Select the *Gear1* tab and click ▷ (Select) in the *Motion Axis* area.
5. Select the rotational joint axis for a pin, cylinder, bearing, or planar joint. Mechanism Design designates the first body in the joint connection as the Carrier and the second body as the Gear. If required, click ⁄ (Flip Gear/Carrier) to switch the body definitions.
6. Enter a value for the diameter of the pitch circle. Mechanism Design displays a circle with the specified diameter, centered around the selected joint axis.
7. Click ▷ (Select) in the *Icon Location* area and select a point or vertex for the offset of the pitch circle. If you press the middle mouse button, the system places the **Gear** icon in a default location.
8. Select the *Gear2* tab and click ▷ (Select) in the *Motion Axis* area.

9. Select a rotational joint axis for a joint. If required, click ⚹ (Flip Rotation Direction) in the *Motion Axis* area to flip the relative rotation direction. You can also click ⚹ (Flip Gear/Carrier) in the *Body* area to switch the body definitions.

10. Enter a value for the diameter of the pitch circle. You can select a new location for the pitch circle.

11. To set a gear ratio, select the *Properties* tab, and select **User Defined** in the drop-down list. Enter real numbers for the pitch circle diameters for **Gear1** and **Gear2**.

12. Click **OK** to complete the connection.

Spur Connection

How To: Create a Spur Connection

1. Click 🦷 (Gears). The Gear Connections dialog box opens.
2. Select the **Spur** gear type in the drop-down list. The Gear Pair Definition dialog box opens as shown in Figure 4–8.

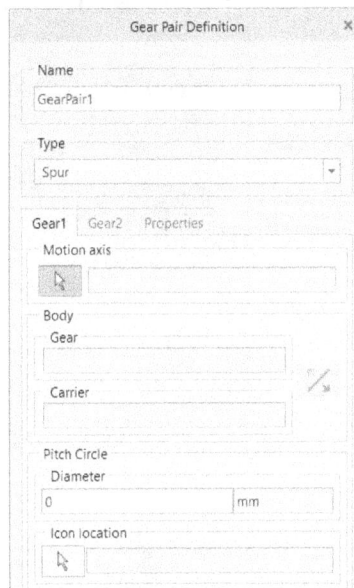

Figure 4–8

3. Enter a name for the new connection in the *Name* field.
4. Select the *Pinion* tab and click ⬚ (Select) in the *Motion Axis* area.
5. Select the rotational joint axis. A double-headed shaded arrow displays, indicating the positive rotation axis. Mechanism Design designates the first body in the joint connection as the Carrier and the second body as the Gear. If required, click ⚹ (Flip Gear/Carrier) to switch the body definitions.

6. Enter a value for the diameter of the pitch circle. Mechanism Design displays a circle with the specified diameter, centered around the selected joint axis.

7. Click ▷ (Select) in the *Icon Location* area and select a point or vertex for the offset of the pitch circle.

8. Select the *Gear2* tab and click ▷ (Select) in the *Motion Axis* area.

9. Select a rotational joint axis for a joint. A shaded arrow displays on the joint, indicating the positive translation direction. If required, click ⚹ (Flip Rotation Direction) in the *Motion Axis* area to flip the relative direction. You can also click ⚹ (Flip Gear/Carrier) in the *Body* area to switch the body definitions.

10. To set a gear ratio, select the *Properties* tab and select **User Defined** in the drop-down list. You can also enter the *Pressure Angle* and *Helix Angle*.

11. Click **OK**.

Bevel Connection

How To: Create a Bevel Connection

1. Click ⚙ (Gears). The Gear Connections dialog box opens.
2. Select the **Bevel** gear type in the drop-down list. The Gear Pair Definition dialog box opens as shown in Figure 4–9.

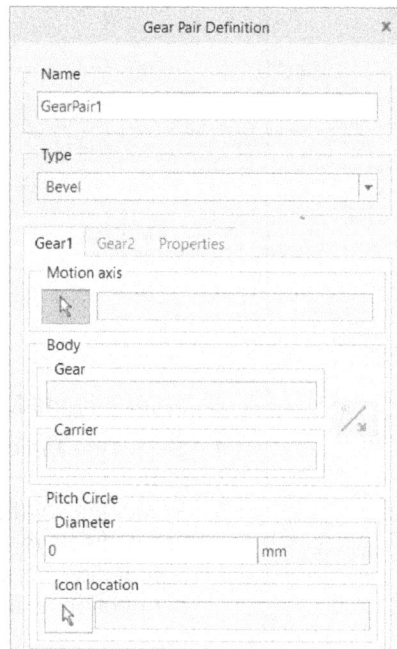

Figure 4–9

3. Enter a name for the new connection in the *Name* field.

4. Select the *Gear1* tab and click ▷ (Select) in the *Motion Axis* area.

5. Select the rotational joint axis. A double-headed shaded arrow displays, indicating the positive rotation axis. Mechanism Design designates the first body in the joint connection as the Carrier and the second body as the Gear. If required, click ⟋ (Flip Gear/Carrier) to switch the body definitions.

6. Enter a value for the diameter of the pitch circle. Mechanism Design displays a circle with the specified diameter, centered around the selected joint axis.

7. Select the *Gear2* tab and click ▷ (Select) in the *Motion Axis* area.

8. Select a rotational joint axis for a joint. A shaded arrow displays on the joint, indicating the positive translation direction. If required, click ⟋ (Flip Rotation Direction) in the *Motion Axis* area to flip the relative direction.

9. To set a gear ratio, select the *Properties* tab and select **User Defined** in the drop-down list. Enter any additional values for the Pressure Angle and Helix Angle.

10. Click **OK**.

Worm Connection

How To: Create a Worm Connection

1. In the Connections group of the *Mechanism* tab, click ⚙ (Gears). The Gear Connections dialog box opens.
2. Select the **Worm** gear type in the drop-down list. The Gear Pair Definition dialog box opens as shown in Figure 4–10.

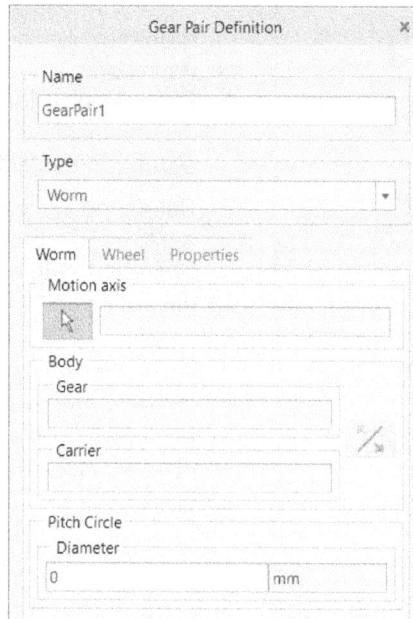

Figure 4–10

3. Enter a name for the new connection in the *Name* field.

4. Select the *Worm* tab and click ⬫ (Select) in the *Motion Axis* area.

5. Select the rotational joint axis. A double-headed shaded arrow displays, indicating the positive rotation axis. Mechanism Design designates the first body in the joint connection as the Carrier and the second body as the Gear. If required, click ⬊ (Flip Gear/Carrier) to switch the body definitions.

6. Enter a value for the diameter of the pitch circle. Mechanism Design displays a circle with the specified diameter, centered around the selected joint axis.

7. Select the *Wheel* tab and click ⬫ (Select) in the *Motion Axis* area.

8. Select a rotational joint axis for a joint. A shaded arrow displays on the joint, indicating the positive translation direction. If required, click ⟋ (Flip Rotation Direction) in the *Motion Axis* area to flip the relative direction. You can also click ⟋ (Flip Gear/Carrier) in the *Body* area to switch the body definitions.

9. To set a gear ratio, select the *Properties* tab and select **User Defined** in the drop-down list. Enter real values for the Worm Spirals and the Wheel Teeth. You can also enter values for the Pressure Angle and Screw Angle.

10. Click **OK**.

Rack & Pinion Connection

How To: Create a Rack & Pinion Connection

1. In the Connections group of the *Mechanism* tab, click ⚙ (Gears). The Gear Connections dialog box opens.

2. Select the **Rack & Pinion** gear type in the drop-down list. The Gear Pair Definition dialog box opens as shown in Figure 4–11.

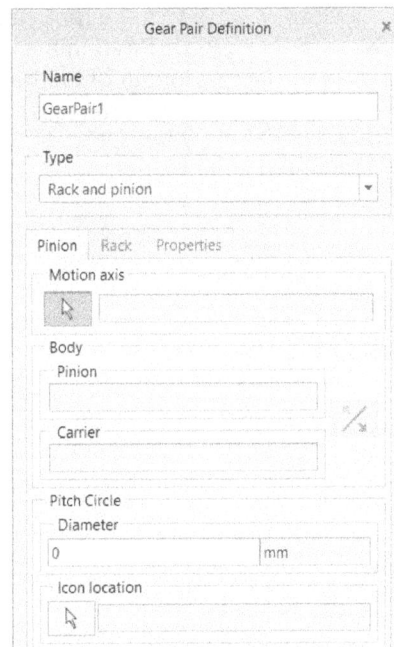

Figure 4–11

3. Enter a name for the new connection in the *Name* field.

4. Select the *Pinion* tab and click ▷ (Select) in the *Motion Axis* area.

5. Select the rotational joint axis for a pin, cylinder, bearing, or planar joint. A double-headed shaded arrow displays, indicating the positive rotation axis. Mechanism Design designates the first body in the joint connection as the Carrier and the second body as the Gear. If required, click ⚞ (Flip Gear/Carrier) to switch the body definitions.

6. Enter a value for the diameter of the pitch circle. Mechanism Design displays a circle with the specified diameter, centered around the selected joint axis.

7. Click ⛏ (Select) in the *Icon Location* area and select a point or vertex for the offset of the pitch circle.

8. Select the *Rack* tab and click ⛏ (Select) in the *Motion Axis* area.

9. Select a translational joint axis for a planar, slider, or cylinder joint. A shaded arrow displays on the joint, indicating the positive translation direction. If required, click ⚞ (Flip Rotation Direction) in the *Motion Axis* area to flip the relative direction. You can also click ⚞ (Flip Gear/Carrier) in the *Body* area to switch the body definitions.

10. To set a rack ratio, select the *Properties* tab and select **User Defined** in the drop-down list. Enter real numbers for the length of the translation of the rack per revolution of the rotational axis.

11. Click **OK**.

4.4 Belt Connections

The Belt feature simulates rotating motion similar to a belt or cable system that connects one pulley to another. The belt connection enables you to connect axes simulating a pulley or belt system. The belt is an assembly feature and can be displayed in both Mechanism and Assembly applications. A part can easily be created from the belt with the correct parameters.

How To: Create a Belt in Mechanism Design

1. In the Connections group of the *Mechanism* tab, click (Belts). The *Belt* dashboard opens as shown in Figure 4–12.

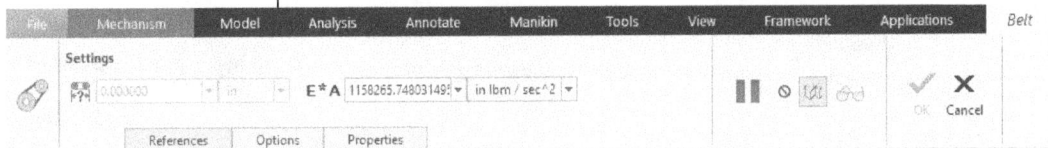

Figure 4–12

2. Press <Ctrl> and select the belt placement references, as shown in Figure 4–13. You can select surfaces, edges, curves, or connections.

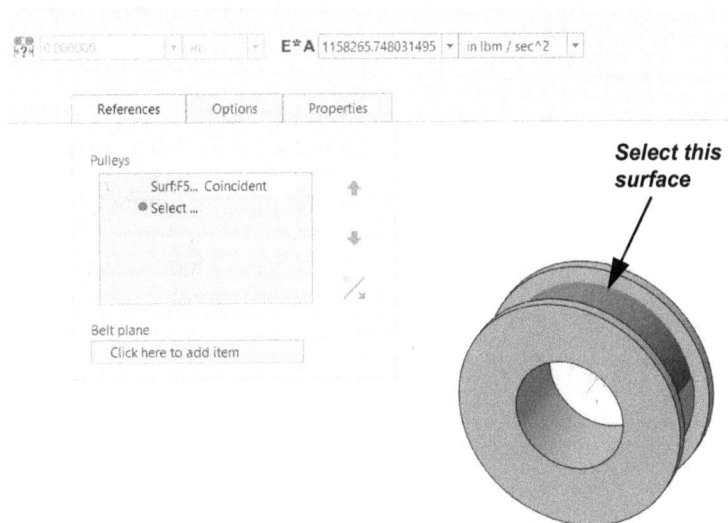

Figure 4–13

3. Flip the belt direction by right-clicking on the hot spot and selecting flip belt direction as shown in Figure 4–14.

Alternatively, you can click ⚒ (Flips Belt Direction) in the reference panel in the Belt dashboard.

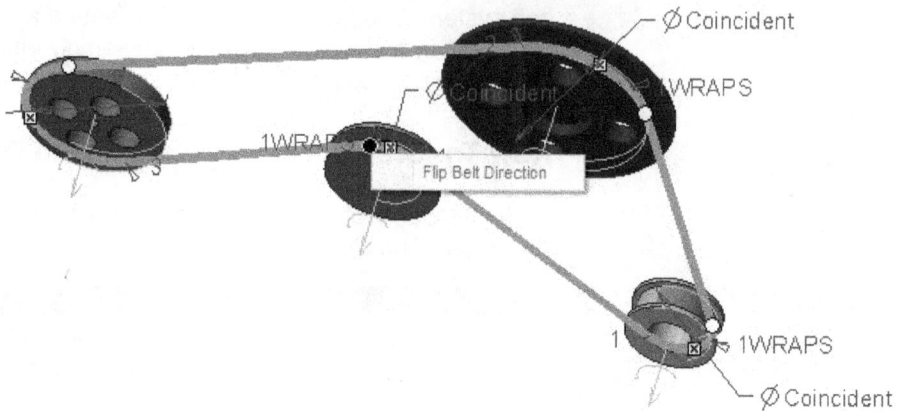

Figure 4–14

4. Click ✓ (OK) to complete the feature.

Some additional options are available in the tab.

• You can enter a value to define Young's modulus multiplied by the area of the belt.

• You can click 🔢 (User Unstretched Belt) to enter a value for the unstretched belt length.

• In the reference panel, you can specify a diameter of the pulley to be independent of the geometry. Select the joint axis in the view window and enter the required value in the reference panel.

Once the belt has been created you can the create a part. Select the belt feature in the Model Tree, right-click and select **Make Part**, as shown in Figure 4–15.

You can also right-click on the Belt connection and select Make part.

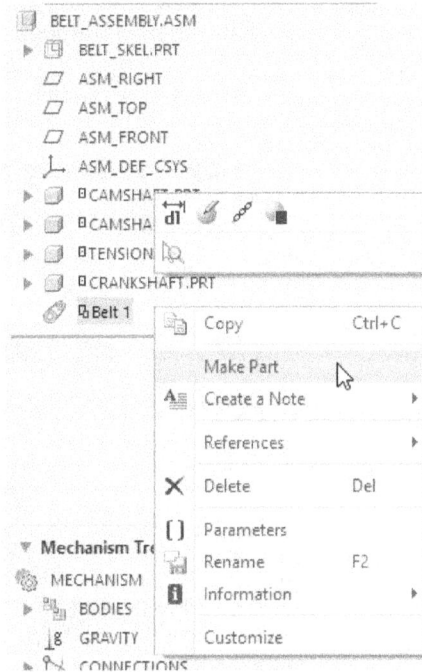

Figure 4–15

4.5 3D Contact Connections

A 3D contact is a connection type that occurs between a single surface or vertex in the first component and one or more surfaces or vertices from the second component. The 3D Contact constrain can be used on planar, cylindrical, and spherical surfaces.

How To: Create a 3D Contact in Mechanism Design

1. In the Connections group of the *Mechanism* tab, click
   (3D Contacts). The *3D Contact* tab opens as shown in Figure 4–16.

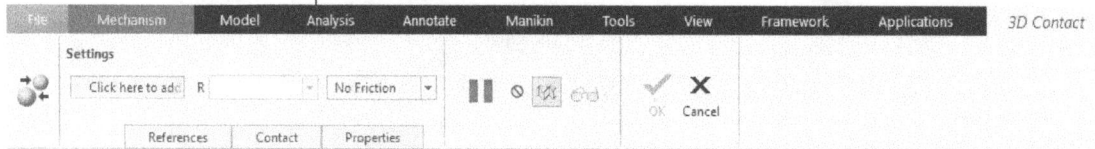

Figure 4–16

2. Select the contact reference on the first model. The reference can be a planar, cylindrical, or spherical surface. A Vertex can also be selected as the reference. When using a vertex you will enter a Vertex Radius and the contact will be with a spherical surface at the specified radius centered on the vertex. The Reference panel is shown in Figure 4–17.

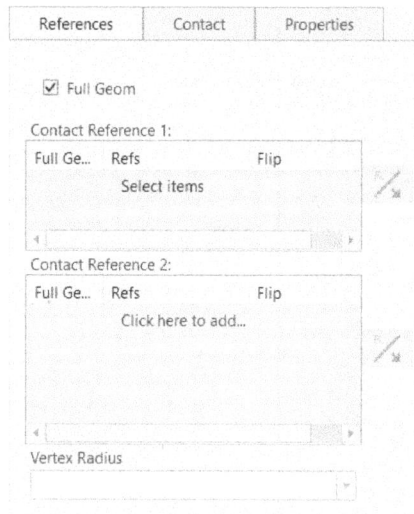

Figure 4–17

If the selected reference is a portion of a cylinder or sphere, you have the option of using the selected portion for the contact reference or the full cylinder or sphere as shown in Figure 4–18.

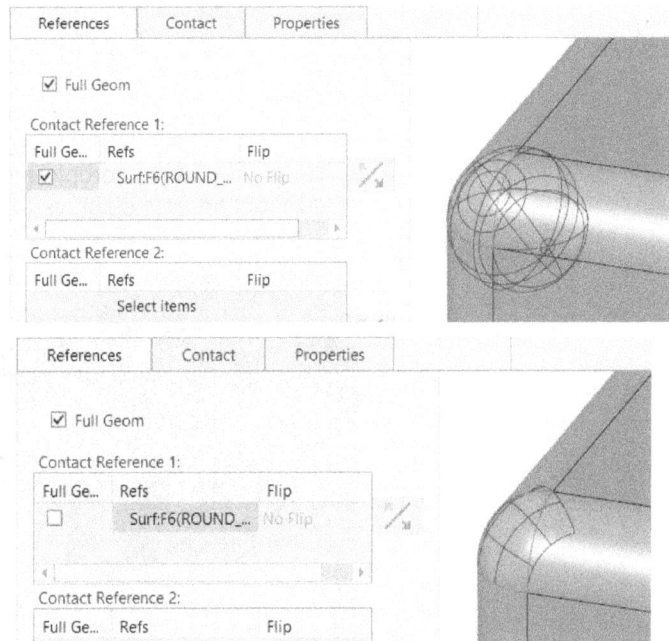

Figure 4–18

3. If a vertex is used, enter a *Vertex Radius* as shown in Figure 4–19.

Figure 4–19

4. Select the Properties panel to enter a name for the 3D Contact, as shown in Figure 4–20.

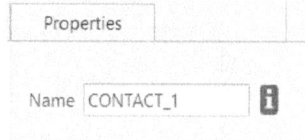

Properties

Name CONTACT_1 ℹ️

Figure 4–20

5. Click ✔️ (OK) to complete the 3D Contact. The 3D Contact connection icon displays as shown in Figure 4–21.

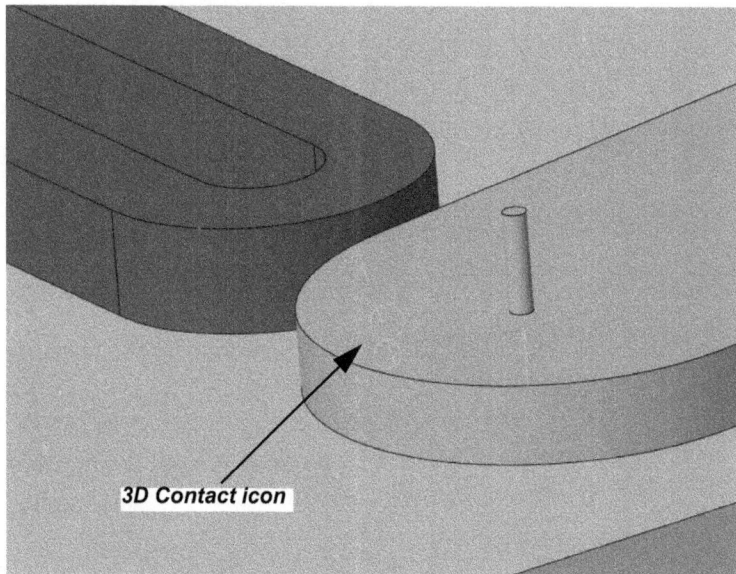

3D Contact icon

Figure 4–21

Practice 4a

Create Slot Connection

Practice Objective

- Create a slot connection

The Slot connection is an advanced connection that enables you to simulate complex motion. It extends the basic motion functionality provided by using the standard assembly connections. In this practice, you will create a simple assembly of a CMM and use the slot connection type to simulate its motion.

Task 1 - Open and add components to a CMM assembly.

1. Set the working directory to the *Create_Slot* folder.

2. Open **measure_machine.asm**.

3. Set the model display as follows:

   - ⅍ *(Datum Display Filters)*: ⁄ₒ (Axis Display)
   - ⅀ *(Spin Center)*: Off
   - ⬜ *(Display Style)*: ⬜ (Shading With Edges)

4. Assemble **carrier.prt** using a cylinder connection. Use the **CL_AXIS** axis in the carrier part and the **A_5** axis in the block part for the axis alignment. If necessary, click ⁄ₓ (Flip Axis constraint) to change the orientation. Click ✍ (Drag) and drag the component to the position shown in Figure 4–22.

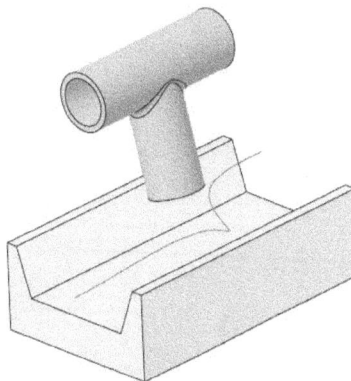

Figure 4–22

5. Assemble **plunger.prt.** Start with a cylinder connection using the **A_8** axis in the carrier part and the **CL_AXIS** axis in the plunger part for the axis alignment references. You may need to flip the constraint to achieve the orientation shown in Figure 4–23.

Note that the plunger may not appear connected to the carrier part. The next step will correct that.

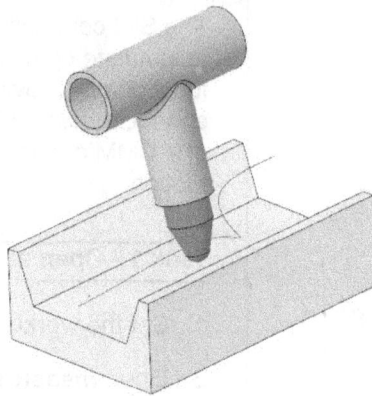

Figure 4–23

6. Select **New Set** in the Placement tab to add a second connection.

7. Click on the second connection in the list and change the second connection type to Slot, as shown in Figure 4–24.

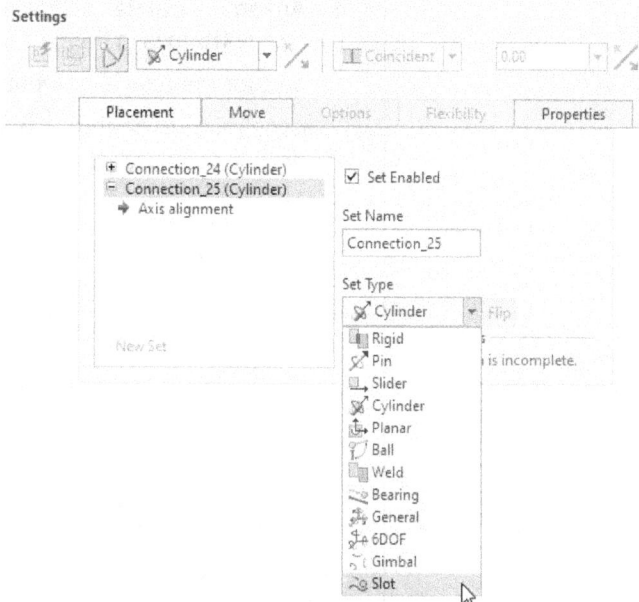

Figure 4–24

8. Select the **TIP** datum point in the plunger part and the blue curve in the base part as the references for the Slot connection.

9. Click ✓ (OK) and, the assembly updates as shown in Figure 4–25.

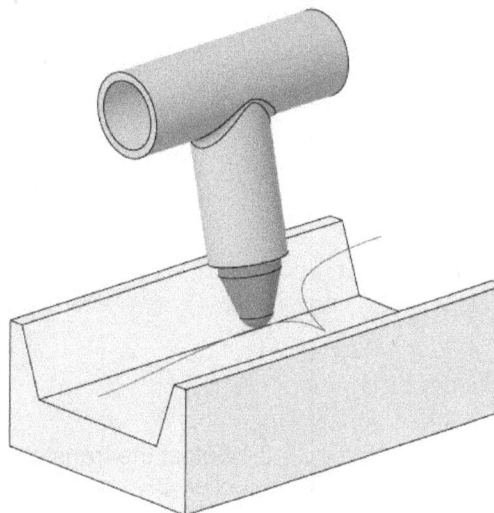

Figure 4–25

10. Click 🖐 (Drag) and drag the carrier part to view the motion. Note that the carrier motion will stop when the tip of the plunger reaches the ends of the blue curve. After testing the motion, click **Close** in the Drag dialog box.

Task 2 - Configure the motion axis settings.

---

1. Active the *Applications* tab and, click 🛠 (Mechanism) to open the *Mechanism* tab.

2. Right-click on the cylinder connection icon shown in Figure 4–26 and, select ⬚ (Pick From List).

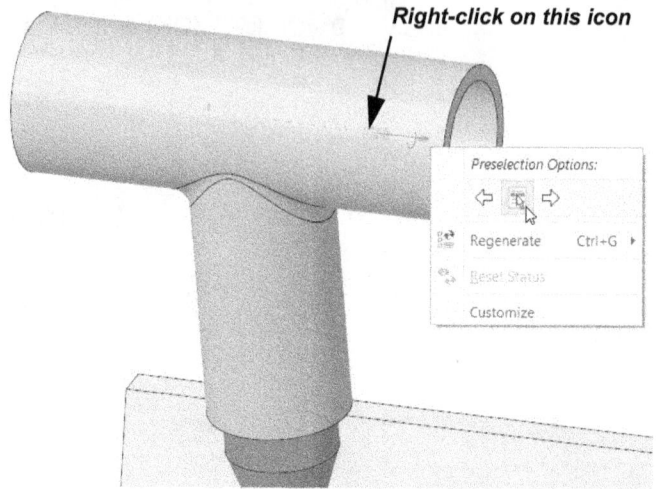

Figure 4–26

3. Select the translation axis as shown in Figure 4–27 and, click **OK**.

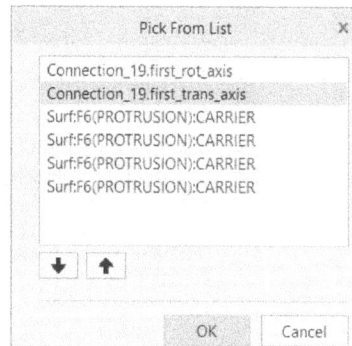

Figure 4–27

4. Right-click and select ⬚ (Edit Definition) in the mini toolbar, as shown in Figure 4–28.

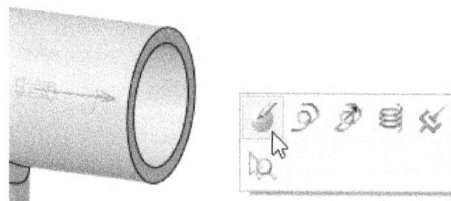

Figure 4–28

5. Select the planar surfaces on the left end of each model, as shown in Figure 4–29, for the translation axis zero references.

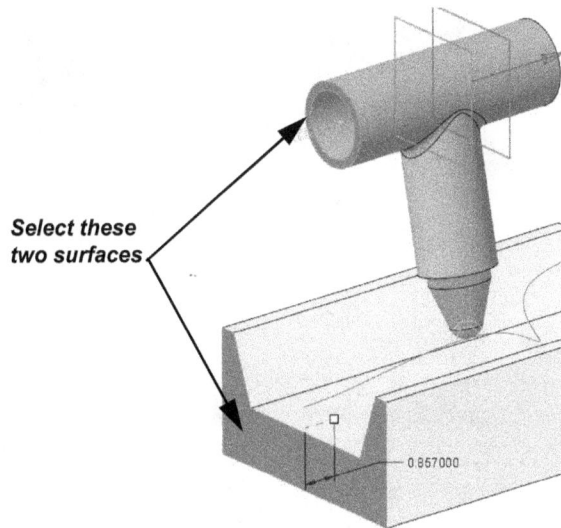

Select these two surfaces

0.857000

Figure 4–29

6. Enter **-3.00** for the *Current Position* and press <Enter>, as shown in Figure 4–30.

Figure 4–30

7. Select **Set Zero Position**, as shown in Figure 4–31.

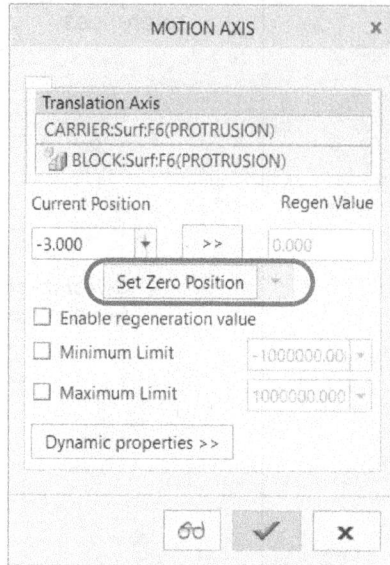

Figure 4–31

8. Verify that the *Regen Value* is set to **0.00** and, enable the regeneration value as shown in Figure 4–32.

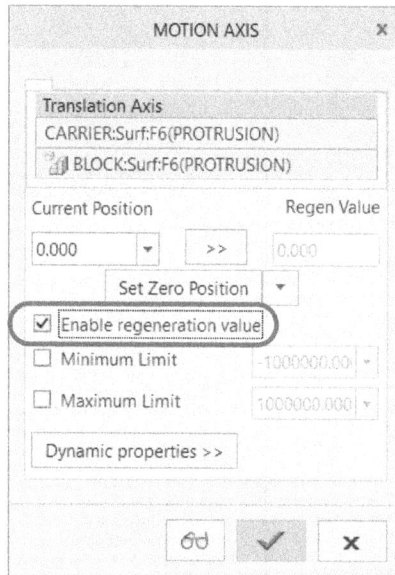

Figure 4–32

9. Click ✓ (OK) to complete the motion axis settings.

10. Drag the carrier component to approximately the middle of the block part, as shown in Figure 4–33

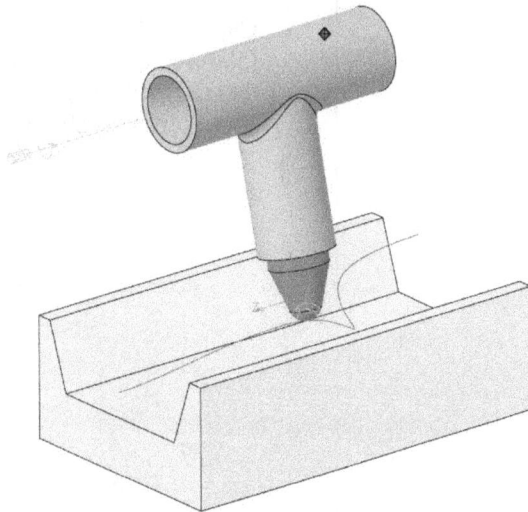

Figure 4–33

11. Regenerate the assembly and, note that the carrier will move to its zero position at the far left of the assembly, as shown in Figure 4–34.

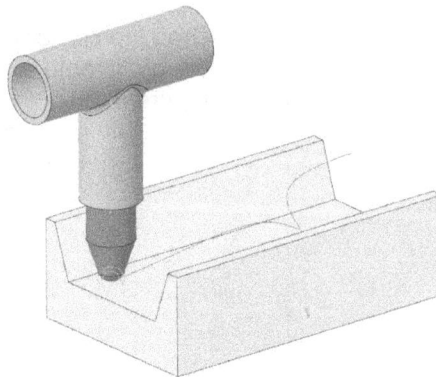

Figure 4–34

Task 3 - Create starting, middle, and ending position snapshots

1. Click 🖑 (Drag Components and click 📷 (Take Snapshot) to take a snapshot of the current configuration. Enter **Start** in the *Current Snapshot* field as its name and press <Enter>. The Start snapshot is shown in Figure 4–35.

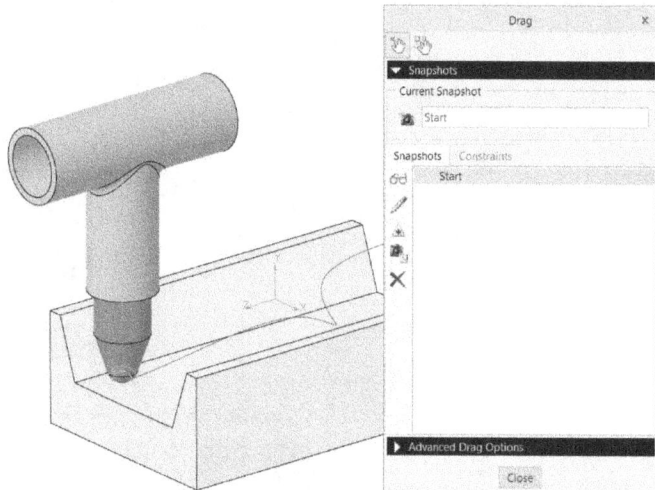

Figure 4–35

2. Drag the carrier part to the other end of the block as far as it will go. Create a snapshot and name it **End**, as shown in Figure 4–36.

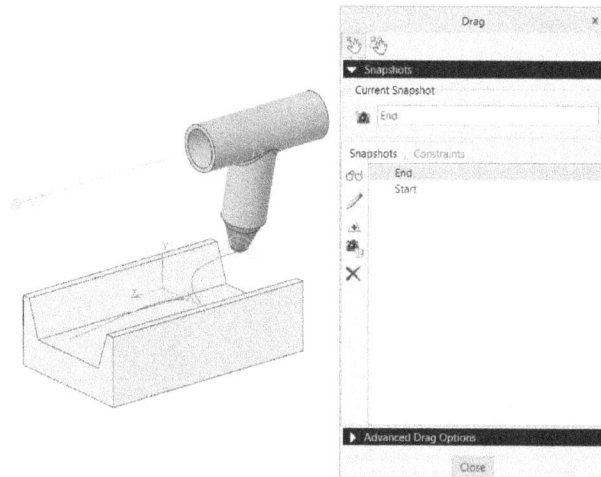

Figure 4–36

3. To create a snapshot exactly in the centered position, select the *Constraints* tab.

4. Click ▦ (Align) and select the two planar surfaces on the left end of the carrier and block parts as shown in Figure 4–37.

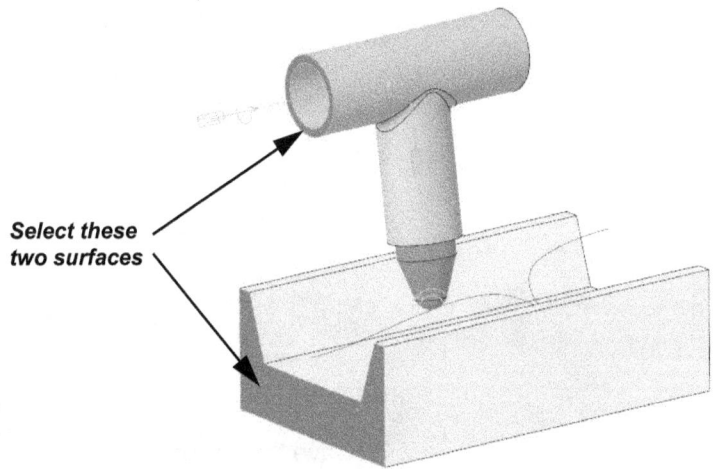

Select these two surfaces

Figure 4–37

5. Note that the length of the block part is 10.00 and the length of the carrier is 6.00. Therefore, an offset of 2.00 will center the parts. Enter **2.00** as the offset at the bottom of the Drag dialog box, as shown in Figure 4–38.

Figure 4–38

6. The assembly will update to the centered position as shown in Figure 4–39. Create a snapshot named **Middle**.

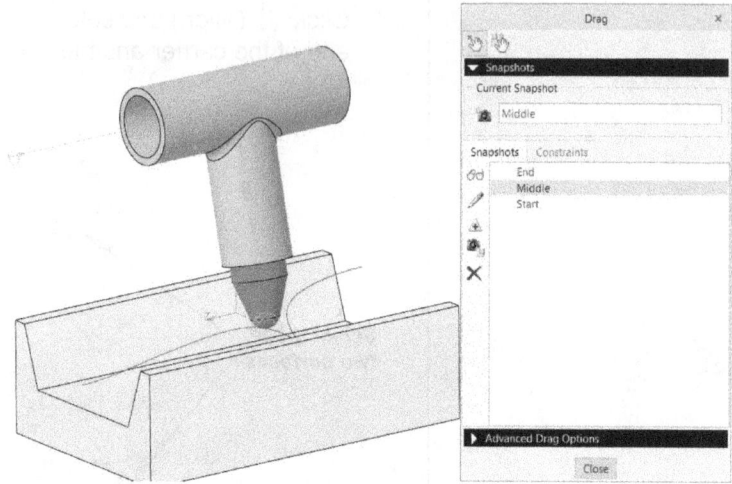

Figure 4–39

7. Save the assembly and erase it from memory.

Practice 4b | Create a Cam Assembly

Practice Objective

- Create an assembly using advanced connections.

In this practice, you will create a cam assembly to be used in an engine assembly. The assembly in this practice contains many datum features that have been created to help you when placing the components. The final assembly displays as shown in Figure 4–40.

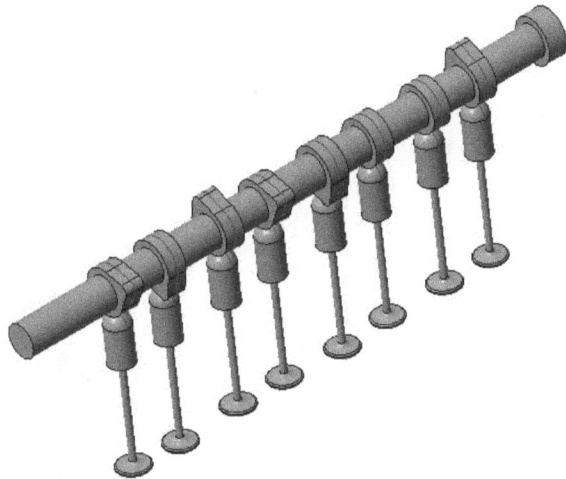

Figure 4–40

Task 1 - Open the cam assembly and assemble camshaft.

1. Set the working directory to the *Create_Cam* folder.

2. Open **cam.asm**. The assembly layout of datum planes has been created for you so that you can easily assemble the components of the cam.

3. Set the model display as follows:

   - *(Datum Display Filters)*: *(Axis Display)*

   - *(Spin Center)*: Off

   - *(Display Style)*: (Shading With Edges)

4. Assemble **camshaft.prt** using the **Pin** connection constraint.

5. In the Model Tree, select the axis **CAMSHAFT_AXIS** in the camshaft and the axis **CAM_AXIS** in the assembly for the axis alignment.

6. Select datum plane **FRONT** in the camshaft and datum plane **ASM_FRONT** in the assembly for the translation reference.

7. If required, click ✗ (Flip Connection) to achieve the default orientation shown in Figure 4–41.

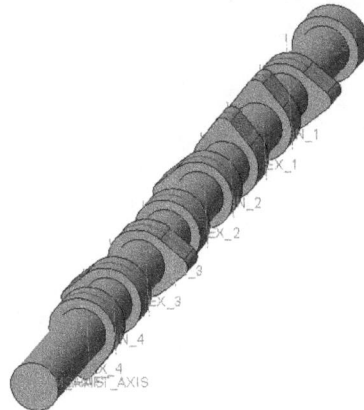

Figure 4–41

8. Complete the component placement.

Task 2 - Assemble the injector part.

---

1. Assemble **valve.prt** using the Slider connection constraint.

2. Select the axis **A_1** in the valve and the axis **IN_1** in the assembly for the axis alignment.

3. Select datum plane **CAM** in the valve and datum plane **VALVE_1** in the assembly for the Rotation reference.

4. Press <Ctrl>+<Alt> and, use the right mouse button to drag the component to the orientation shown in Figure 4–42.

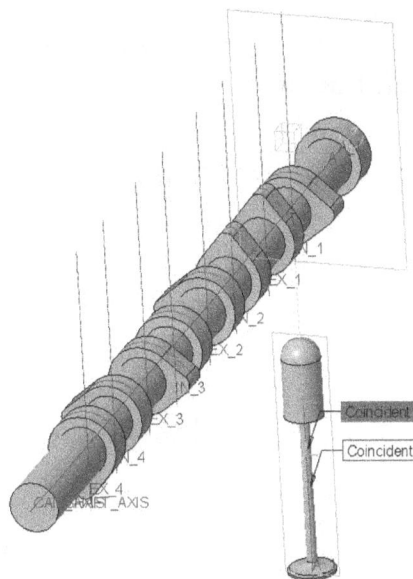

Figure 4–42

5. Complete the component placement.

The repeat command could also be used to assemble the other valve parts.

6. Repeat the steps in this task to connect the remaining valves. The assembly displays as shown in Figure 4–43.

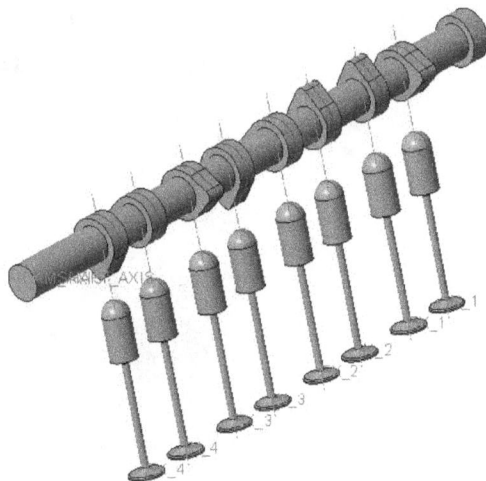

Figure 4–43

7. Save the assembly.

Task 3 - Create a cam connection between the valves and the camshaft.

Design Considerations

In this task, you will add a cam-follower connection between a valve and the camshaft. This is done by selecting the curves on both components that will be followed. The selected curves define the motion for the connection. Once the connection has been added, you can drag the camshaft component to display the motion.

1. Select the *Applications* tab and click 🕸 (Mechanism) to enable Mechanism mode.

2. Click 👃 (Cams).

3. Click ↳ (Select) in the *Surfaces/curves* area.

4. Set the Selection Filter to **Curve**.

5. Hold <Ctrl> and then select the two parts of the datum curve on the first valve. Press the middle mouse button to accept the selection. Both parts of the curve should be highlighted, as shown in Figure 4–44.

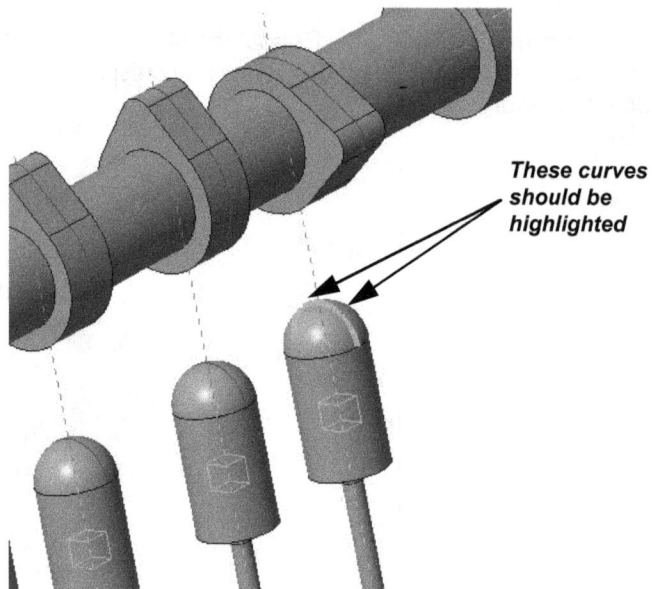

These curves should be highlighted

Figure 4–44

6. Select the *Cam2* tab.

7. Hold <Ctrl> and then select the corresponding four parts of the datum curve on the cam. Press the middle mouse button to accept the selection. The entire curve should be highlighted, as shown in Figure 4–45.

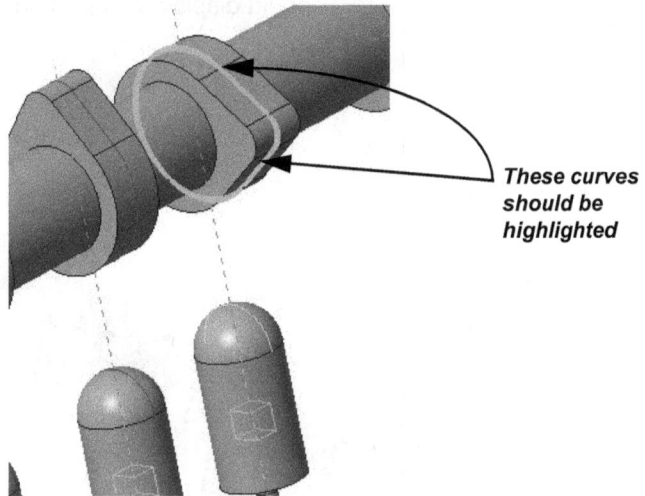

These curves should be highlighted

Figure 4–45

8. Click **OK** to complete the cam follower, as shown in Figure 4–46.

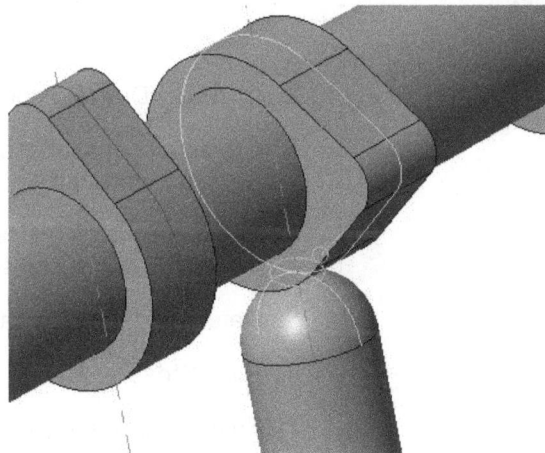

Figure 4–46

9. Save the assembly.

Task 4 - Add cam connections to the remaining valves.

1. Add 7 more cam connections to the valves and the cam by repeating Steps 2 to 7 in Task 3. The completed assembly should display as shown in Figure 4–47.

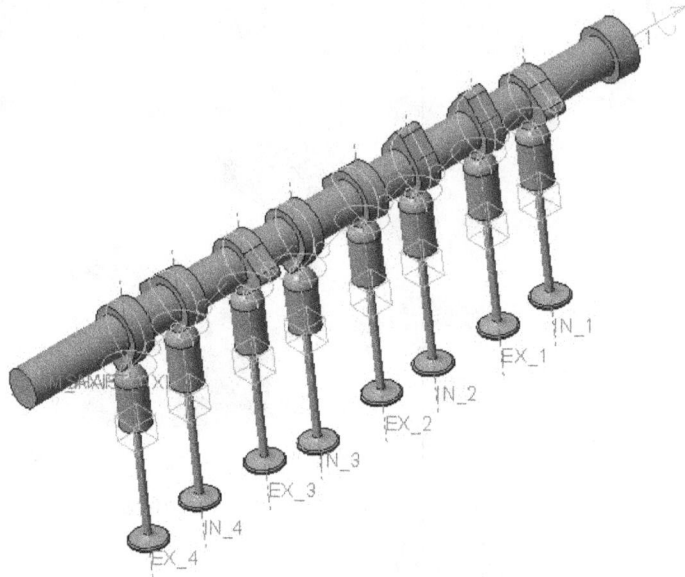

Figure 4–47

2. Click 🖑 (Drag Components).

3. Create a snapshot of the current configuration and set the *Name* to **camstart**.

4. Select a point on the camshaft and drag it. Note that all of the valves follow the camshaft motion.

5. Return to the saved camstart snapshot.

6. Click **Close**.

7. Save the assembly and erase it from memory.

Practice 4c

Pantograph

Practice Objective

- Create a cylinder and slot connection.

In this practice, you will add a pencil component to a pantograph assembly using a Cylinder and a Slot connection. The final assembly displays as shown in Figure 4–48.

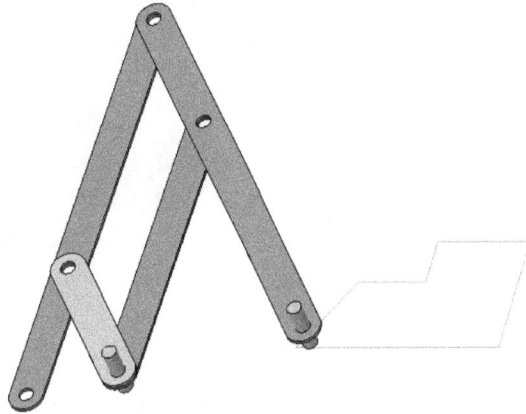

Figure 4–48

Task 1 - Open an existing assembly.

1. Set the working directory to *Pantograph_I*.

2. Open **pantograph.asm**.

3. Set the model display as follows:

   - ⁘ *(Datum Display Filters)*: All Off

   - ⌖ *(Spin Center)*: Off

   - ▢ *(Display Style)*: ▢ (Shading With Edges)

Task 2 - Add a component with a Cylinder and Slot connection

1. Click ▆ (Assemble) in the *Model* tab.

2. Double click on **pencil.prt**.

3. Select **Cylinder** as the connection type.

4. Select the two cylindrical surfaces shown in Figure 4–49.

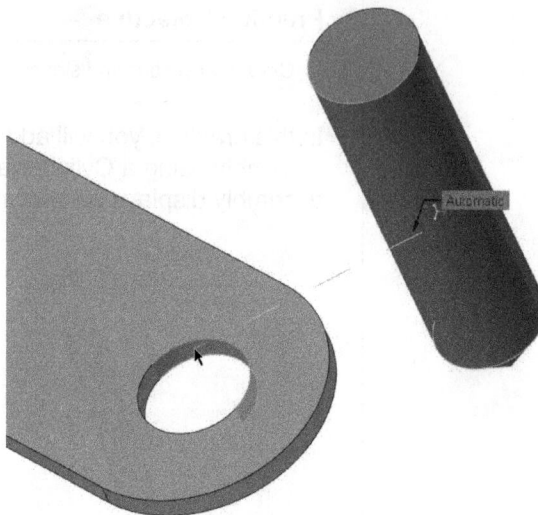

Figure 4–49

5. Select **New Set** in the *Placement* tab to add a second connection. Click on the second connection in the list and change the second connection type to **Slot**, as shown in Figure 4–50.

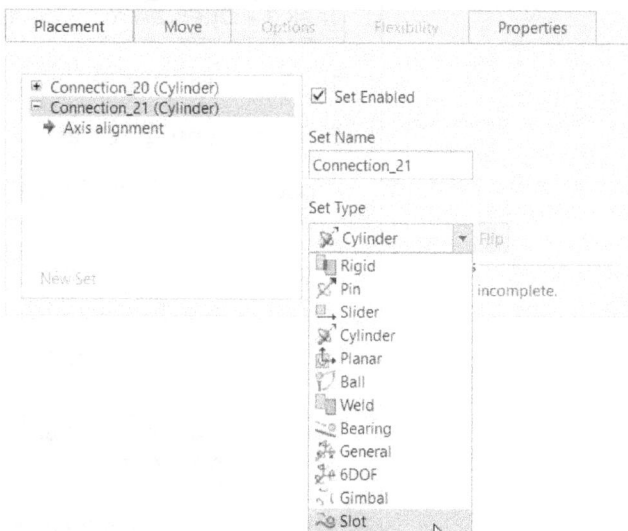

Figure 4–50

6. In the *View* tab of the ribbon, enable ⁙ (Point Display) and ⁙ (Point Tag Display).

7. Select the *Component Placement* tab.

8. Hold <Ctrl> and, select the 6 lines of the sketch as shown in Figure 4–51.

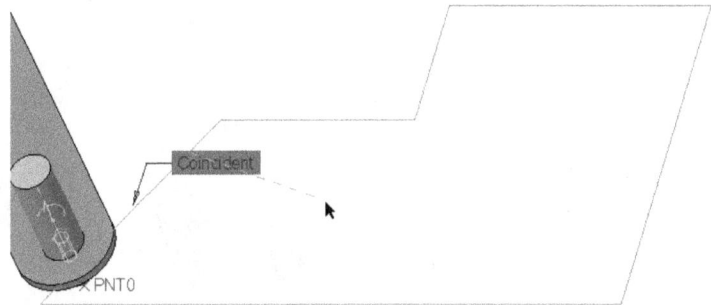

Figure 4–51

9. Select datum point **PNT0** in the pencil part, as shown in Figure 4–52.

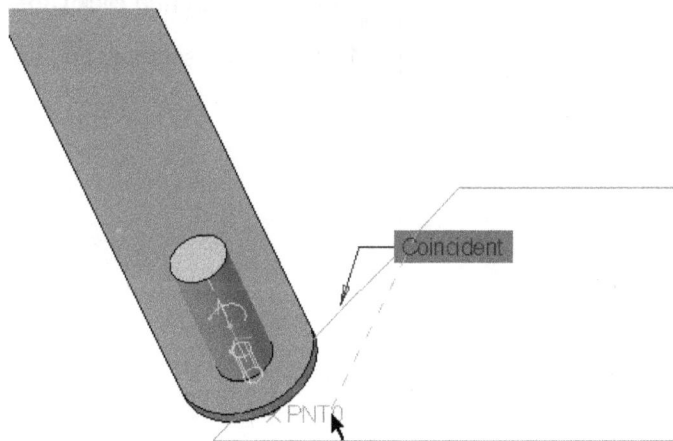

Figure 4–52

10. Click ✓ (OK).

11. Turn off the display of datum points, The assembly updates as shown in Figure 4–53.

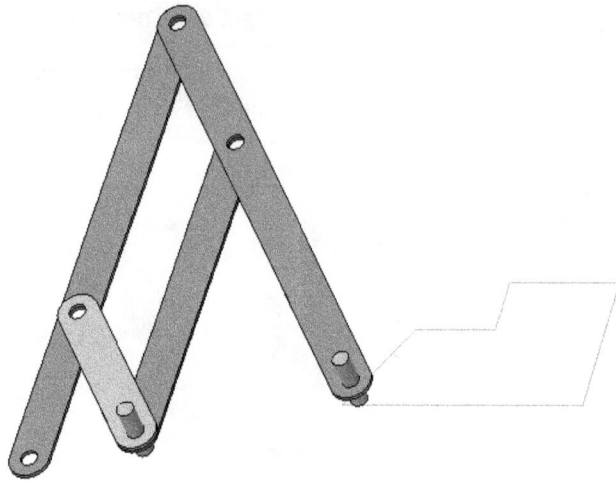

Figure 4–53

12. Click ✋ (Drag Components) to verify the motion.

13. Middle-click and click **Close** in the Drag dialog box.

14. Save the assembly and erase it from memory.

Practice 4d	# Create a Gear Pair Connection

Practice Objective

- Create gear connections.

Similar to the slot and cam connections, a Gear connections enables you to simulate complex motions. In this practice, you will create gear connections for a gear train assembly. The gear train assembly is assembled with pin joint connections. The final assembly displays as shown in Figure 4–54.

Figure 4–54

Task 1 - Open the spur_gear assembly and investigate the joint connections.

1. Set the working directory to the *Gear_Pair* folder.

2. Open **spur_gear.asm**.

3. Set the model display as follows:

   - ⅟⅄ *(Datum Display Filters)*: All Off

   - ⊱ *(Spin Center)*: Off

   - ▱ *(Display Style)*: ▱ (Shading With Edges)

4. Activate Mechanism mode. The model's pin joint icons display as shown in Figure 4–55.

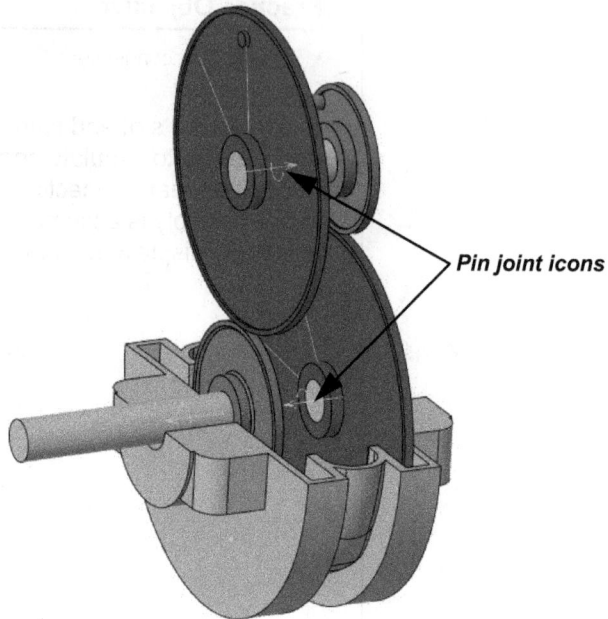

Pin joint icons

Figure 4–55

Design Considerations

Understanding the ground and body components that make up a joint is important for gear pairs so that you can define which component drives the motion.

5. In the mechanism tree, expand the **CONNECTIONS** node and the **JOINTS** node. The three joint connections that were used to assemble the components display. Expand each of the connections. Select the **Ground** and **Body** components in the mechanism tree to display them in green in the model.

Task 2 - Create a gear pair in the mechanism.

Design Considerations

Gear pairs are used to control the velocity ratio between two joint axes. Gear pairs consist of two gear connections. Each gear connection requires two bodies (components) that are connected by a joint connection. The first body (known as carrier) remains stationary and the second body (known as gear) moves. The gear pairs in MDX are velocity constraints and are not based on the geometry of the model. You can specify and change the gear ratios easily without modifying or creating new geometry.

You can also select **GEARS** *in the mechanism tree, select*

✴ *(New) in the mini toolbar.*

1. In the Connections group in the ribbon, click ⚙ (Gears) to create a gear pair connection. The Gear Pair Definition dialog box opens, as shown in Figure 4–56.

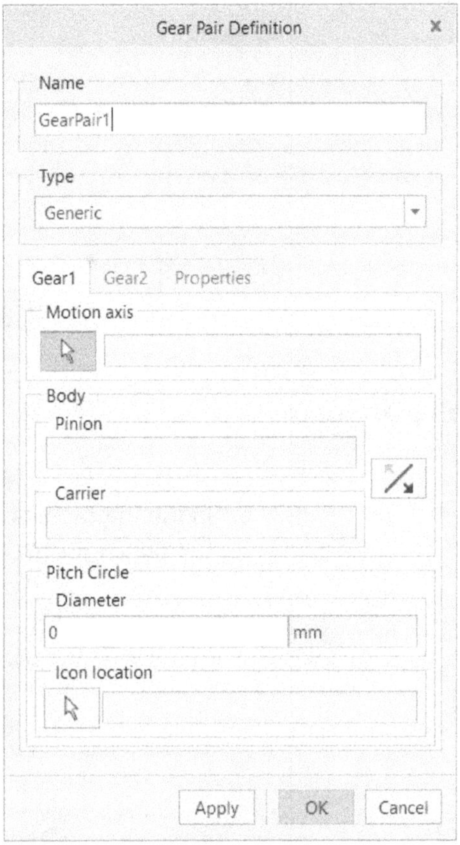

Figure 4–56

2. Set the Gear Pair connection *Name* to **spur_1**.

3. Select **Spur** in the Type drop-down list as the type of Gear Pair connection.

4. The *Motion Axis* field in the *Gear1* tab is the default selection. Select the pin joint shown in Figure 4–58, as the Motion Axis reference for **Gear 1**.

Connection_5.first_rot_axis

Figure 4–57

5. In the In-graphics toolbar, enable ▱ (No Hidden). Observe the purple arrow, as shown and described in Figure 4–58.

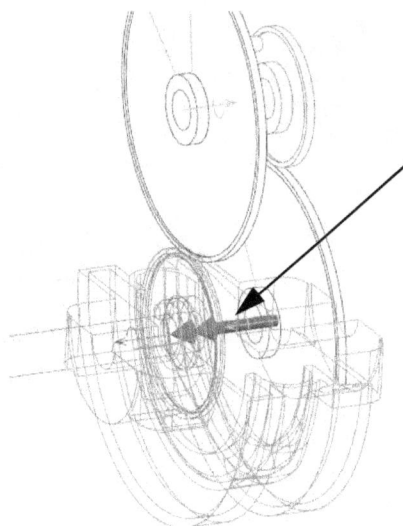

The double-headed arrow displays once the pin joint has been selected. It indicates the positive direction of the axis, (you can use the right rule to determine the rotation). The arrow is best displayed in No Hidden rather than Shaded.

Figure 4–58

The *Body* area in the Gear Pair Definition dialog box automatically populates with the Body information based on the joint connection, as shown in Figure 4–59.

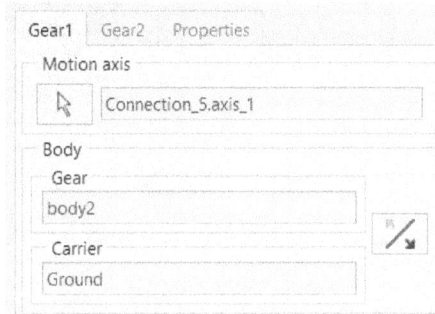

Figure 4–59

The Gear is body2, **GEAR_A_ASSEM.asm**. The Carrier is ground, **BLOCK_BOTTOM.prt**, which displays in green in the model.

6. In the Gear Pair Definition dialog box, edit the *Diameter* for the **Pitch Circle** to **34**.

7. Select the *Gear2* tab.

Review the carrier and ground bodies for this joint axis.

8. Select **Connection_7.axis_1** as the Motion Axis reference for Gear2, as shown in Figure 4–60.

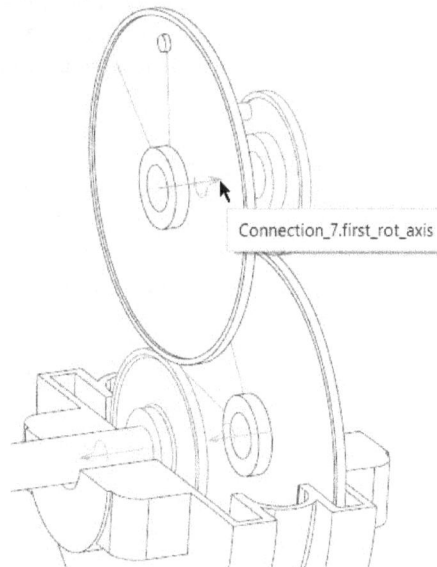

Figure 4–60

9. Select the *Properties* tab. The Gear Pair Definition dialog box opens as shown in Figure 4–61.

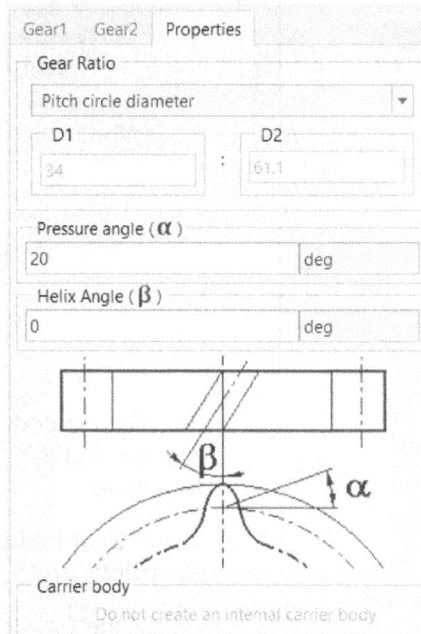

Figure 4–61

Design Considerations

The other option in the Gear Ratio drop-down list is **User Defined**. This option enables you to directly specify a user-defined gear ratio, so that you can change gear ratios easily without modifying or creating new geometry.

10. In the In-graphics toolbar, enable ⬚ (Shading With Edges).

11. Click **OK** to complete the gear pair definition. The model displays as shown in Figure 4–62. The **spur_1** gear displays in the mechanism tree. Expand its sub-tree to display the detailed information.

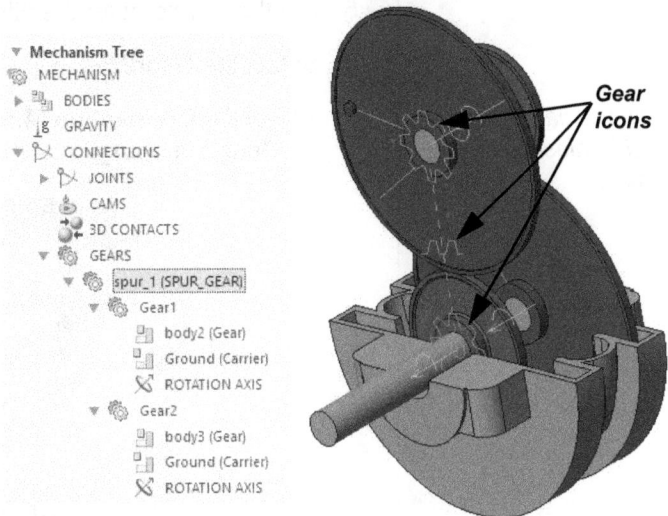

Figure 4–62

Task 3 - Create a second gear pair in the mechanism.

1. Click 🐾 (Gears) and set the *Name* to **spur_2**.

2. Select **Spur** in the *Type* field.

3. Select the **Connection_7.axis_1** pin joint as the Motion Axis for **Gear 1** in **spur_2**, as shown in Figure 4–63.

Figure 4–63

4. The Gear is body4(**GEAR_C_ASSEM.asm**), which displays in green in the model. The Carrier is **body3 (GEAR_D_ASSEM.asm)**, which displays in orange in the model.

5. Set the *Diameter* for the pitch circle to **31**.

6. Select the *Gear2* tab.

Review the carrier and ground bodies for this joint axis.

7. Select the **Connection_4.axis_1** pin joint as the Motion Axis for Gear 2 in **spur_2**, as shown in Figure 4–64.

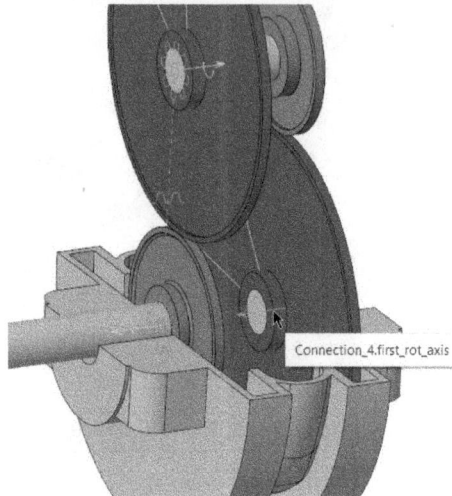

Figure 4–64

8. Click **OK** to complete the operation. The model displays as shown in Figure 4–65.

Figure 4–65

Task 4 - Display the gear motion using the Drag function.

1. Click ✋ (Drag Components).

2. Select a point on the outer edge of any of the four gears (two gear pairs). A black dot should display on the edge. Drag the cursor around the circular path for the gear.

3. Cancel the movement of the component by pressing the middle mouse button.

4. Click **Close**.

5. Save the assembly and erase it from memory.

Practice 4e | Create a Belt Connection

Practice Objectives

- Create a belt connection.
- Create a belt part.

In this practice, you will create a belt connection for an assembly to simulate a pulley type motion. The belt assembly is assembled with pin joint connections. The final assembly displays as shown in Figure 4–66.

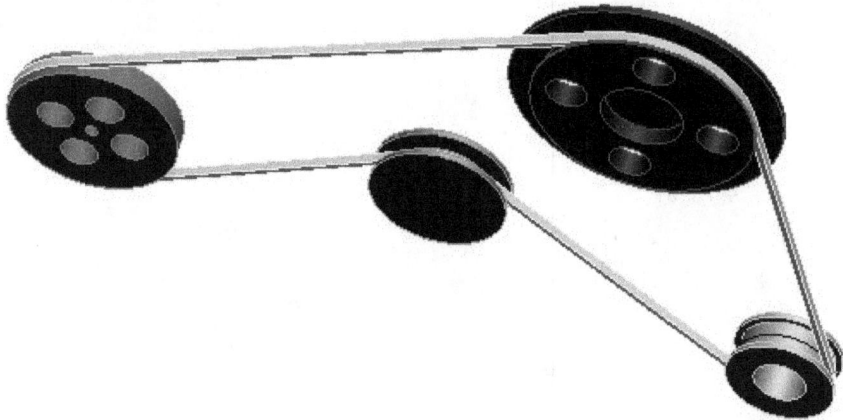

Figure 4–66

Task 1 - Open the belt assembly and investigate the joint connections.

1. Set the working directory to the *Create_Belt* folder.

2. Open **belt_assembly.asm**.

3. Set the model display as follows:

    - ⁂ *(Datum Display Filters)*: All Off

    - ⊱ *(Spin Center)*: Off

    - ▱ *(Display Style)*: ▱ (Shading With Edges)

4. Activate the Mechanism mode. The model's pin joint icons display, as shown in Figure 4–67.

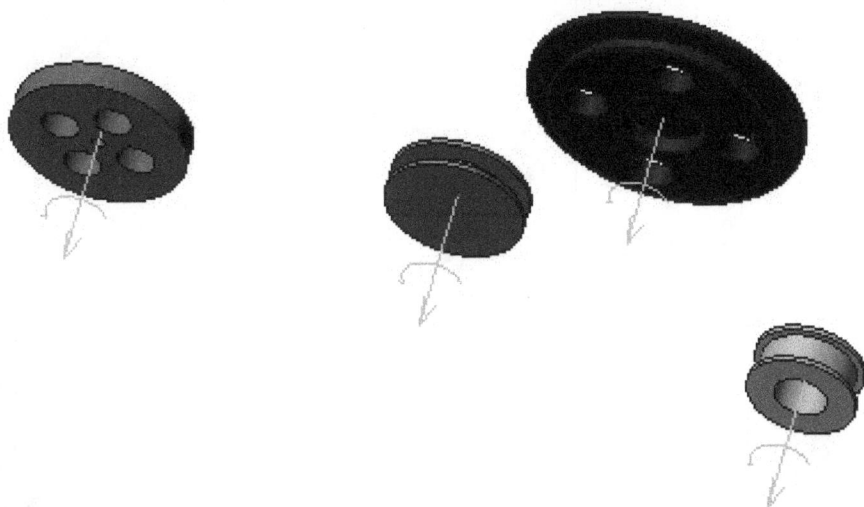

Figure 4–67

5. In the mechanism tree, expand the *CONNECTIONS* node and the *JOINTS* node. The four joint connections that were used to assemble the components display.

Task 2 - Create a belt connection in the mechanism.

1. The Belt connection is used to control the velocity ratio between joint axes. In the Connections group in the ribbon, click ✐ (Belts). The Belt dashboard activates, as shown in Figure 4–68.

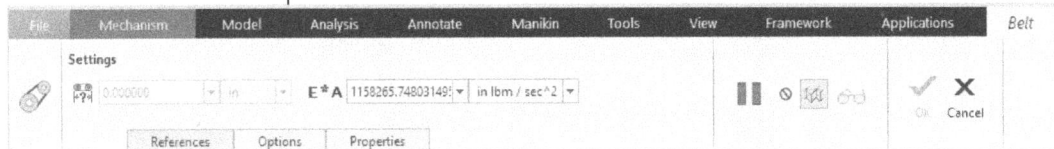

Figure 4–68

2. Select the cylinder surface on the **CRANKSHAFT.prt** as
   shown in Figure 4–69. This adds the surface to the
   Reference panel.

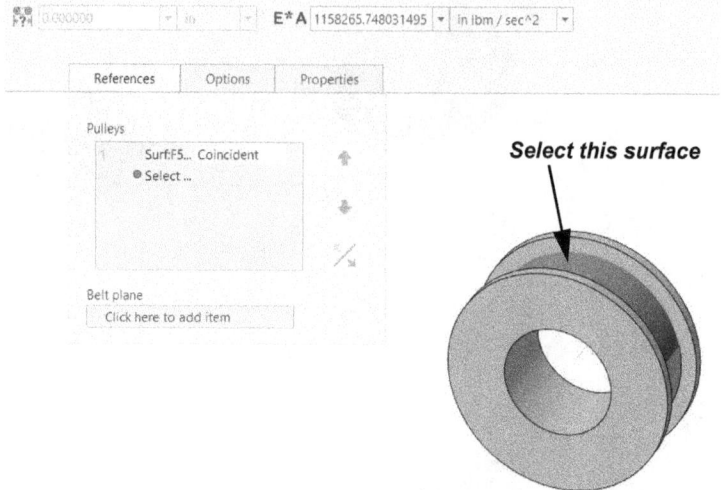

Select this surface

Figure 4–69

3. The belt will wrap around the references in the order they are
   selected in. Hold <Ctrl> and select the surfaces on
   CAMSHAFT2 (blue), **CAMSHAFT** (red), and
   TENSIONER_PULLEY (brown). This adds the surfaces to
   the reference panel, as shown in Figure 4–70.

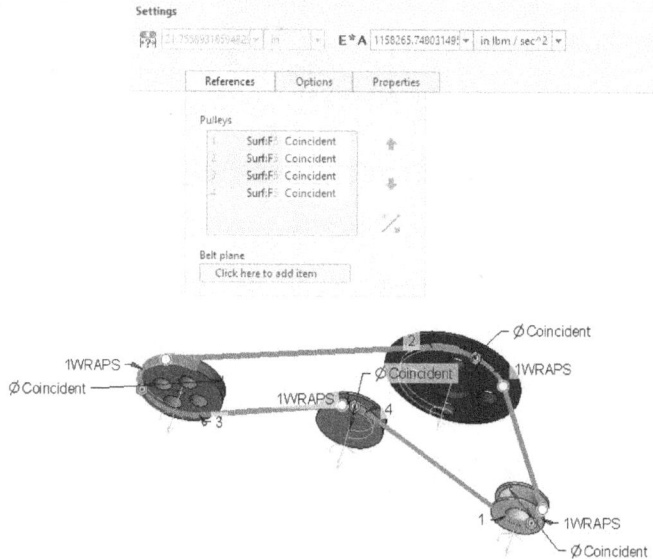

Figure 4–70

You can also flip the belt direction by clicking

⚞ *(Flips Belt Direction) in the References panel.*

4. If required, right-click on the white hot spot and select **Flip Belt Direction** to change the direction of the belt. Flip the directions to achieve the result shown in Figure 4–71.

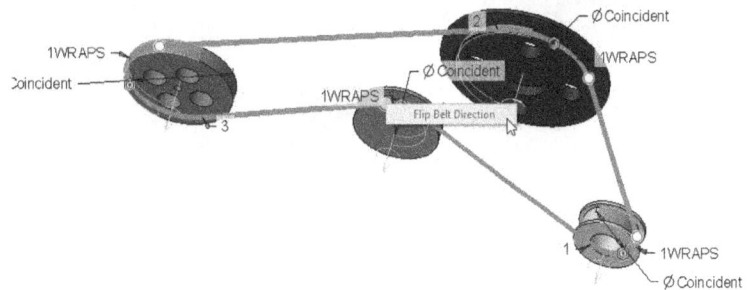

Figure 4–71

5. Select the **Options** panel to display the four pulleys listed.

6. Hover over each pulley listed to highlight the Pulley Body and the Carrier Body references.

7. Complete the feature.

8. Click ✋ (Drag Components). Select a point on one of the models and drag to view the motion.

Task 3 - Create a part.

1. Select the Belt feature in the Mechanism Tree, right-click, and select **Make Part**, as shown in Figure 4–72.

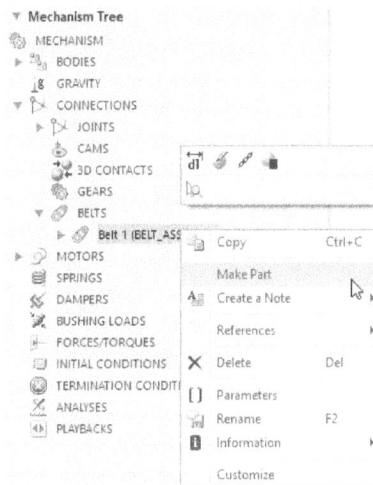

Figure 4–72

2. The Create Component dialog box opens. Enter **belt_solid** as the name of the new part, as shown in Figure 4–73.

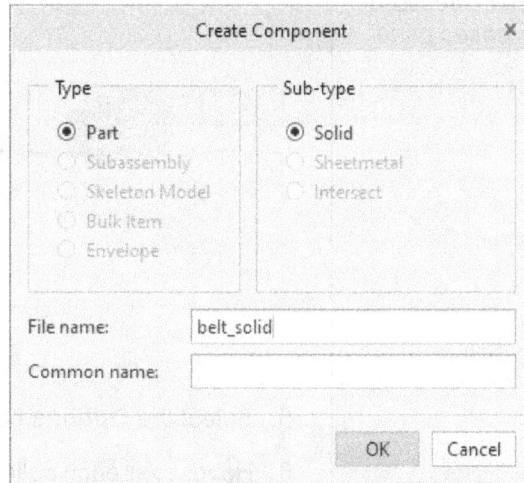

Create Component   ✕

Type   Sub-type

⦿ Part   ⦿ Solid
○ Subassembly   ○ Sheetmetal
○ Skeleton Model   ○ Intersect
○ Bulk Item
○ Envelope

File name: belt_solid

Common name:

OK   Cancel

Figure 4–73

3. Click **OK** in the dialog box.

4. Select **Empty** in the Creation Options dialog box. Click **OK**. The part is created and displays in the Model Tree.

5. Expand **belt_solid** in the Model Tree. Note that the belt curve is already a feature in the part.

6. In the *Mechanism* tab, click ✕ (Close).

7. Save the assembly and erase it from memory.

Practice 4f

Create a Bevel Gear

Practice Objectives

- Create a bevel gear assembly

In this practice, you will create an assembly with two bevel gears. The gears are mounted to a bracket with their axis normal to each other. The gears have been assembled to the mounting bracket with Pin connections and you will add a Bevel Gear connection to connect the two gears. The final assembly displays as shown in Figure 4–74.

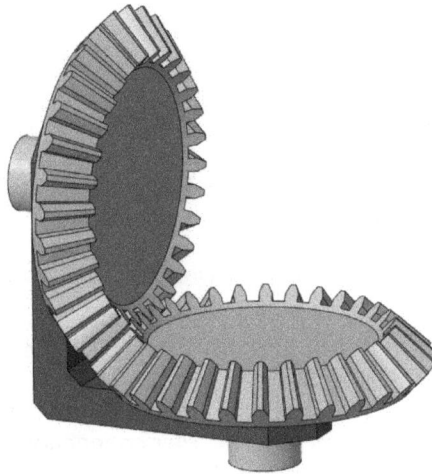

Figure 4–74

Task 1 - Open the assembly and a create a Bevel Gear

1. Set the working directory to the *Create_Bevel_Gear* folder.

2. Open **bevel_gear.asm**.

3. Set the model display as follows:

   - *(Datum Display Filters)*: All Off

   - *(Spin Center)*: Off

   - *(Display Style)*: (Shading With Edges)

4. Select the *Applications* tab and click (Mechanism) to enable Mechanism mode.

5. Click 🛞 (Gears) to create a gear pair connection. The Gear Pair Definition dialog box opens as shown in Figure 4–75.

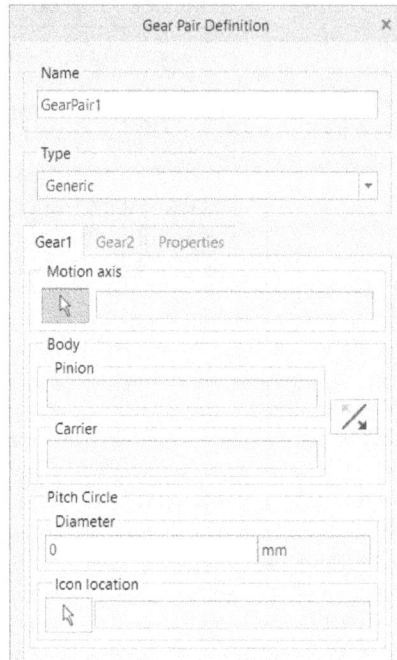

Figure 4–75

6. Select **Bevel** in the Type drop-down list as the type of Gear Pair connection.

7. Select the **Connection_2.first_rot_axis** as the Motion Axis for **Gear 1** in the left hand gear, as shown in Figure 4–76.

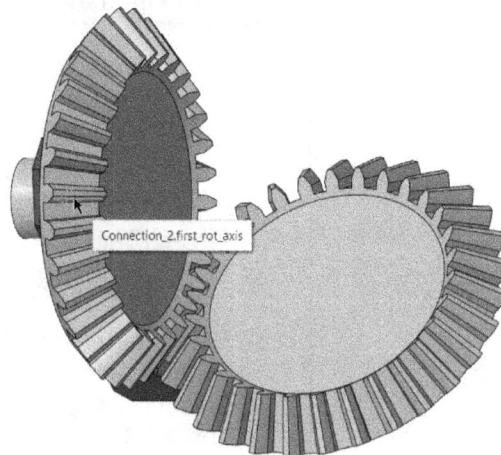

Figure 4–76

8. Enter **50.00** as the Pitch Circle Diameter for **Gear1**.

9. Select the *Gear2* tab.

10. Select the **Connection_3.first_rot_axis** as the Motion Axis for **Gear 2** in the lower right gear, as shown inFigure 4–77.

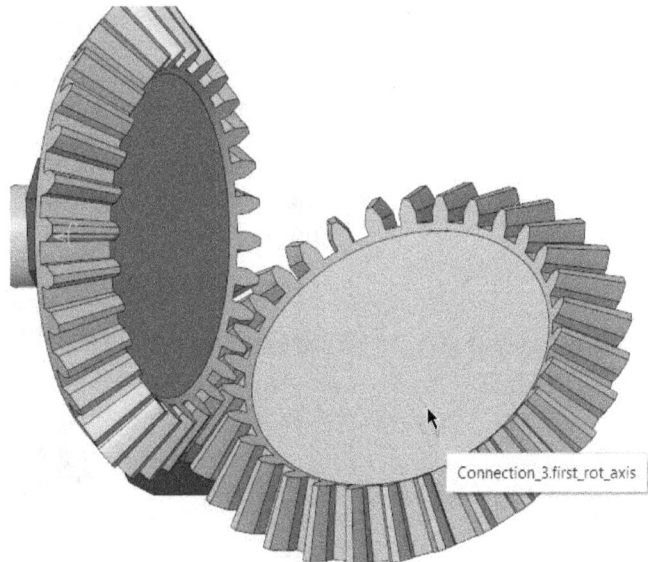

Figure 4–77

11. Click ✕ (Flip) in the *Gear2* tab, as shown in Figure 4–78.

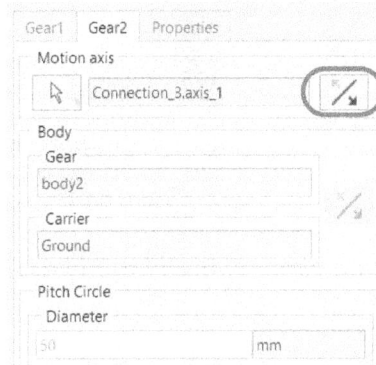

Figure 4–78

12. Select **OK** to complete the gear connection.

13. Click 🖑 (Drag Components). Select a point on one of the gears and drag to view the motion.

14. Save the assembly and erase from memory.

Practice 4g	**(Optional) Project - Create a Worm Gear**

Practice Objectives

- Create a worm gear assembly

In this practice, you will create an assembly with a worm and wheel gear. The gears are mounted with their axis normal to each other. The worm and wheel have been assembled with Pin connections and you will add a Worm Gear connection to connect the two gears. The final assembly displays as shown in Figure 4–79.

Figure 4–79

Task 1 - Open the assembly and a create a Worm Gear

1. Set the working directory to the *Create_Worm_Gear* folder.

2. Open **worm_gear_m26.asm**.

3. Set the model display as follows:

   - ⅍ *(Datum Display Filters)*: All Off

   - ⅌ *(Spin Center)*: Off

   - ▢ *(Display Style)*: ▢ (Shading With Edges)

4. Select the *Applications* tab and click ⚙ (Mechanism) to enable Mechanism mode.

5. Click ⚙ (Gears) to create a gear pair connection. The Gear Pair Definition dialog box opens as shown in Figure 4–80.

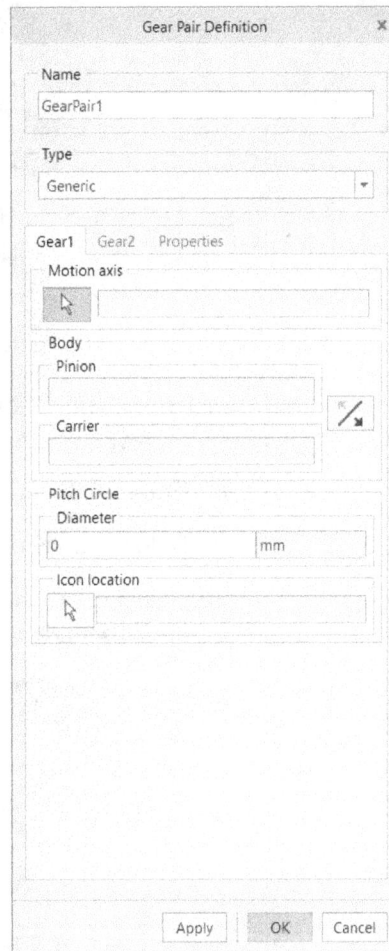

Figure 4–80

6. Select **Worm** in the Type drop-down list as the type of Gear Pair connection.

7. Select the **Connection_1.first_rot_axis** as the Motion Axis for **Worm** as shown in Figure 4–81.

Figure 4–81

8. Enter **26.00** as the Pitch Circle Diameter.

9. Select the *Wheel* tab.

10. Select the **Connection_1.first_rot_axis** as the Motion Axis for **Wheel**, as shown in Figure 4–82.

Figure 4–82

11. Click ✎ (Flip) in the *Wheel* tab as shown in Figure 4–83 and verify the purple arrow is pointing into the wheel as shown in Figure 4–84.

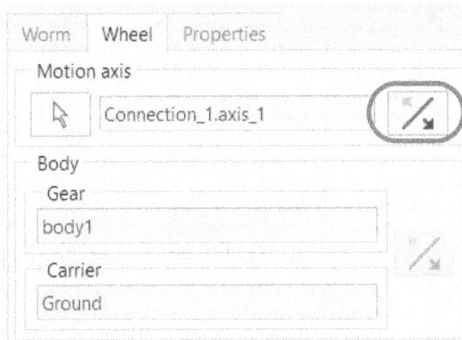

Figure 4–83

Figure 4–84

12. Select the *Properties* tab.

13. Select **User Defined** for the *Gear Ratio*, as shown in Figure 4–85.

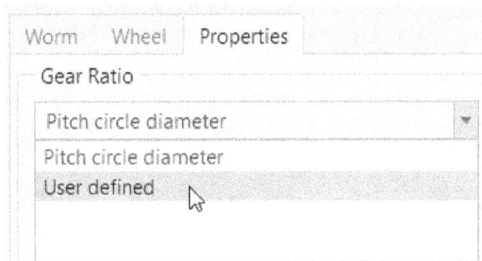

Figure 4–85

14. Enter **5** for the *Worm spirals* and **42** for the *Wheel teeth*, as shown in Figure 4–86.

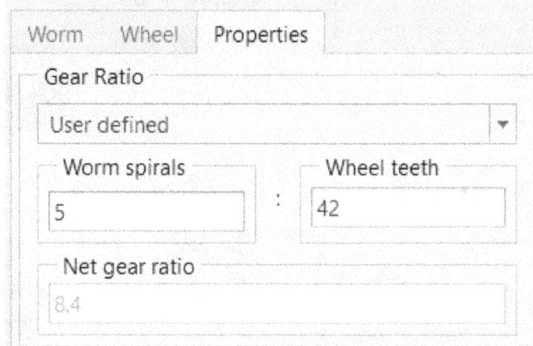

Worm	Wheel	Properties

Gear Ratio

User defined   ▼

Worm spirals   Wheel teeth

5   :   42

Net gear ratio

8.4

Figure 4–86

15. Note the resulting gear ratio is 8.4. Click **OK** to complete the Bevel Gear connection.

16. Click 🖐 (Drag Components). Select a point on one of the gears and drag to view the motion.

17. Save the assembly and erase from memory.

Practice 4h

(Optional) Project - Create a 3D Contact Assembly

Practice Objective

- Create a 3D Contact assembly

In this practice, you will create an assembly where two rotating cams will push a slider back and forth when the cams contact the slider. As cam rotates away from the slider the contact between the parts will separate. The 3D Contact connection enables for this type of motion. The final assembly displays as shown in Figure 4–87.

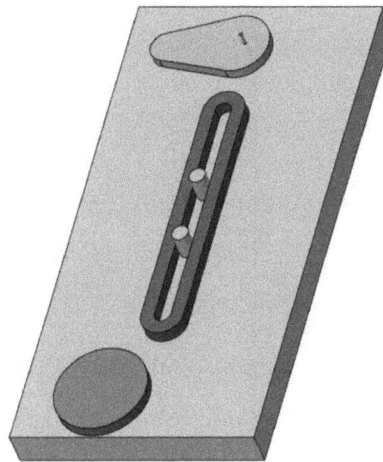

Figure 4–87

Task 1 - Open the assembly and add 3D Contact connections.

1. Set the working directory to the *Project_3D_Contact* folder.

2. Open **3d_contact.asm**.

3. Set the model display as follows:

- *(Datum Display Filters)*: All Off

- *(Spin Center)*: Off

- *(Display Style)*: (Shading With Edges)

4. Select the *Applications* tab and click ⚙ (Mechanism) to enable Mechanism mode.

5. In the Connections group in the ribbon, click 🔩 (3D Contact) to create a 3D Contact connection. The *3DContact* tab opens as shown in Figure 4–88.

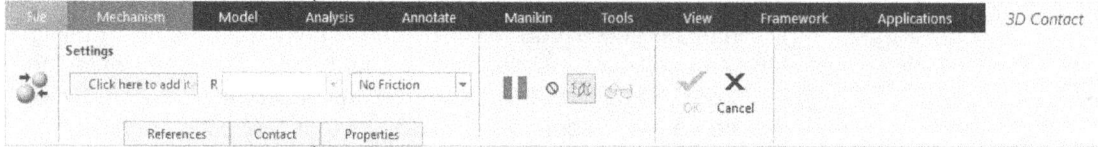

Figure 4–88

6. Click **References** in the dashboard, as shown in Figure 4–89.

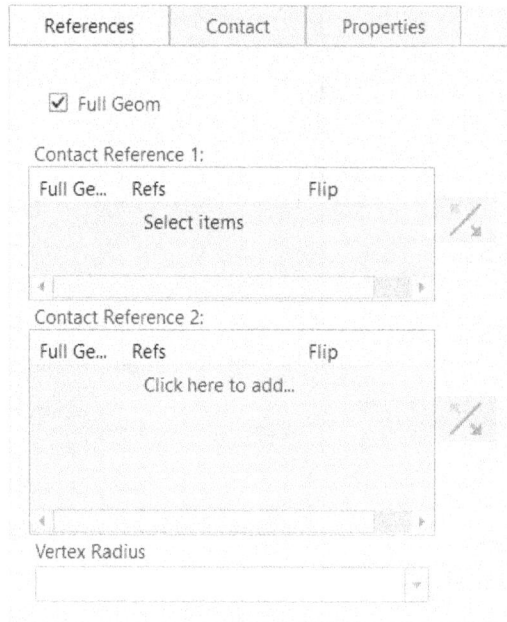

Figure 4–89

7. Select the cylindrical surface from **3D-GEAR1**, as shown in Figure 4–90.

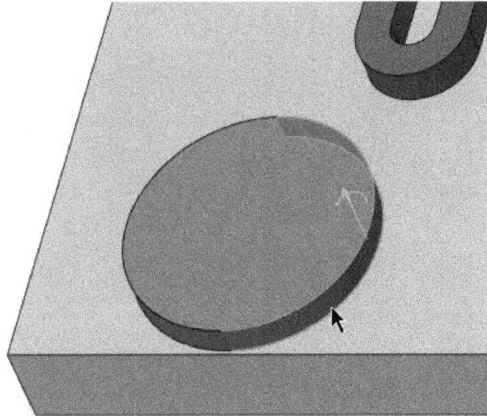

Figure 4–90

8. In References panel, click in the box for **Contact Reference 2** and select the cylindrical surface on 3D-contact slider bar, as shown in Figure 4–91.

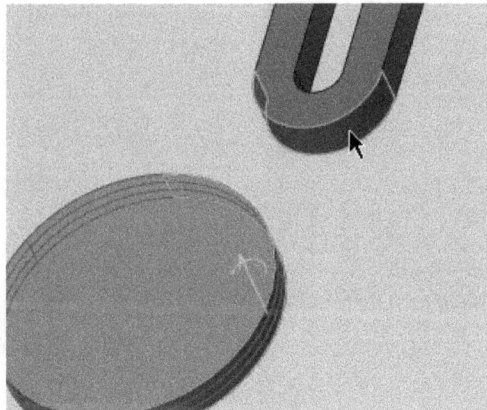

Figure 4–91

9. In the Reference panel, clear the checkbox in the *Full Geom* column for **Contact Reference 2**, as shown in Figure 4–92.

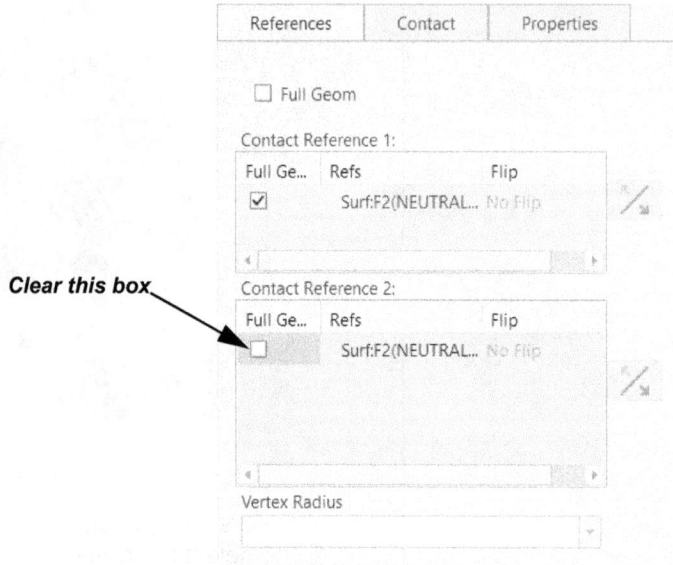

Figure 4–92

10. Ensure that the full cylinder is selected for the first reference and, only half of a cylinder for the second reference, as shown in Figure 4–93. Click ✓ (OK) to complete the 3D Contact connection.

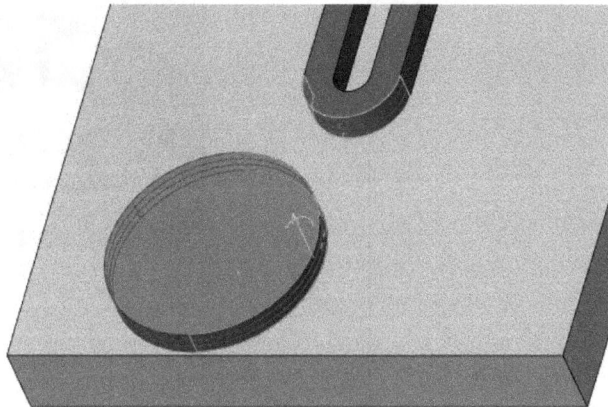

Figure 4–93

11. Click ⛶ (3D Contact) to a create a second 3D Contact connection.

12. Clear the checkbox for **Full Geometry**, as shown in Figure 4–94.

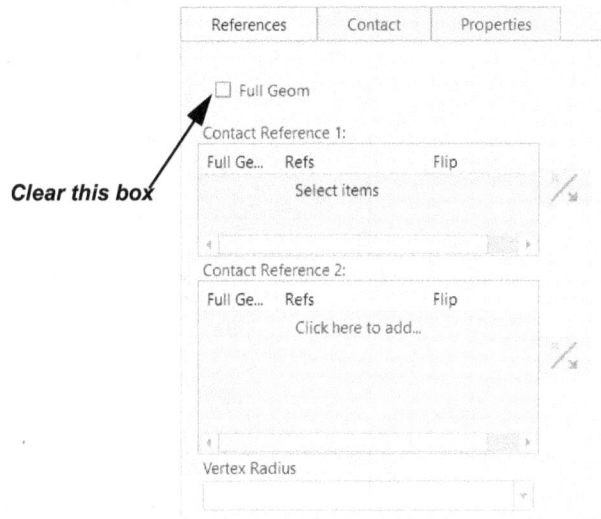

References	Contact	Properties

☐ Full Geom

Contact Reference 1:

Full Ge...	Refs	Flip
	Select items	

Clear this box

Contact Reference 2:

Full Ge...	Refs	Flip
	Click here to add...	

Vertex Radius

Figure 4–94

13. Select the cylindrical surface shown in Figure 4–95 for **Contact Reference 1**.

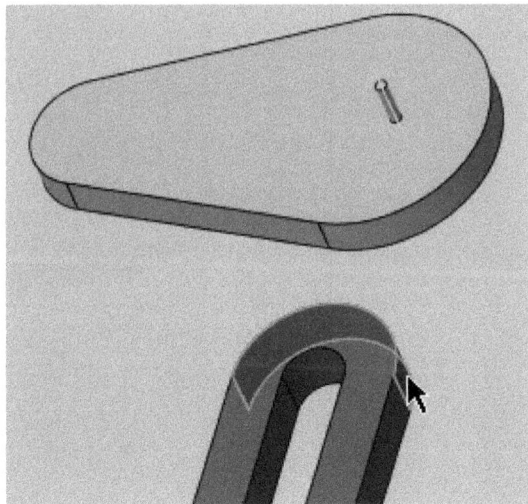

Figure 4–95

14. In References panel, click in the checkbox for **Contact Reference 2** and select the cylindrical surface on 3D-gear2, as shown in Figure 4–96.

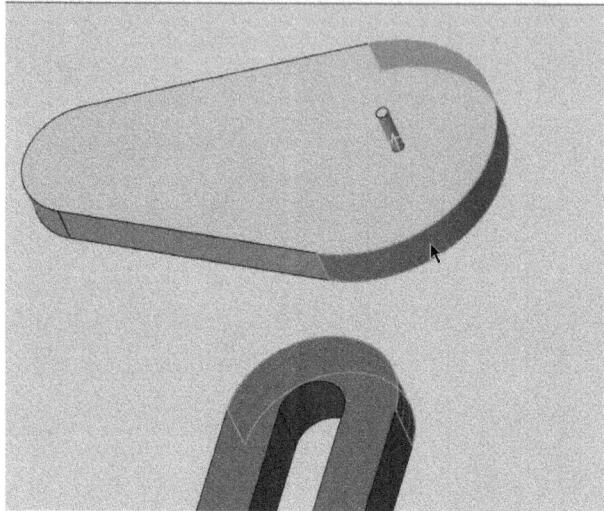

Figure 4–96

15. Hold <Ctrl> and select the other 3 side surfaces of 3D-gear2, as shown in Figure 4–97.

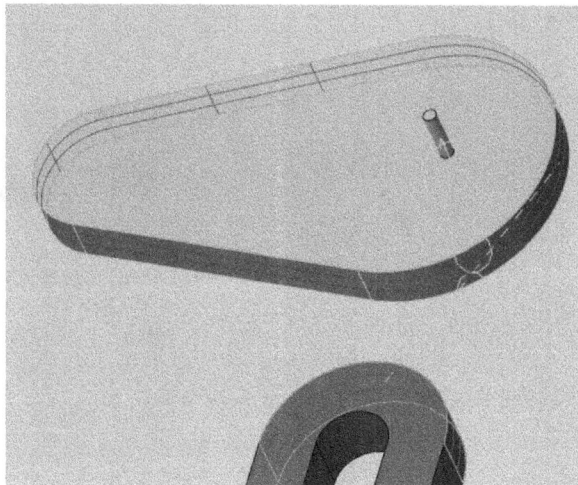

Figure 4–97

Note that adding the 3D Contact constrains did not move the geometry into a contacting position like the Cam connections did. The 3D Contact will push the component once the contact occurs by moving a component until they touch.

16. Click ✔ (OK) to complete the 3D Contact connection. The assembly updates as shown in Figure 4–98.

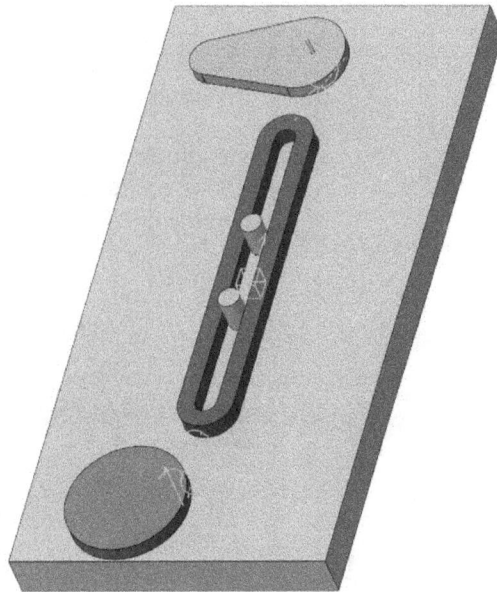

Figure 4–98

Viewing the intended motion of this assembly will not be possible with the drag components command as you must move two parts simultaneously. Two motors will be added in the next chapter to rotate both cam parts at the same time and push the slider bar back and forth.

17. Save the assembly and erase from memory.

Practice 4i	(Optional) Project - Geneva Mechanism

Practice Objective

- Create a 3D Contact connection in the geneva mechanism.

In this practice, you will create a 3D Contact connection between surfaces on the driving pin and the slots on the wheel. The final assembly displays as shown in Figure 4–99.

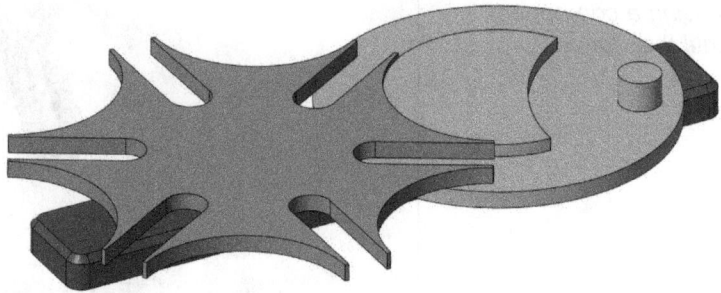

Figure 4–99

Task 1 - Open an existing assembly and create a 3D Contact connection.

1. Set the working directory to the *Create_Geneva* folder.

2. Open **geneva_mechanism.asm**.

3. Set the model display as follows:

   - ✕ *(Datum Display Filters)*: ⟋ (Axis Display)

   - *Datum Tag Display:* 🔲 (Plane Tag Display), ⟋ (Axis Tag Display), ᪲ (Csys Tag Display)

   - ⤷ *(Spin Center)*: Off

   - ▢ *(Display Style)*: ▢ (No Hidden)

4. Select the *Applications* tab and click ⚙ (Mechanism) to activate the Mechanism application.

5. Click ⚙ (3D Contact) to a create a second 3D Contact connection.

6. Select the cylindrical surface shown in Figure 4–100 for **Contact Reference 1**.

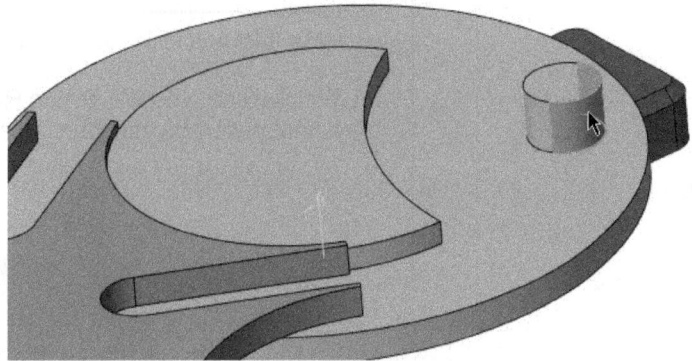

Figure 4–100

7. Now hold <Ctrl> and select the 12 planar side surfaces of the slots, as shown in Figure 4–101.

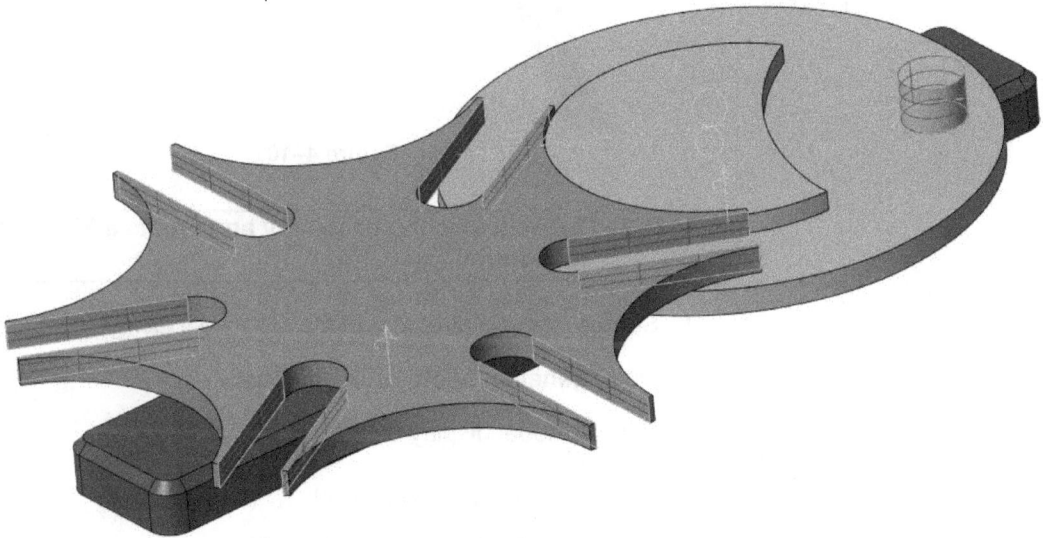

Figure 4–101

8. Click ✓ (OK) to complete the 3D Contact connection.

9. Save the assembly and erase it from memory.

Practice 4j

(Optional) Project - Geneva with Rack Pinion Gear

Practice Objective

- Add a Rack and Pinion gear to the Geneva Mechanism

In this practice, you will create Rack and Pinion gear connection. The final assembly displays as shown in Figure 4–102.

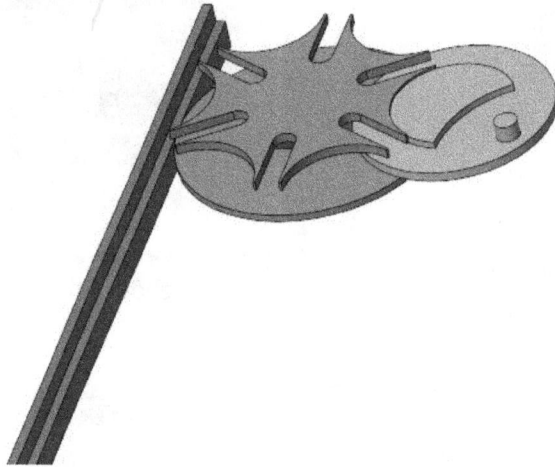

Figure 4–102

Task 1 - Open an existing assembly and create a 3D Contact connection.

1. Set the working directory to the *Geneva_Rack_Pinion* folder.

2. Open **geneva_mech_rack_gear.asm.**

3. Set the model display as follows:

   - *(Datum Display Filters)*: /◉ (Axis Display)
   - *Datum Tag Display:* 🔲 (Plane Tag Display), /◔ (Axis Tag Display), 🔲 (Csys Tag Display)
   - *(Spin Center)*: Off
   - *(Display Style)*: 🗇 (No Hidden)

4. Select the *Applications* tab and click 🔧 (Mechanism) to activate the Mechanism application.

5. Click 🦷 (Gears) to create a gear pair connection. The Gear Pair Definition dialog box opens, as shown in Figure 4–103.

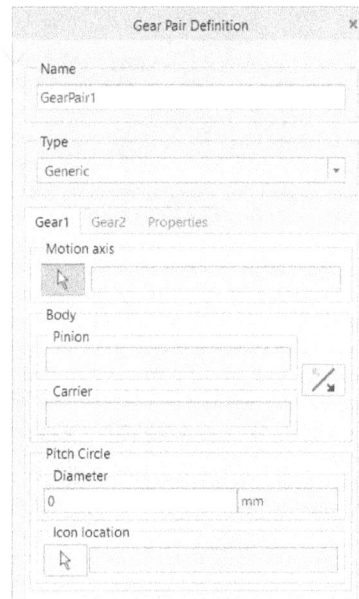

Figure 4–103

6. Select **Rack and pinion** in the Type drop-down list as the type of Gear Pair connection.

7. Select the pin connection icon as shown in Figure 4–104.

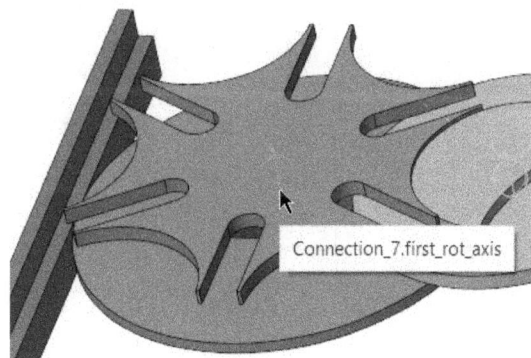

Figure 4–104

8. Enter **13.7** as the Pitch Circle Diameter.

9. Select the *Rack* tab.

10. Select the slider connection icon as shown in Figure 4–105.

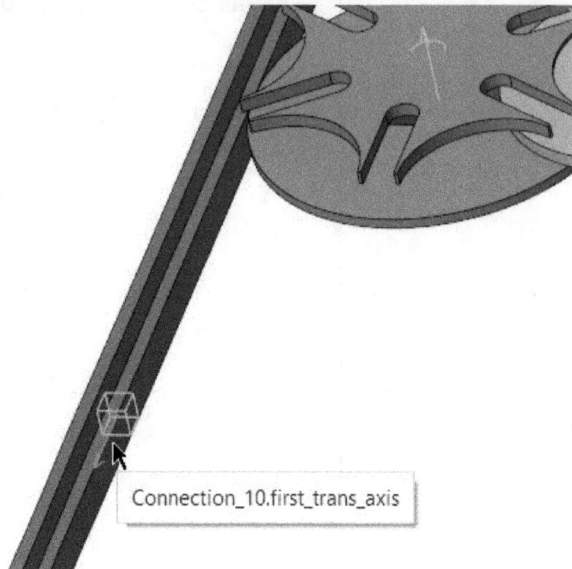

Connection_10.first_trans_axis

Figure 4–105

11. Click **OK** to complete the Rack and Pinion gear.

12. In the Mechanism Tree, expand **ANALYSIS**, select **AnalysisDefinition1 (POSITION)** and click ⚑ (Run), as shown in Figure 4–106.

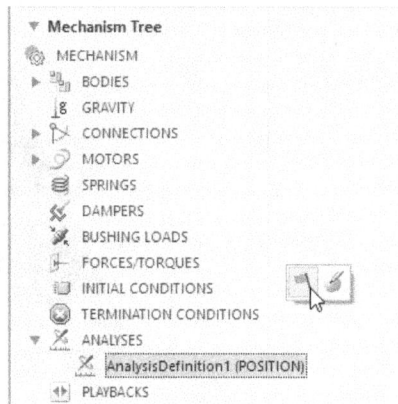

Figure 4–106

13. Save the assembly and erase it from memory.

Practice 4k

(Optional) Project - Scotch Yoke

In this practice, you will add a 3D Contact constraint to the Scotch yoke assembly. The final assembly displays as shown in Figure 4–107.

Figure 4–107

Task 1 - Open an existing assembly and add a 3D Contact constraint.

1. Set the working directory to the *Create_Yoke* folder.

2. Open **scotch-yoke.asm**.

3. Set the model display as follows:

   - ⁺ *(Datum Display Filters)*: All Off

   - ✂ *(Spin Center)*: Off

   - ▢ *(Display Style)*: ▢ (Shading With Edges)

4. Select the *Applications* tab and click ⚙ (Mechanism) to enable the Mechanism application.

5. Click ⚙ (3D Contact) to create a 3D Contact connection. Select the cylindrical surface of the post in the s-wheel part as **Contact Reference 1**, as shown in Figure 4–108.

Figure 4–108

6. Now select the two planar surfaces on the inside of the slot in the yoke part, as shown in Figure 4–109.

Figure 4–109

7. Click ✓ (OK).

8. Save the assembly and erase it from memory.

Chapter Review Questions

1. Which connection type will move two surfaces into contact with each other and keep them in contact?

   a. Slot

   b. Cam-follower

   c. Gear pairs

   d. 3-D Contact

2. Which connection type will constrain a point or vertex on one component to a non-linear curve or edge on the other component?

   a. Slot

   b. Cam-follower

   c. Gear pairs

   d. Belt

3. Which connection type is used to control the velocity ratio between two joint axes independent from the actual model geometry?

   a. Slot

   b. Cam-follower

   c. Gear pairs

   d. Belt

4. When a Slot connection is created, Creo Parametric does not check for interference between two moving components.

   a. True

   b. False

5. The curve selected for a Slot connection can be any continuous datum curve or edge on a component.

   a. True

   b. False

6. When using a Gear connection, you can change the velocity ratio without changing the model geometry.

   a. True

   b. False

7. When using a Belt, you can change the velocity ratios of the pulleys without changing the model geometry.

    a. True

    b. False

Servo Motors and Analyses

The Drag function provides a quick and easy way to visualize the mechanism in motion and to analyze specific moments of the motion. If you want to create a specific type of motion or to analyze the entire range of motion, you can apply servo motors and create analysis definitions.

Learning Objectives in this Chapter

- Learn to define a servo motor on joint axes or on geometric entities, and use the dialog box to determine the motion path and magnitude type.
- Learn create analysis definitions to specify time domains and the servo motors.

5.1 Servo Motors

Servo motors force a specific type of motion to occur between two components in one degree of freedom. Servo motors can specify positions as a function of time, velocity, or acceleration. The profile of the motion can be specified using a selected function.

*Alternatively, you can expand **MECHANISM** and **MOTORS** in the Mechanism Tree, select **SERVO**, right-click and select **New**.*

How To: Create a Servo Motor

1. In the Insert group in the ribbon, click ⟲ (Servo Motors). The *Servo Motor* tab opens as shown in Figure 5–1.

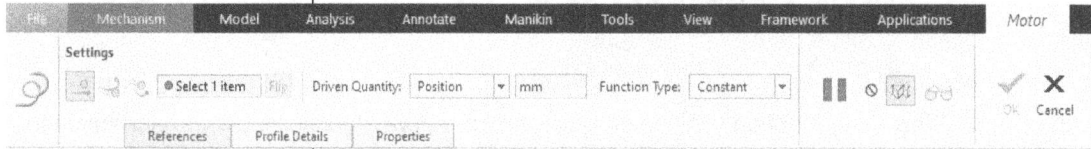

Figure 5–1

The maximum length of a servo motor name is 31 characters.

2. Enter a name for the servo motor in the Properties panel.
3. Servo motors are placed on joint axes or on geometric entities, such as planar surfaces and points. You can select the Geometry as Driven entity types in the *Driven Entity* area as shown in Figure 5–2.

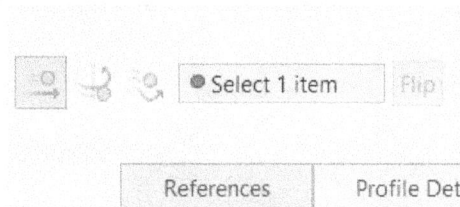

Figure 5–2

Some servo motors might conflict with others during a motion run and need to be deactivated.

Motion axis drivers are used to create a translational or rotational motion in one direction. If you select points and planes to define the motor, you are creating a geometric motor. Geometric drivers are used to create motion that is difficult to simulate with joint axis drivers. Geometric drivers can be used for 3D helix motion or movement about a curve. There are five combinations of geometric drivers and more than one driver type is required to restrict the degrees of freedom and create the motion. To use geometric drivers, you must select a reference entity and a motion entity in either a translation or rotation direction.

4. If required, click **Flip** to flip the selected driven entity as shown in Figure 5–3.

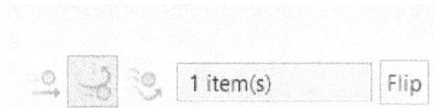

Figure 5–3

5. Select the Profile Details panel.

6. The specification profile of the servo motor is used to create the motion path. This information is available in the Specification drop-down list, as shown in Figure 5–4. The analysis depends on position, velocity, or acceleration.

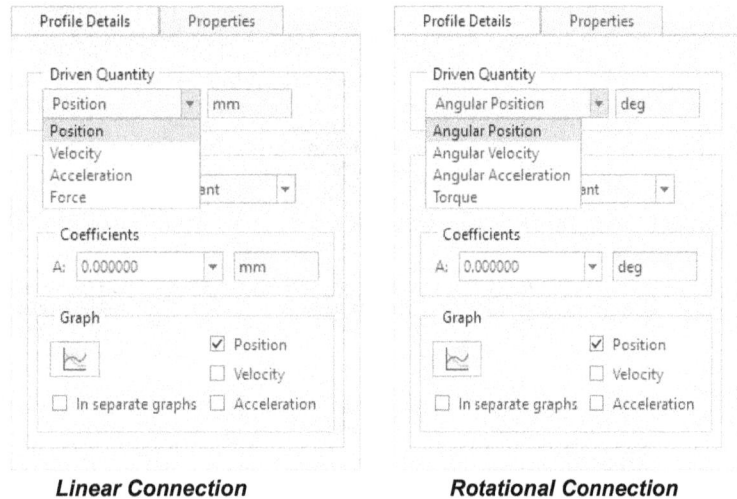

Linear Connection   *Rotational Connection*

Figure 5–4

The Driven Quantity drop-down list options are described as follows:

Option	Description
Position/Angular Position	Specifies the position of the component.
Velocity/Angular Velocity	Specifies the velocity of the component. A starting or zero reference must be defined. The current position or joint axis zero can be the zero reference.
Acceleration/Angular Acceleration	Specifies the acceleration of the component. The initial position and initial velocity must be defined.

| Force/Torque | Specifies the linear or rotational force at a joint. |

7. Nine types of servo motor functions can be selected as the Motor Function, as shown in Figure 5–5.

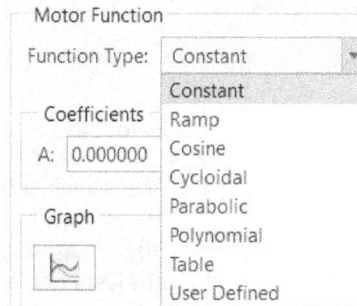

Figure 5–5

The Motor Function options and their equation inputs are described as follows:

Servo Motor Profile Type	Description	Equation (t=time) Inputs Required
Constant	Use to simulate constant motion.	$y=A$ A is constant for all time.
Ramp	Use to simulate linearly changing motion.	$y=A+B*t$ A is constant. B is the slope.
Cosine	Use to simulate oscillation.	$y=A*\cos(360*t/T+B)+C$ A is the amplitude. B is the phase. C is the offset. T is the period.
SCCA	Use to simulate a cam.	Refer to the *Sine-Constant - Cosine Acceleration Drivers* area.
Cycloidal	Use to simulate a cam.	$y=L*t/T-L*\sin(2*PI*t/T)/2*PI$ L is the total rise. T is the period.
Parabolic	Use to simulate a trajectory.	$y=A*t+1/2*B*t^2$ A is the linear coefficient. B is the quadratic coefficient.

Polynomial	Use to simulate generic motion.	$y=A+B*t+C*t^2+D*t^3$ A is the constant coefficient. B is the linear coefficient. C is the square coefficient. D is the cubic coefficient.
Table	Use to simulate a complex profile. For example, if a measurement has been outputted as a file, it can be imported into Mechanism using this option.	File with two columns of data. First column is time and the second column is value.
User Defined	Use to specify any kind of complex profile defined by multiple expression segments.	File with two columns of data. First column is Expression: You can edit the default expression directly in the table cell. For example, to enter cosine function, enter **A*cos(360*t/T+B)+C**. Second column is Domain: You can specify the domain values directly in the cell. For example, to enter a range of time between 0 and 10, enter **0 <= t <= 10**.

Sine-Constant-Cosine Acceleration Profile

This profile is only available for acceleration servo motors. The equation consists of five separate equations evaluated at different times. You must enter the following inputs:

A = Percentage of normalized time for increasing acceleration

B = Percentage of normalized time for constant acceleration

H = Amplitude of the profile

T = Period of the profile

Creo Parametric automatically calculates the percentage of normalized time for decreasing acceleration based on:

A + B + C = 1, where C is decreasing acceleration.

The value of the function is computed by:

$y = H * \sin\{(t * PI) / (2 * A)\}$ for time between 0 and A

$y = H$ for time between A and A+B

$y = H * \cos\{(t - A - B) * PI / (2 * C)\}$ for time between A + B and A + B + 2C

$y = -H$ for time between A + B + 2C and A + 2B + 2C

$y = -H * \cos\{(t - A - 2B - 2C) * PI / (2 * A)\}$ for time between A + 2B + 2C and 2A + 2B + 2C

8. Click ⬓ (Graph Motor Profile) to graph the profile to examine and compare the position, velocity, or acceleration characteristics of the Servo Motor profile.

9. Click ✓ (OK) to finish the servo motor definition.

5.2 Analysis Definition

After you create servo motors, you can create Analysis definitions to specify the time domain settings and which servo motors to use. The analysis definition can be saved for future reference.

How To: Define an Analysis

*Alternatively, you can expand MECHANISM in the mechanism tree, select **ANALYSES**, right-click and select **New**.*

1. In the Analysis group of the *Mechanism* tab in the ribbon, click ⚒ (Mechanism Analysis). The Analysis Definition dialog box opens as shown in Figure 5–6.

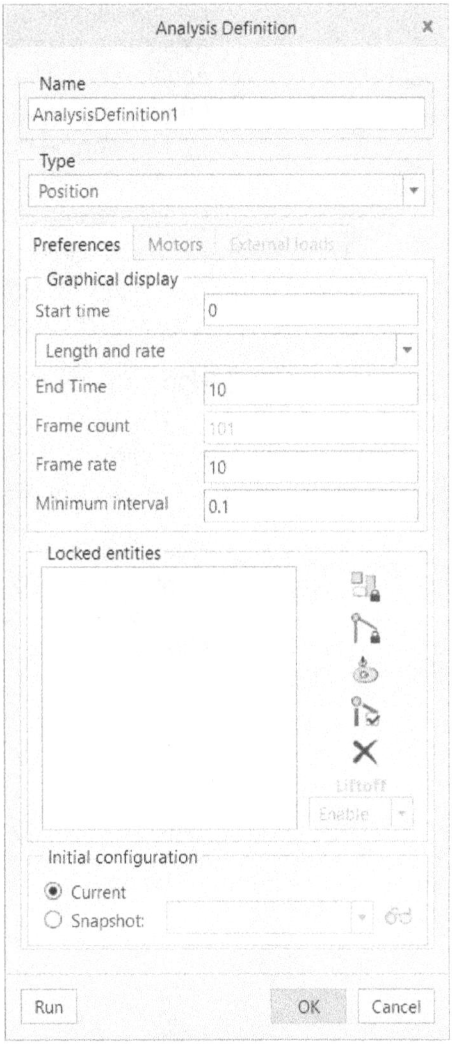

Figure 5–6

2. Select an analysis type in the Type drop-down list, as shown in Figure 5–7. The **Kinematic** and **Position** analysis types are covered in this learning guide.

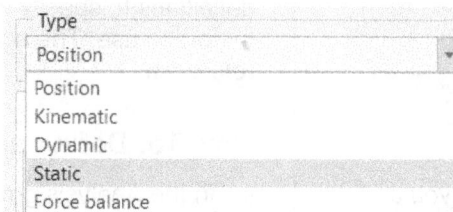

Type
Position
Position
Kinematic
Dynamic
Static
Force balance

Figure 5–7

Use a **Kinematic** analysis to evaluate the motion of your mechanism as driven by servo motors. You can use any joint axis servo motors with a profile that results in finite acceleration. Use a Kinematic analysis to obtain information on any of the following:

- Position, velocity, and acceleration of geometric entities and connections
- Interference between components
- Trace curves of the mechanism's motion
- Motion envelopes that capture the mechanism's motion as a Creo Parametric part

Use a **Position** analysis to study:

- Positions of components over time
- Interference between components
- Trace curves of the mechanism's motion

3. Creo Parametric automatically sets the time domain. If you want to use another time domain, specify the time domain type in the drop-down list in the *Graphical Display* area, as shown in Figure 5–8.

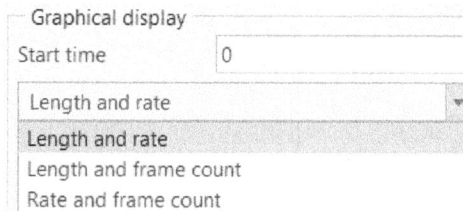

Graphical display	
Start time	0
Length and rate	
Length and rate	
Length and frame count	
Rate and frame count	

Figure 5–8

There are three time domain options. They depend on the following three separate parts of the analysis run:

- **Length:** Length is the total time of the motion run in seconds from beginning to end. Specify a Start Time and an End Time.
- **Frame count:** Frame count is the total number of frames calculated for the analysis run.
- **Frame rate:** Frame rate is the number of frames produced each second.

Only the Length and Frame rate need to be defined. The following relation calculates the Frame count:

Frame Count = Rate * Length + 1

4. Select the *Motors* tab. The dialog box opens as shown in Figure 5–9.

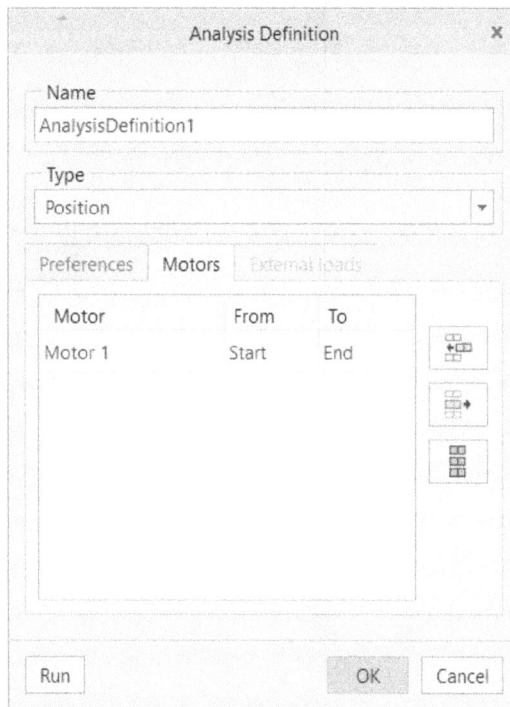

Figure 5–9

---

5. Select the appropriate servo motor for the analysis. By default, all of the servo motors defined for the mechanism display. Click ⊞ (Add Row) to add a servo motor or click ⊞ (Add All Motors) to add all servo motors. To remove a servo motor, click ⊞ (Delete Row). Servo motors can be activated at specific times and deactivated at other times by changing the values in the *From* and *To* columns. This gives you more flexibility when you create the analysis. Only one servo motor can be active for an entity at a specific time. After selecting the appropriate servo motors, you can review the analysis playback by clicking **Run**.

6. To complete the analysis, click **OK**. Once completed, the results can be viewed and analyzed.

Practice 5a

Applying Servo Motors I

Practice Objective

- Apply servo motors to a mechanism.

Servo motors enable you to assign a specific motion to your mechanism. In this practice, you will apply two separate servo motors to the four-bar linkage mechanism. After the servo motors have been applied, you will run an analysis to drive the motion.

Task 1 - Open the pin assembly and create a servo motor.

1. Set the working directory to the *Apply_Servo_I* folder.

2. Open **pin_5.asm**.

3. Set the model display as follows:

   - ⅔, *(Datum Display Filters)*: All Off

   - ✣ *(Spin Center)*: Off

   - ⬚, *(Display Style)*: ⬚ (Shading With Edges)

4. Activate Mechanism mode.

Alternatively, you can create a Servo Motor by clicking on the link_to_base connection on the model and selecting ☞ (Servo Motor) in the mini toolbar.

5. In the Insert group in the ribbon, click ☞ (Servo Motors).

6. Select the **link_to_base** connection axis on the model, as shown in Figure 5–10. The Driven Quantity switches to Angular Position in the *Motor* tab.

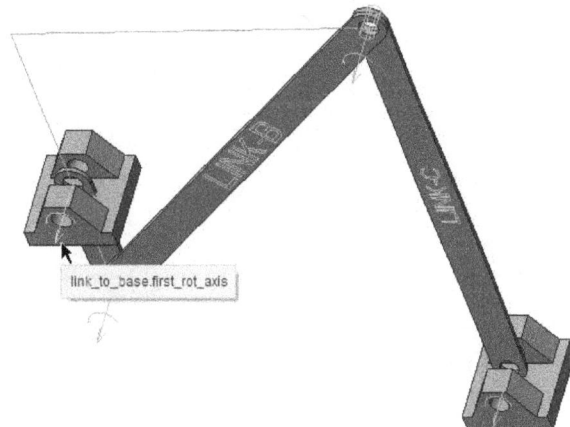

Figure 5–10

Design Considerations

When assigning a Servo Motor to a connection, a motion axis setting should be specified to assign the zero references and regeneration position. This can be done while in Servo Motor creation instead of having to exit and assign a Motion Axis Setting using an independent creation option.

7. Select the References panel.

8. Motion axis settings must be specified for this connection and a consistent starting position is required. Click 🖉 (Motion Axis Settings) to open the MOTION AXIS dialog box and set a starting position.

9. Select the thin surface on the link and the horizontal surface of the base, as shown in Figure 5–11.

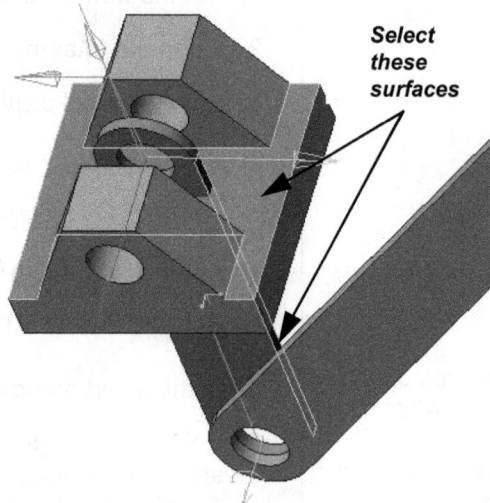

Select these surfaces

Figure 5–11

10. Specify the regeneration position to be **45** degrees. Click
   👓 (Preview). The model displays as shown in Figure 5–12.

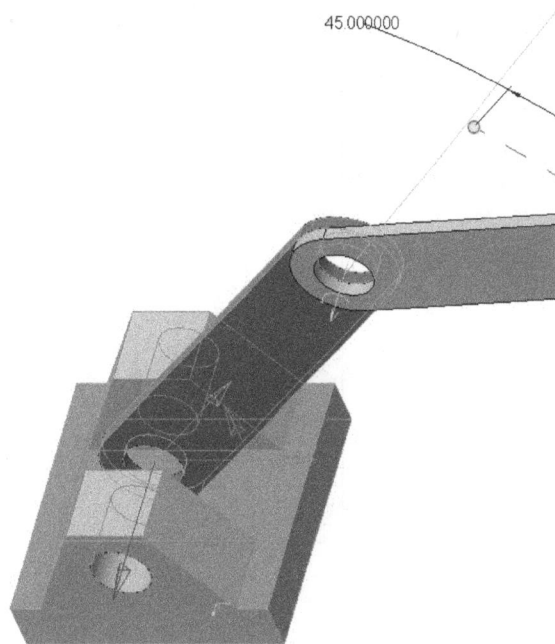

Figure 5–12

11. Click ✓ (OK).

Design Considerations

The default magnitude for a Servo Motor is a constant value.
This motor will be defined using a Ramp magnitude. The value of
the ramp is determined using the following equation:
y = A + B x t, where A is a constant and B is the slope.

12. Select the Profile Details panel and select **Ramp** in the
   Function Type drop-down list to define the magnitude as
   linearly changing motion.

13. Enter **45** for *A* and **36** for *B*. The starting position at time zero
   is equal to the regeneration position (45°) and is incremented
   by 36° every second, based on the following equation:

   y=A+B*t

   A is constant.

   B is the slope.

14. Select **Position**, **Velocity** and **Acceleration** in the graph
   area.

15. Click ⬚ (Graph Motor Profile). The Servo Motor profile graph displays as shown in Figure 5–13.

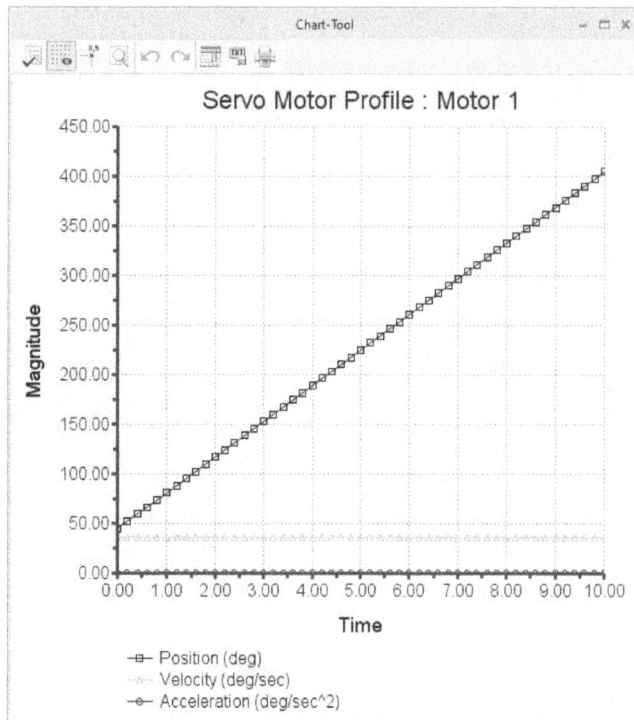

Figure 5–13

16. This is the motion that is required. Close the graph.

17. Click ✔ (OK) to complete the servo motor.

Task 2 - Create a new analysis definition.

1. Click ⬚ (Mechanism Analysis). The Analysis Definition dialog box opens.

2. Select **Kinematic** in the Type drop-down list to change the default analysis type.

3. Examine the settings. The motion is set to run for 10 seconds and requires 101 frames.

4. Select the *Motors* tab. The servo motor begins moving at the beginning of the run and stops moving at the end of the run.

5. Click **Run**.

6. Creo Parametric begins to calculate all 101 frames of the analysis. The analysis is one complete revolution based on the servo motor and time domain settings.

7. Click **OK**.

Task 3 - Create another servo motor.

In this task, you will define a second Servo Motor. Multiple Servos can be used to drive the same joint axis. The Servo Motors that are added to any analysis are controlled using the Analysis Definition dialog box.

1. Select the **link_to_base** connection axis on the model and select ✏️ (Servo Motor) in the mini toolbar.

2. Select the Profile Details panel and select **Angular Acceleration** in the Driven Quantity drop-down list.

3. Clear the **Use Current Position as Initial** option and set the Initial Angle to **45**.

4. Set the Initial Angular Velocity to **45**.

5. Select **SCCA** in the FunctionType drop-down list.

Design Considerations

The **SCCA** option defines the magnitude using the following parameters:

A = Percentage of period that the magnitude is increasing

B = Percentage of period that the magnitude is constant

H = Amplitude

T = Period

6. Change the values of A to **0.25**, B to **0.5**, H to **3** and T to **5**.

7. Graph the results for just the Acceleration using ⬚ (Graph Motor Profile). The graph should display as shown in Figure 5–14.

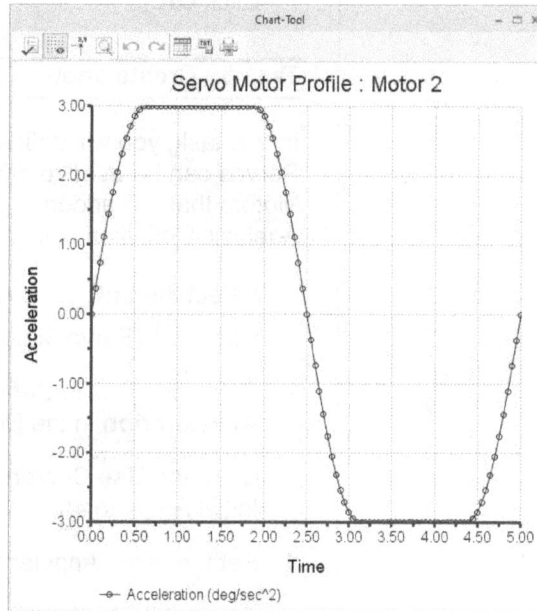

Figure 5–14

8. Close the graph and Click ✓ (OK).

Task 4 - Create a new analysis definition.

1. Click ⬚ (Mechanism Analysis).

2. Change the *End Time* from *10 seconds* to **20 seconds**.

*The Frame Count can only be edited when using the **Length and frame count** or **Rate and frame count** options.*

3. The Frame count automatically updates from *101* to **201**.

4. Select the *Motors* tab. Both servo motors are listed.

5. Select **ServoMotor1** and click ⬚ (Delete Row) to delete it. This operation removes the Servo Motor from the analysis, not from the model.

6. Click **Run**.

7. If prompted regarding a result set already being in session, click **Yes** to overwrite it.

8. When the run is complete, click **OK**.

9. Save the assembly and erase it from memory.

Practice 5b | Applying Servo Motors II

Practice Objective

- Apply servo motors to a mechanism.

In this practice, you will apply a Servo Motor to the engine assembly to drive the motion of the crankshaft. You will also assemble the cam assembly and apply a Servo Motor to it. Once the Servo Motors have been applied, you will create an analysis definition.

Task 1 - Open the engine assembly and apply a servo motor.

1. Set the working directory to the *Apply_Servo_II* folder.

2. Open **engine_5.asm**.

3. Set the model display as follows:

    - *(Datum Display Filters)*: All Off

    - *(Spin Center)*: Off

    - *(Display Style)*: (Shading With Edges)

4. Activate Mechanism mode.

5. Select on the crankshaft pin joint axis and, click (Servo Motor) in the mini toolbar, as shown in Figure 5–15.

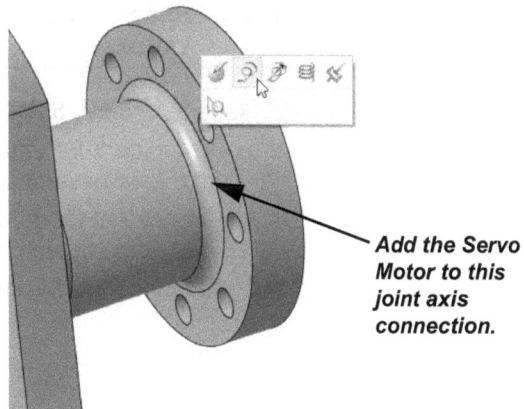

Add the Servo Motor to this joint axis connection.

Figure 5–15

6. The *Motor* tab opens. Edit the *Name* to **crank**.

7. Select the Profile Details panel and select **Angular Velocity** in the Driven Quantity drop-down list.

8. Clear the Use Current Position as Initial option and specify the initial angle as **0** where 0 is the position that is used during regeneration.

9. Select **Constant** in the Function Type drop-down list.

10. Specify the value of A as **72**.

The units for the constant magnitude of an Angular Velocity Servo Motor are deg/sec.

11. Click ✔ (OK).

Task 2 - Create the analysis definition.

1. Select **ANALYSES** in the mechanism tree and click ✴ (New) in the mini toolbar. The Analysis Definition dialog box opens.

2. Verify that the Crank servo motor is listed in the *Motors* tab. Maintain the remaining default options.

3. Click **Run**.

4. When the run is finished, click **OK**.

5. Save the assembly.

6. Click ☒ (Close) in the *Mechanism* tab. Click **Save** in the Save Playbacks dialog box to ensure the motion analysis results will be saved.

Task 3 - Assemble the cam assembly and set joint axis settings.

1. Assemble **cam_5.asm** using the following constraints:
   - Coincident for datum planes **ASM_RIGHT** on the engine and cam assemblies.
   - Coincident for datum planes **ASM_FRONT** on the engine and cam assemblies.
   - Distance for datum planes **ASM_TOP** on the engine and cam assemblies and offset them by **375**.

The assembly should display as shown in Figure 5–16.

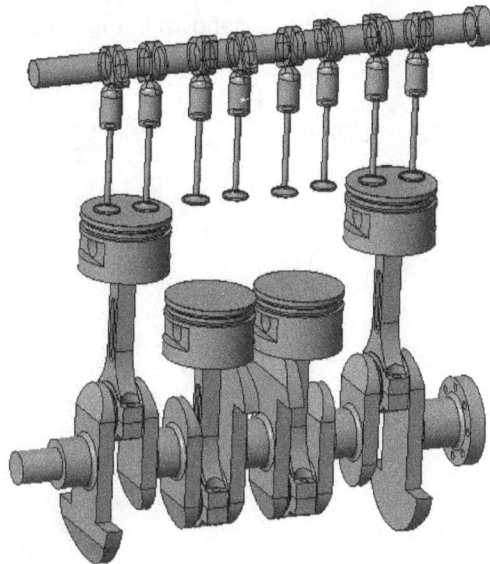

Figure 5–16

Design Considerations

The cam subassembly consists of a cam shaft and valve components. This assembly moves independently of the mechanism created in the engine assembly. Therefore, the subassembly will be opened in a new window and brought into Mechanism mode. This subassembly mechanism can then be driven by the top-level assembly.

2. Click on **cam_5.asm** in the Model Tree and select **Open** in the mini toolbar.

3. Activate Mechanism mode.

Task 4 - Create a servo motor for the camshaft.

---

1. Select the pin connection on the camshaft and add a new servo motor called **cam**.

2. In the *Profile* tab, click ⬚ (Motion Axis Settings) to open the MOTION AXIS dialog box.

3. Specify the zero references. Select the **ZERO_REF** datum plane in the camshaft and **ASM_TOP** in the assembly.

4. Set the regeneration position to **-95** and enable the Regeneration Value. Click ✓ (OK).

5. Select **Angular Velocity** as the Driven Quantity and set its Initial Angle to **-95** with an A Coefficient value of **-36** as shown in Figure 5–17.

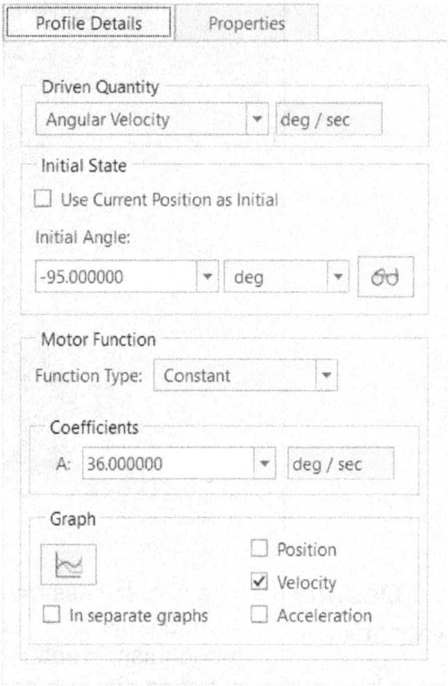

Figure 5–17

6. Click ✔ (OK).

Task 5 - Edit the existing analysis definition.

Design Considerations

In this task, you will return to the engine assembly and edit the Analysis definition to add the new Servo Motor that was created in the cam sub-assembly. Once this has been added, both motors will run at the same time to display the motion of the engine.

1. Return to the **ENGINE_5.ASM** window.

2. Activate Mechanism.

3. Select **AnalysisDefiniton1** under **ANALYSES** in the Mechanism tree and select **Edit Definition** in the mini toolbar. The Analysis Definition dialog box opens.

4. Select the *Motors* tab. The newly created servo motor is not part of the analysis.

5. Click ⊞ (Add All Motors) to add the cam servo motor, and click **Run**.

6. Click **OK**.

7. Save the assembly. Do not save the motion.

Practice 5c | Applying Servo Motors III

Practice Objective

- Apply servo motors to a mechanism.

In this practice, you will apply a Servo Motor to the sliding carriage assembly. The motor will drive rotation of the brown **link_d** model, as shown in Figure 5–18.

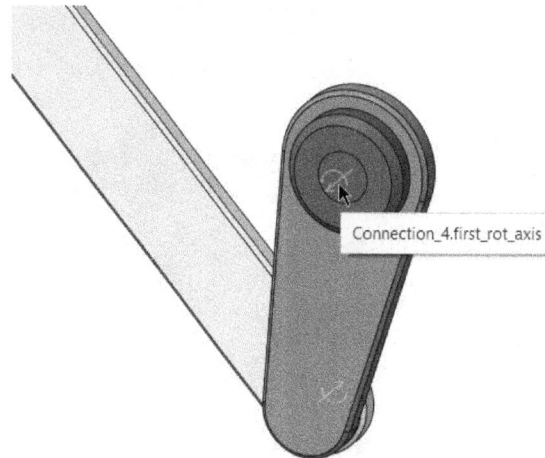

Figure 5–18

1. Set the working directory to the *Apply_Servo_III* folder.

2. Open **pause_slider.asm**.

3. Set the model display as follows:

   - ⤴ *(Datum Display Filters)*: All Off

   - ⤴ *(Spin Center)*: Off

   - ⬚ *(Display Style)*: ⬚ *(No Hidden)*

4. Activate Mechanism mode.

5. Click ⤵ *(Servo Motors)* to create a Servo Motor.

6. Change the motor Name to **Rotation**.

7. Select the rotation axis of the **link_d** to mount-1 pin joint as shown in Figure 5–19.

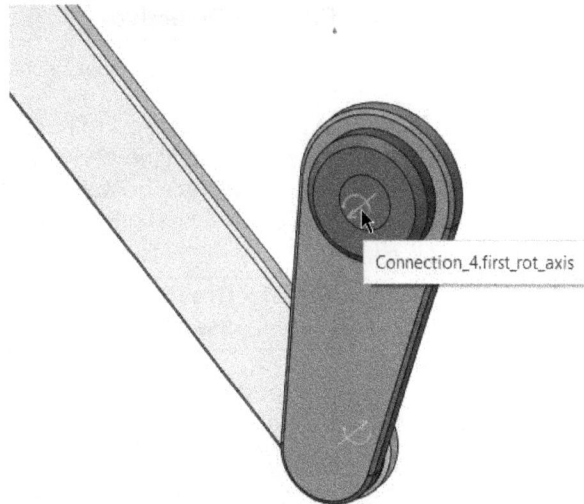

Connection_4.first_rot_axis

Figure 5–19

8. Set the *Driven Quantity Type* to **Angular Velocity**.

9. Set the *Function Type* to **Constant** and enter **36** for the *A* coefficient.

10. Click ✔ (OK).

11. Click ✕ (Mechanism Analysis).

12. Change the *End Time* to **20**.

13. Click **Run**.

14. Save the assembly and erase it from memory.

Practice 5d | Applying Servo Motors IV

Practice Objective

- Apply servo motors to a mechanism.

In this practice, you will apply Servo Motors to the tractor assembly. Multiple servo motors are created. Some servo motors will only be active during certain portions of the analysis. The analysis definition will be defined to include this intent.

Task 1 - Create the first servo motor in the hydraulic boom assembly.

1. Set the working directory to the *Apply_Servo_IV* folder.

2. Open **hydraulic_boom_5.asm**.

3. Set the model display as follows:

   - ⁺⁄⁺ *(Datum Display Filters)*: All Off

   - ⋟ *(Spin Center)*: Off

   - ⬚ *(Display Style)*: ⬚ (No Hidden)

4. Activate Mechanism mode.

5. Click ⌕ (Servo Motors) to create a Servo Motor.

6. Set the Servo Motor *Name* to **rotation**.

7. Select the rotation axis of the pin connection used to connect the pivot-arm and the base, as shown in Figure 5–20.

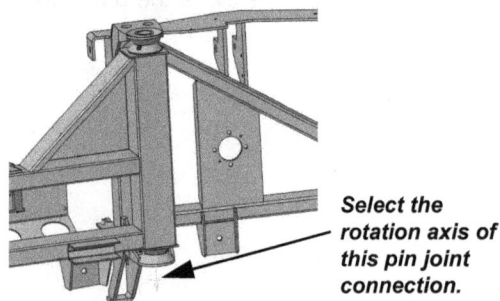

Select the rotation axis of this pin joint connection.

Figure 5–20

By clicking ⌇ (Graph Motor Profile), you can display a position, velocity, or acceleration graph of the selected motor.

8. In the Profile Details panel, select **Angular Position** as the *Driven Quantity*, and select **Ramp** as the *Function Type*.

9. Set *A* to **175** and *B* to **-35**. This takes the pivot arm from 175 degrees down to its preferred position of zero degrees in 5 seconds during the run.

10. Click ✔ (OK).

Task 2 - Create a servo motor for piston1.

---

1. Click ✑ (Servo Motors) and select the translation axis of the cylinder connection for **piston1**, as shown in Figure 5–21. You will need to right-click or use Pick From List to select the translation axis instead of the rotation axis.

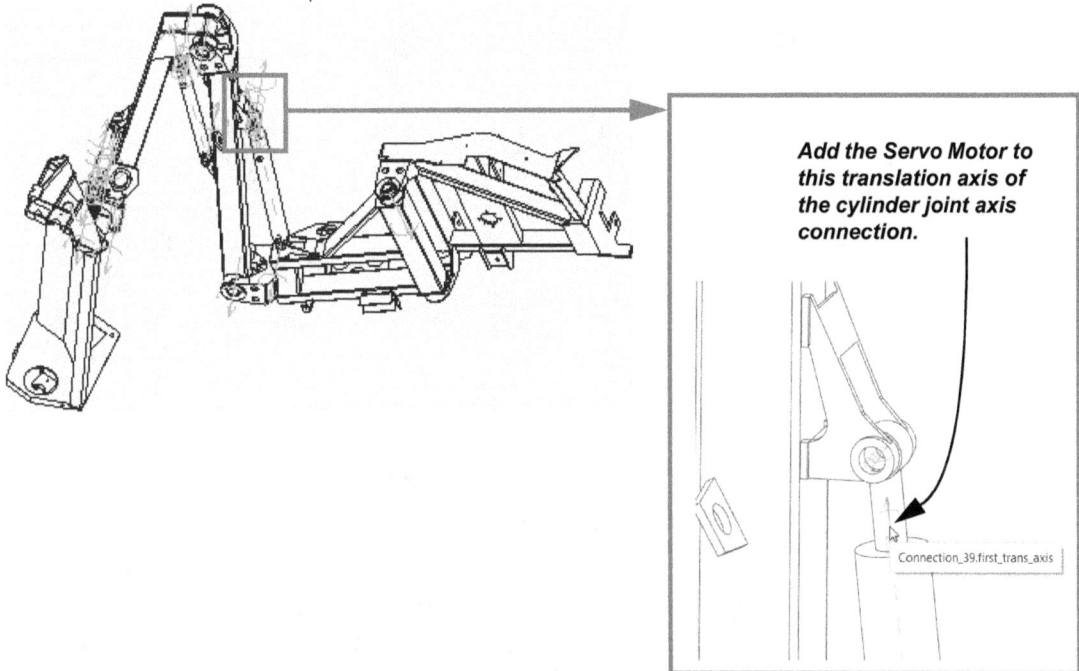

Add the Servo Motor to this translation axis of the cylinder joint axis connection.

Connection_39.first_trans_axis

Figure 5–21

2. Set the Servo Motor *Name* to **piston1**.

3. In the Profile Details panel, select **Position** as the *Driven Quantity*, and select **Ramp** as the *Function Type*.

   Note: If Angular Position is listed instead of Position, the rotation axis of the connection was selected.

---

4. Enter **-700** for *A* and **120** for *B*. This takes **boom1** from its contracted position to its extended position in 5 seconds during the run.

5. Click ✔ (OK).

Task 3 - Create a servo motor for piston2.

1. Click 🖉 (Servo Motors) and select the translation axis of the cylinder connection for **piston2**, as shown in Figure 5–22. You will need to right-click or use **Pick From List** to select the translation axis instead of the rotation axis.

Add the Servo Motor to this translation axis of the cylinder joint axis connection.

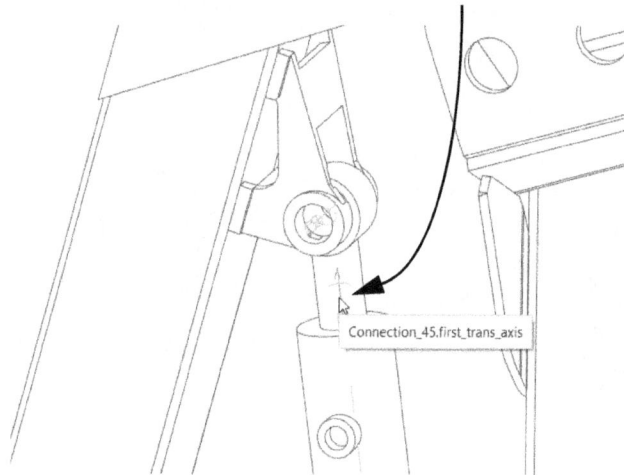

Connection_45.first_trans_axis

Figure 5–22

2. In the Profile Details panel, select **Ramp** as the Function Type.

3. Set *A* to **-575** and *B* to **250**. This takes **boom2** from its contracted position to its extended position in 2 seconds during the run.

4. Click ✔ (OK).

Task 4 - Create a servo motor for piston3.

1. Click (Servo Motors) and select the translation axis of the cylinder connection for piston3, as shown in Figure 5–23.

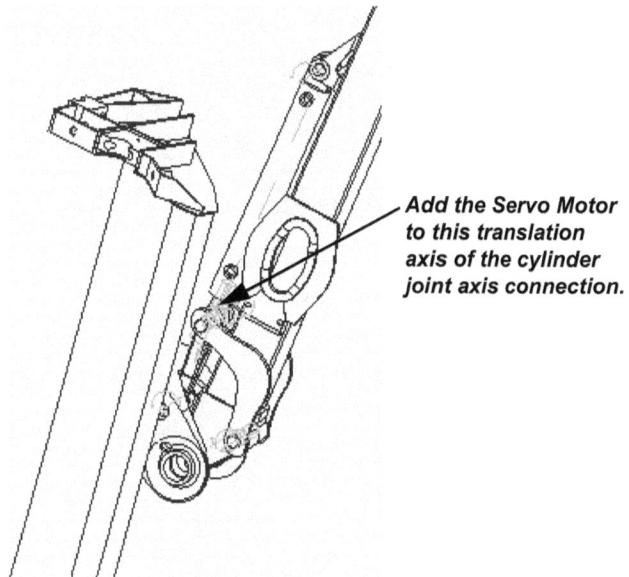

Add the Servo Motor to this translation axis of the cylinder joint axis connection.

Figure 5–23

2. Enter **piston3** as the name of the Servo Motor.

3. In the Profile Details panel, select **Ramp** as the Function Type.

4. Set *A* to **-450** and *B* to **79**. This takes the bucket attachment from its contracted position to its extended position in 3 seconds during the run.

5. Click (OK).

Task 5 - Set up the analysis definition.

1. Add a new analysis definition.

2. Verify that the *End Time* is set to **10**.

3. Select the **Snapshot** option in the *Initial Configuration* area and set the 3-1 snapshot as the starting point.

4. Click (Preview Snapshot).

5. Select the *Motors* tab.

All four servo motors are included in the run. However, all of the servo motors start at the beginning of the run and end at the end of the run. This is not wanted in this case because of the servo motor definition.

6. Set the motor start and end time, as shown in Figure 5–24.

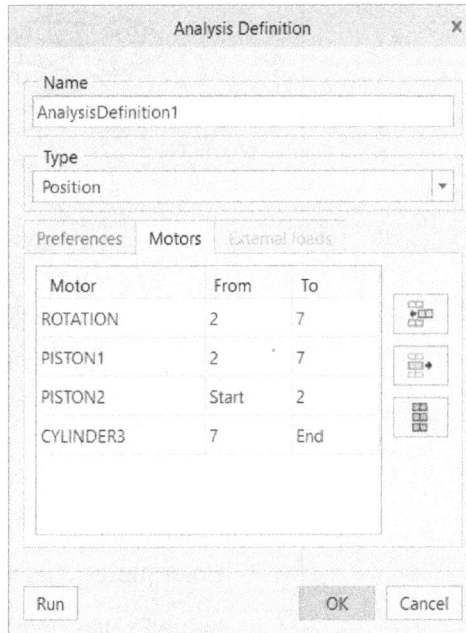

Analysis Definition   ✕

Name

AnalysisDefinition1

Type

Position

Preferences | Motors | External loads

Motor	From	To
ROTATION	2	7
PISTON1	2	7
PISTON2	Start	2
CYLINDER3	7	End

Run   OK   Cancel

Figure 5–24

Shaded models run more quickly than the other display options (wireframe, hidden-line, or no-hidden line model).

7. Click **Run**.

8. Click **OK**.

9. Save the assembly and erase it from memory.

Practice 5e

Pantograph

Practice Objectives

- Add a servo motor.

In this practice, you will add a servo motor to drive the pencil along the curve in the Slot connection. The final assembly displays as shown in Figure 5–25.

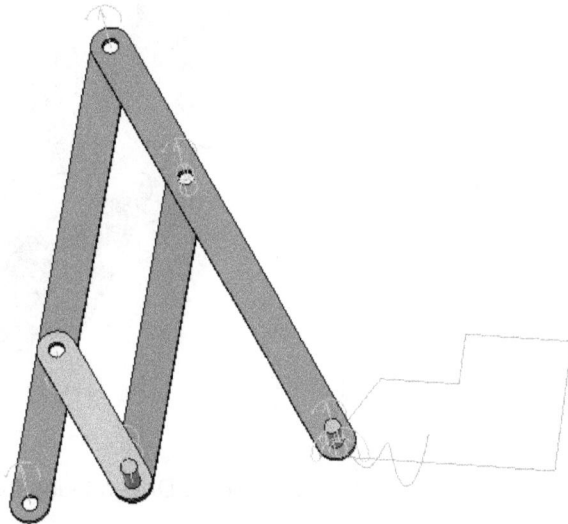

Figure 5–25

Task 1 - Open an existing assembly.

1. Set the working directory to *Pantograph_II*.

2. Open **pantograph.asm**.

3. Set the model display as follows:

- ⁺⁄⁎ *(Datum Display Filters)*: All Off

- ⤙ *(Spin Center)*: Off

- ⬜ *(Display Style)*: ⬜ (Shading With Edges)

Task 2 - Add a servo motor on the Slot axis.

1. Select the *Applications* tab and click ❄ (Mechanism).

2. Click ⌇ (Servo Motors) to create a Servo Motor.

3. In the Properties panel, set the Servo Motor *Name* to **curve**.

4. Select the Slot icon as shown in Figure 5–26.

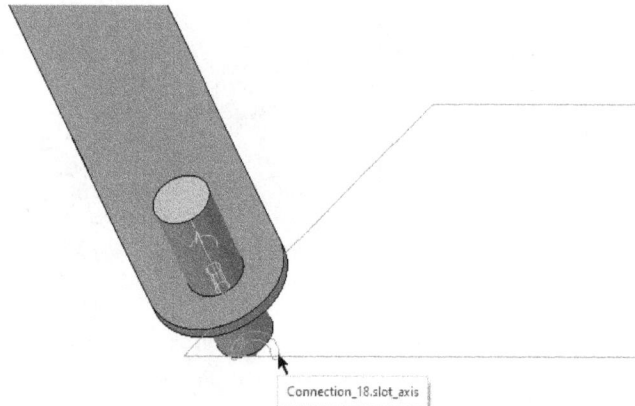

Connection_18.slot_axis

Figure 5–26

5. Set the Driven Quantity Type to **Velocity**.

6. In the Profile Detail panel, set the Function Type to **Constant** and enter **44** for the A coefficient.

7. Click ✓ (OK).

8. Click ⋈ (Mechanism Analysis).

9. Set the Frame Rate to **50**.

10. Click **Run**.

11. Save the assembly and erase it from memory.

Practice 5f | (Optional) Project - 3D Contact Assembly

Practice Objective

- Apply servo motors to a mechanism.

In this practice, you will apply Servo Motors to the 3D Contact assembly shown in Figure 5–27. Two motors will be created. One to drive each of the two rotation cam parts in the assembly. An analysis will be setup running both motors simultaneously.

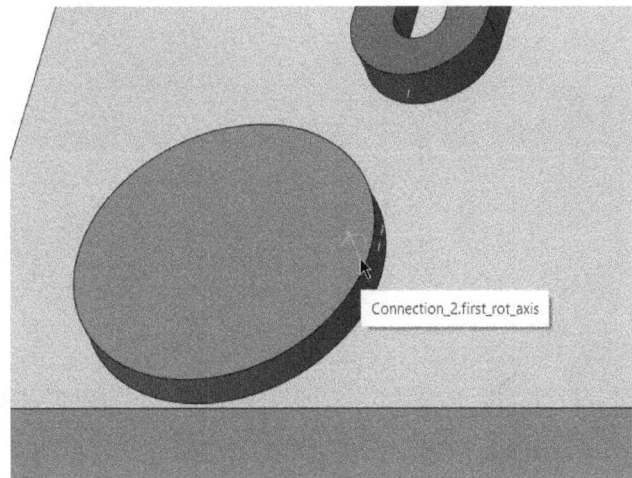

Figure 5–27

1. Set the working directory to the *Project_3D_Contact* folder.

2. Open **3d_contact.asm**.

3. Set the model display as follows:

    - ⚓ *(Datum Display Filters)*: All Off

    - ⤳ *(Spin Center)*: Off

    - ▱ *(Display Style)*: ▱ (No Hidden)

4. Activate Mechanism mode.

5. Click ⌖ (Servo Motors) to create a Servo Motor.

6. Set the Servo Motor *Name* to **rotation-gear1**.

7. Select the rotation axis of the pin connection used to connect the 3D-gear1 part and the 3D-contact-plate part, as shown in Figure 5–28.

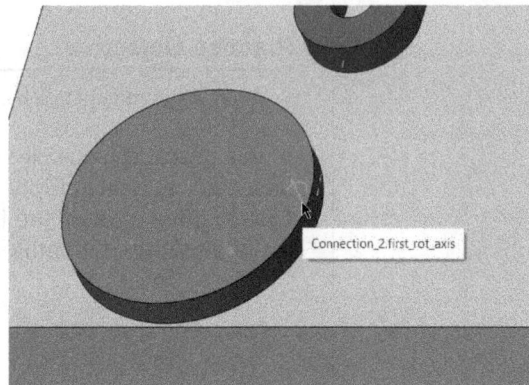

Connection_2.first_rot_axis

Figure 5–28

8. Set the *Driven Quantity Type* to **Angular Velocity**.

9. Set the Function Type to **Constant** and enter **36** for the A coefficient.

10. Click ✓ (OK).

11. Click ⌒ (Servo Motors) to create a second Servo Motor.

12. Set the Servo Motor *Name* to **rotation-gear2**.

13. Select the rotation axis of the pin connection used to connect the 3D-gear2 part and the 3D-contact-plate part, as shown in Figure 5–29.

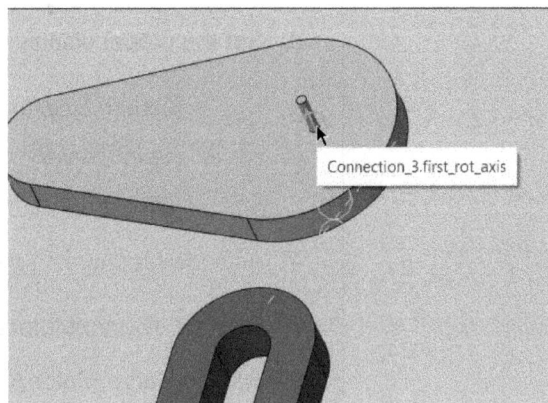

Connection_3.first_rot_axis

Figure 5–29

14. Set the *Driven Quantity Type* to **Angular Velocity**.

15. Set the *Function Type* to **Constant** and enter **36** for the *A* coefficient.

16. Click ✓ (OK).

17. Click ⚒ (Mechanism Analysis).

18. Change the *End Time* to **20**.

19. Select **Snapshot** in the *Initial Configuration* area and set the **Starting Position** snapshot as the starting point.

20. Click 👓 (Preview Snapshot).

21. Active the *Motors* tab. Note that both motors are listed and set to run from start to end.

22. Click **Run**.

23. Save the assembly and erase it from memory.

Practice 5g

(Optional) Project - Applying Servo Motors

Practice Objective

• Apply servo motors to a mechanism.

In this practice, you will apply a Servo Motor to the worm gear assembly. The motor will drive rotation of the worm model shown in Figure 5–30.

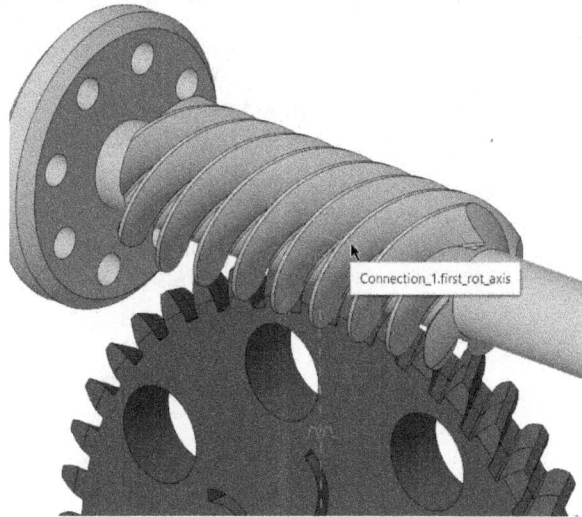

Figure 5–30

1. Set the working directory to the *Project_Servo* folder.

2. Open **worm_gear_m10.asm**.

3. Set the model display as follows:

   • *(Datum Display Filters)*: All Off

   • *(Spin Center)*: Off

   • *(Display Style)*: (No Hidden)

4. Activate Mechanism mode.

5. Click *(Servo Motors)* to create a Servo Motor.

6. Change the motor name to **Rotation**.

7. Select the rotation axis of the **link_d** to mount-1 pin joint, as shown in Figure 5–31.

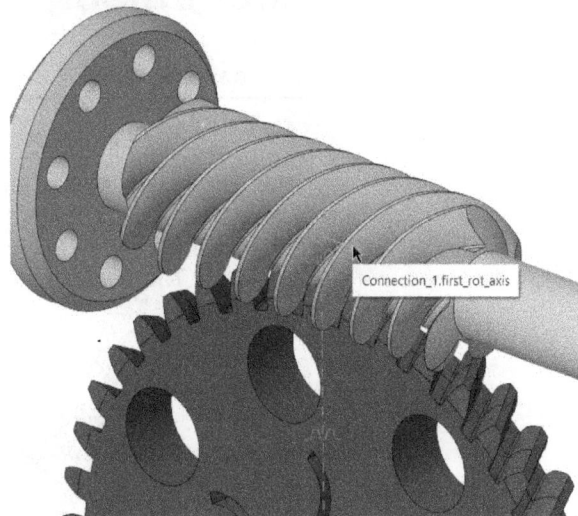

Figure 5–31

8. Set the *Driven Quantity Type* to **Angular Velocity**.

9. Set the *Function Type* to **Constant** and enter **36** for the A coefficient.

10. Click ✔ (OK).

11. Click 📐 (Mechanism Analysis).

12. Change the *End Time* to **20**.

13. Select **Snapshot** in the *Initial Configuration* area and set the **Starting Position** snapshot as the starting point.

14. Click 👓 (Preview Snapshot)

15. Click **Run**.

16. Save the assembly and erase it from memory.

Practice 5h | (Optional) Project - Geneva Mechanism

Practice Objective

- Create a Servo Motor to drive rotation in the geneva mechanism.

In this practice, you will create a rotational motor to drive the geneva mechanism. The motor will be defined using a constant angular velocity and applied to the rotation axis of a pin connection. The final assembly displays as shown in Figure 5–32.

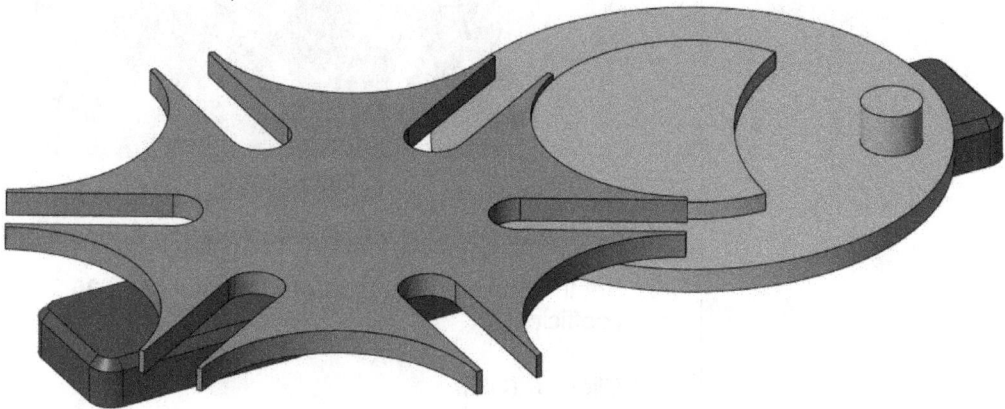

Figure 5–32

Task 1 - Open an existing assembly and create a 3D Contact connection.

1. Set the working directory to the *Project_Geneva* folder.

2. Open **geneva_mechanism.asm**.

3. Set the model display as follows:

    - *(Datum Display Filters)*: *(Axis Display)*

    - *Datum Tag Display:* (Plane Tag Display), (Axis Tag Display), (Csys Tag Display)

    - *(Spin Center)*: Off

    - *(Display Style)*: (No Hidden)

4. Select the *Applications* tab and click ⚙ (Mechanism) to activate the Mechanism application.

5. Select on the gm-driver pin joint axis and, click 🔧 (Servo Motor) in the mini toolbar, as shown in Figure 5–33.

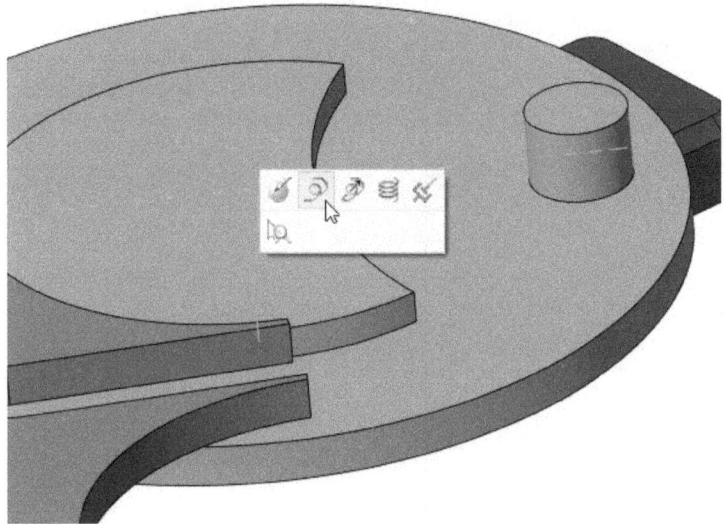

Figure 5–33

6. Change the motor name to **Rotation**

7. Set the *Driven Quantity Type* to **Angular Velocity**.

8. Set the *Function Type* to **Constant** and enter **21.6** for the *A* coefficient, as shown in Figure 5–34.

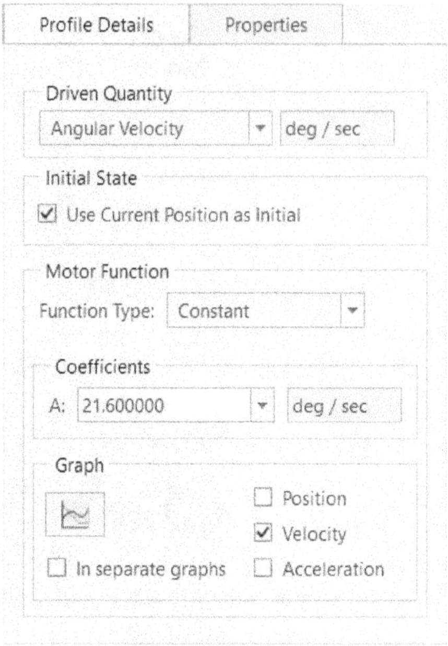

Figure 5–34

9. Click ✔ (OK).

10. Click ✂ (Mechanism Analysis).

11. Change the *End Time* to **100**. At an angular velocity of 21.6 deg/sec run for 100 seconds the driver will rotate total of 2160 degrees or 6 full revolutions (6 times 360 is 2160).

12. Click **Run**.

13. Save the assembly and erase it from memory.

Practice 5i

(Optional) Project - Scotch Yoke

Practice Objective

- Create a Servo Motor to drive the scotch yoke.

In this practice, you will create a rotational motor to drive the scotch yoke mechanism. The final assembly displays as shown in Figure 5–35.

Figure 5–35

Task 1 - Open an existing assembly and add a 3D Contact constraint.

1. Set the working directory to the *Project_Yoke* folder.

2. Open **scotch-yoke.asm**.

3. Set the model display as follows:

    - (*Datum Display Filters*): All Off

    - (*Spin Center*): Off

    - (*Display Style*): ⬜ (Shading With Edges)

4. Select the *Applications* tab and click ⚙ (Mechanism) to enable the Mechanism application.

5. Click ⟳ (Servo Motors) to create a Servo Motor.

6. Set the Servo Motor name to **rotation**.

7. Select the rotation axis of the pin connection used to connect the s-wheel to the mounting-plate as shown in Figure 5–36.

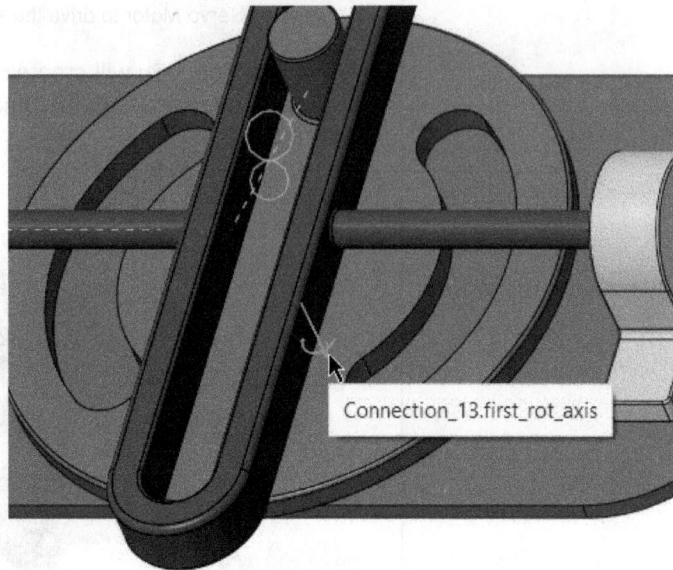

Connection_13.first_rot_axis

Figure 5–36

8. Set the *Driven Quantity Type* to **Angular Velocity**.

9. Set the *Function Type* to **Constant** and enter **36** for the *A* coefficient.

10. Click ✔ (OK).

11. Click ⟋ (Mechanism Analysis).

12. Click **Run**.

13. Save the assembly and erase it from memory.

Practice 5j

(Optional) Project - Quick Return Mechanism

Practice Objective

- Create a Servo Motor to drive the quick return mechanism.

In this practice, you will add a servo motor to rotate the driving-wheel of the quick return mechanism. The final assembly displays as shown in Figure 5–37.

Figure 5–37

Task 1 - Open an existing assembly and create a rotational servo motor on a pin joint axis.

1. Set the working directory to the *Project_Quick_Return* folder.

2. Open **whitworth.asm**.

3. Set the model display as follows:

   - ⤬⤬ *(Datum Display Filters)*: All Off

   - ➤ *(Spin Center)*: Off

   - ▢ *(Display Style)*: ▢ (Shading With Edges)

4. Select the *Applications* tab and click ⚙ (Mechanism) to enable the Mechanism application.

5. Click ⟳ (Servo Motors) to create a Servo Motor.

6. Set the Servo Motor name to **rotation**.

7. Select the rotation axis of the pin connection used to connect the driving-wheel to the assembly, as shown in Figure 5–38.

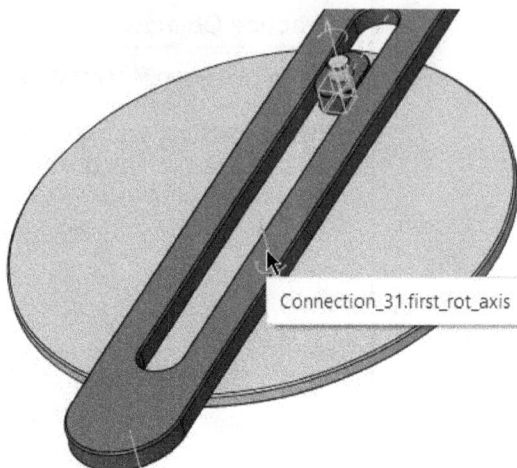

Connection_31.first_rot_axis

Figure 5–38

8. Set the *Driven Quantity Type* to **Angular Velocity**.

9. Set the *Function Type* to **Constant** and enter **36** for the A coefficient.

10. Click ✔ (OK).

11. Click ✕ (Mechanism Analysis).

12. Change the *End Time* to **30**.

13. Click **Run**. Note that the bar slides to the left much faster than it does to the right.

14. Save the assembly and erase it from memory.

Chapter Review Questions

1. Servo motors can be used to drive which of the following as a function of time? (Select all that apply.)

   a. Position

   b. Velocity

   c. Acceleration

2. Which servo motor function type has a non-linear equation?

   a. Constant

   b. Ramp

   c. Cosine

3. Multiple servo motors can run simultaneously in a Mechanism Analysis.

   a. True

   b. False

4. A single servo motor can drive both the rotation and translation axis of Cylinder connection.

   a. True

   b. False

5. Which of the following would be valid units for a servo motor assigned to a Slider connection driving the velocity?

   a. m/sec^2

   b. in/sec

   c. degree/sec

   d. ft-lb

Answers: 1abc, 2c, 3a, 4b, 5b

Playback Results

Once an analysis has been created, you can use playback tools to help analyze the results. These include checking the mechanism for interference, creating curves, creating motion envelopes (which create new parts that display the full extent of motion), and enabling users who might not have access to Creo Parametric to record the motion. In addition, you can use a standard Creo Parametric analysis feature to create measurements in your mechanism that can also be evaluated.

Learning Objectives in this Chapter

- Learn to create a Playback to review the motion of the mechanism without re-running the motion.
- Learn to export the analysis in the Playback dialog box, and create a movie and image file.
- Use the Playback results to check for interference between parts.
- Use the **Playback** command to create a swept volume that a mechanism claims in space throughout its motion using a motion envelope.
- Use measurements in mechanisms to compare the measurement against an analysis result and display the comparison graphically.
- Learn to generate trace curves to capture the movement of a point or vertex with respect to a component in the mechanism.
- Use a Cam Synthesis Curve to represent the motion of a curve or edge relative to a part in the assembly.

6.1 Playback

*You can also open the Playbacks dialog box directly from the Mechanism tree. Select **PLAYBACKS** in the Mechanism tree, right-click and select **Play**.*

After an analysis has been run, the results of it are temporarily stored in memory. Click ◀▶ (Playback) in the *Mechanism* tab to display the results. The Playbacks dialog box opens as shown in Figure 6–1.

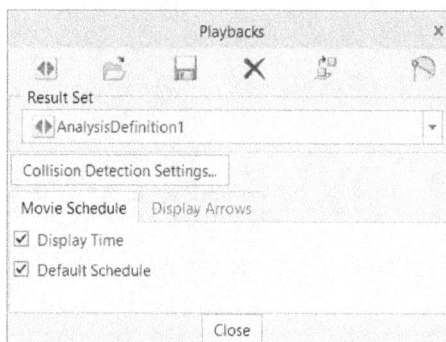

Figure 6–1

Select the appropriate analysis definition in the Result Set drop-down list. If no analysis definitions are available, you must rerun the analysis or import a result set from the hard disk by clicking 🗁 (Restore Result Set). To save an analysis definition for later use, click 🖫 (Save Result Set). The analysis definition files are saved with a .PBK extension.

To run the mechanism through the analysis, click ◀▶ (Play Result Set) in the Playbacks dialog box. The Animate dialog box opens as shown in Figure 6–2.

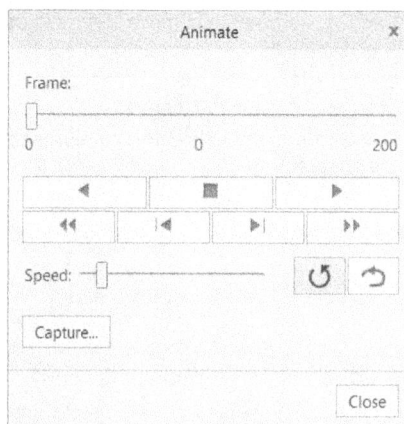

Figure 6–2

The Animate dialog box icons are described as follows:

Button	Action
◀	Enables you to play the animation in reverse.
▦	Enables you to stop the animation.
▶	Enables you to play the animation.
◀◀	Enables you to reset the animation to the beginning.
⏮	Enables you to move to the previous frame of the animation.
⏭	Enables you to move to the next frame of the animation.
▶▶	Enables you to advance the animation to the end.
↺	Enables you to loop the animation (selected by default).
↩	Enables you to automatically run the motion in reverse when the animation is complete.

You can also use the two sliders in the Animate dialog box to adjust the animation. Use the Speed slider to adjust the speed of the animation. Use the Frame slider to move to a specific frame in the animation.

6.2 Movie and Image Files

You might want to share the results of an analysis with colleagues or clients who do not have Creo Parametric. To do so, you can create a movie or image file of the analysis by clicking **Capture** in the Animate dialog box. The Capture dialog box opens as shown in Figure 6–3.

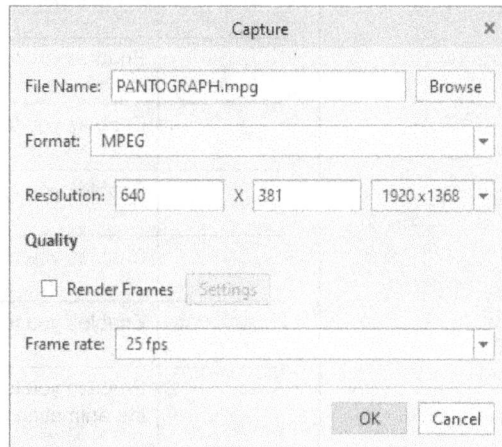

	Capture ✕
File Name:	PANTOGRAPH.mpg Browse
Format:	MPEG ▼
Resolution:	640 X 381 1920 x 1368 ▼
Quality	
	☐ Render Frames Settings
Frame rate:	25 fps ▼
	OK Cancel

Figure 6–3

To create an MPEG movie file that contains the entire range of motion, select the **MPEG** type in the drop-down list. To create images of specific frames in the animation, select the **JPEG**, **TIFF**, or **BMP** option. JPEG, TIFF, and BMP files are created for each frame in the motion.

The higher the resolution, the larger the file size.

You can increase or decrease the resolution of the frames by entering custom values in the *Width* (pixels) and *Height* (pixels) fields. This creates larger or smaller images and movies.

In the *Quality* area in the dialog box, the **Render Frames** option enables you to record the movie or images with a variable number samples.

The *Frame Rate* area enables you to change the frame rate. However, it can only be used for MPEG movies. You can select **25**, **30**, or **50 fps** (frame per seconds).

6.3 Checking for Interference

During playback, Creo Parametric can check for interference between parts. The interference options can be specified by clicking **Collision Detection Settings...** in the Playbacks dialog box. The Interference options are described as follows:

- The **Global Interference** option might result in longer model generation times.

- Global settings can also be defined by selecting **File> Prepare>Model Properties** and clicking **change** beside Collision Detection.

Option	Description
No Collision Detection	Creo Parametric does not check the model for interference (default option).
Global Collision Detection	Checks for any interference in the model. Any interference in the model is highlighted in red.
Partial Collision Detection	Enables you to look for interference between two selected parts. Creo Parametric checks for interference between the two parts and highlights any interference in red.

In large assemblies, the advanced collision detection options can cause very slow movement of the assembly.

Additional settings can be applied to the Collision detection when the **enable_advance_collision** configuration option is set to **yes**. The Collision Detection Settings dialog box with the **enable_advance_collision** configuration option enabled is shown in Figure 6–4.

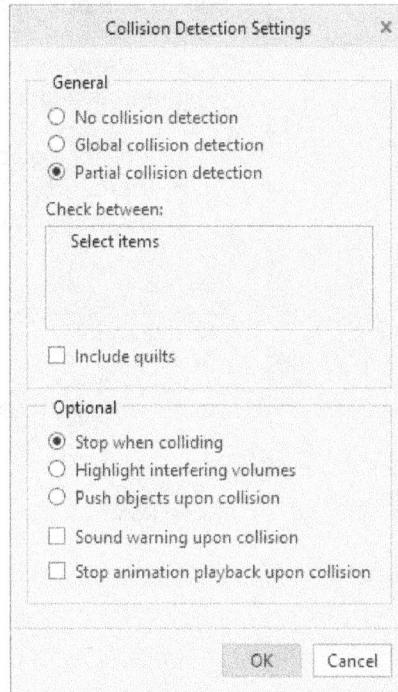

Figure 6–4

The Optional Settings enable you to control how Creo Parametric prompts you about a collision. For example, select **Ring Message Bell When Colliding** to sound a warning bell when a collision happens.

6.4 Motion Envelope Creation

A motion envelope created using assembly analysis features and the Behavioral Modeling Extension only produces a surface feature.

A motion envelope is a surface that is created to describe the swept volume that a mechanism claims in space throughout its motion. You can create motion envelopes using MDX or using assembly analysis features and the Behavioral Modeling Extension. You can use the exported motion envelope (surface) in the same manner as a standard Creo Parametric part.

How To: Create an Envelope Using MDX

1. Click (Motion Envelope) in the Playbacks dialog box. A result set must be available in the current session, or you can restore a saved .PBK file. The Create Motion Envelope dialog box opens as shown in Figure 6–5.

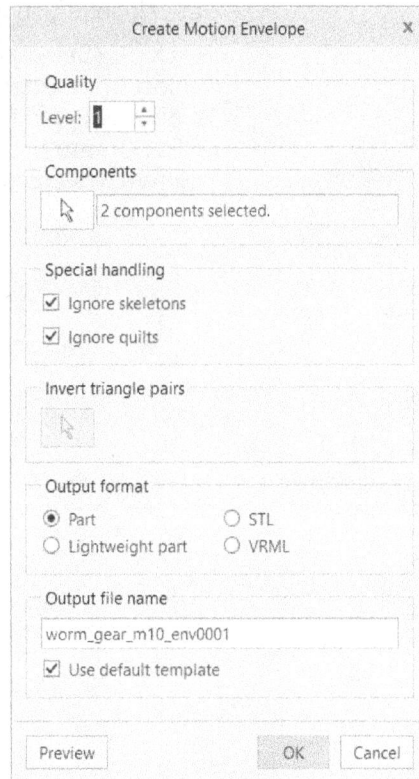

Figure 6–5

Mechanism Design selects all of the components in your assembly by default, and displays the number of components in the text box.

2. Specify the quality level of the envelope. The higher the level, the longer it takes to generate. However, the higher the level, the better the geometry is rendered.

3. Click ⌕ (Select) in the *Components* area to select parts or bodies in the assembly to include in the motion envelope.

4. The *Special Handlings* area enables you to set whether the skeletons and quilts will be ignored during motion envelope creation.

5. Specify an *Output Format*. Part is the default selection; it creates a Creo Parametric part with surface geometry. LW creates a Creo Parametric part with faceted and lightweight geometry. STL creates an .STL file and VRML creates a .VRML file.

6. Enter an *Output File Name* and select whether or not the envelope will be created using the default template.

7. Click **Preview** to preview a shaded display of the motion envelope. If you want to adjust the motion envelope model, click ⌕ (Select) in the *Invert triangle pairs* area. When you select the shaded representation, the triangular edges are highlighted and inverted with other pairs.

8. Click **Create** to create the motion envelope part/file in the current working directory.

6.5 Analyzing Measures

Measures are used in mechanisms to compare a defined measurement against an analysis result. The comparison displays graphically for you to evaluate whether the mechanism needs modification or redesign.

The measures that can be studied can be created in one of the following ways:

- Create analysis features using the standard Creo Parametric functionality (Select the *Analysis* tab, expand ✐ (Measure) and select ⊓ (Distance), or ⋈ (Length), ⟁ (Angle), etc.). Once the analysis feature has been created, it generates parameters that can be used in the study of the mechanism (e.g., distance or angular measurements).

Measurement parameters created in Mechanism Design are available for use in a BMX motion analysis.

- Create mechanism design measurements for position, velocity, or acceleration using the Measure Results dialog box. To use these measurement tools, click ⋈ (Measures) in the tab and click ▢ (Create New Measure) to create a measurement.

Measures for different types of analyses are described as follows:

Analysis	Measures
Kinematic	Position, Velocity, Acceleration, and Creo Parametric features.
Repeated Assembly	Position and Creo Parametric features.

How To: Tack a Defined Measurement for the Total Range of Motion

1. Click ⬰ (Measures). The Measure Results dialog box opens as shown in Figure 6–6.

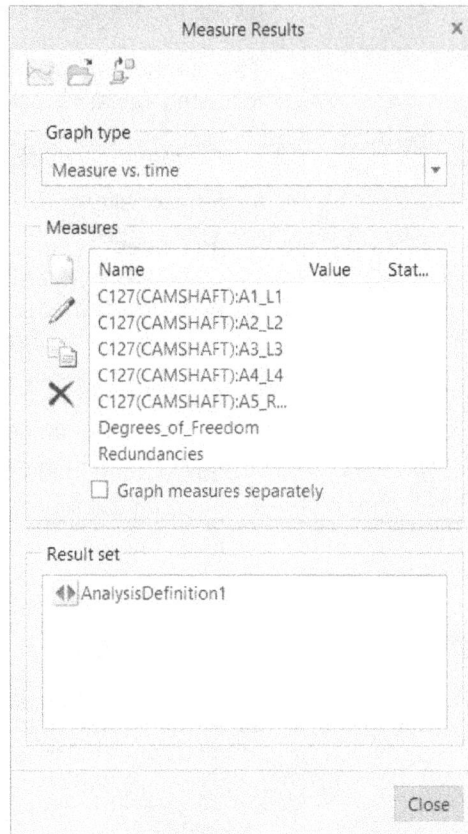

Figure 6–6

2. Select one or more measures from the list of available measurements for which you want to graph the results. This list consists of measurements created using this dialog box or any measurements that were created as Analysis features.

3. Select a Result Set to analyze. If your results are saved on your hard drive, click 🗁 (Load Result Set) and load them.

*You can alter the graph using the **Graph** tool's drop-down list options and icons.*

4. To display the plot, click ⬓ (Graph Selected Measures). The graph displays in a new window, similar to that shown in Figure 6–7.

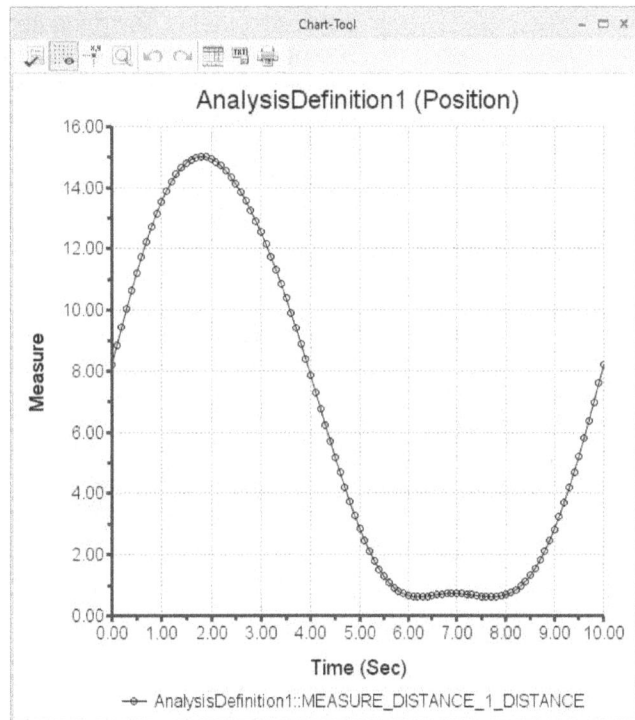

Figure 6–7

5. By default, the results display in a graph window. To share the results with others, you can export the content of the graph window into an Excel file (*.XLS) or into a text file (*.GRT) using **Export Excel** and **Export Text** in the File drop-down list in the Graph tool window.

6. Once you have reviewed the graph, you can close the Graph tool window. Alternatively, if you want to simultaneously view an analysis playback and track the value of your measure, close the Measure Results dialog box. However, do not close the Graph tool window. When you run a playback, a tracking bar indicates the progression through the graph.

6.6 Trace Curves

Trace curves are used to capture the movement of a point or vertex, with respect to a component in the mechanism. The point or vertex that is being studied can be selected from any component in the mechanism. In addition, the resulting trace curve can be stored in any component, including the component to which the selected point or vertex belongs. The selected component to which the curve is stored is called the Paper Part. Once created, the trace curve can be used to create solid geometry or for measurements.

How To: Create a Trace Curve

1. Select **Analysis>Trace Curve**. The Trace Curve dialog box opens as shown in Figure 6–8.

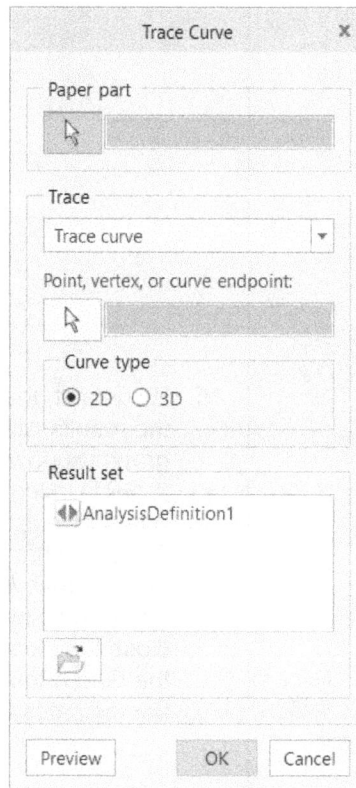

Figure 6–8

2. Select the part (Paper Part) in which the curve becomes created.

3. Select the type of trace that is to be created in the Trace drop-down list. The options include **Trace Curve** and **Cam Synthesis Curves**.

4. Select the trace point or vertex that is going to be used to generate the curve. This point does not have to exist in the Paper Part.

5. Select **2D** or **3D** as the Curve Type. 2D trace curves are created as sketched datum curves in the Part. 3D trace curves are created as a series of points in a group that are used to create a curve through these points. These points can be redefined to get the profile that you want to use. The Model Trees for both 2D and 3D trace curves are shown in Figure 6–9.

Figure 6–9

6. Before you create a trace curve, a result set must be in session or you can load one using (Load Result Set).

7. Click **Preview** to preview the trace curve that is going to be generated.

8. Click **OK** to complete the trace curve and create it in the Paper Part. To save the datum curve feature in the Paper Part, you must save the part. If the Paper Part is used multiple times in the mechanism, the trace curve displays in each instance because it is stored in that file.

9. To delete the trace curve, open the Paper Part in the Model Tree and delete it in this component.

6.7 Cam Synthesis Curves

Cam Synthesis curves represent the motion of a curve or edge relative to a part in your assembly. The process of creating Cam Synthesis curves is similar to creating Trace curves. However, only a 2D curve can be generated. Select **Cam Synthesis Curves** in the Trace drop-down list. The resulting curve can be used to generate a cam profile.

Practice 6a

Pantograph

Practice Objectives

- Run an analysis.
- Create a trace curve.

In this practice, you will create a trace curve of the follower pencil in the pantograph assembly. The final assembly displays as shown in Figure 6–10.

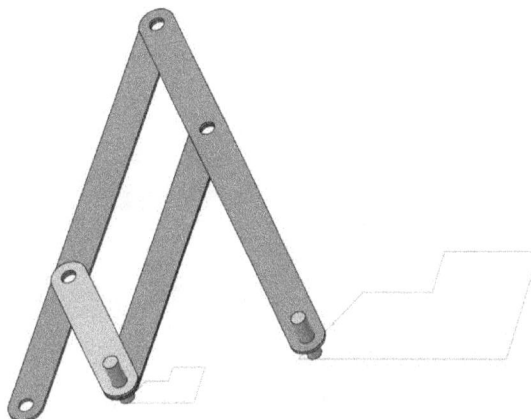

Figure 6–10

Task 1 - Open an existing assembly.

1. Set the working directory to *Pantograph_III*.

2. Open **pantograph.asm**.

3. Set the model display as follows:

- ✲ *(Datum Display Filters)*: All Off

- ⊶ *(Spin Center)*: Off

- ▢ *(Display Style)*: ▢ (Shading With Edges)

Task 2 - Create a Trace Curve.

1. Select the *Applications* tab and click ⚙ (Mechanism) to enable the Mechanism application.

2. Expand ANALYSIS in the Mechanism Tree, click on AnalysisDefinition1 (POSITION) and select click ⚑ (Run) in the mini toolbar, as shown in Figure 6–11.

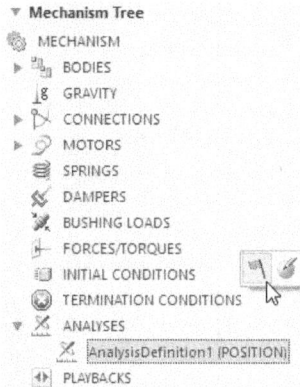

Figure 6–11

1. In the *Mechanism* tab, select **Analysis>Trace Curve**. The Trace Curve dialog box opens.

2. Select the **PAPER-CURVES** part as the Paper Part.

3. Maintain **Trace curve** in the drop-down list as the type of tracing that will be created.

4. Select datum point **PNT0** on the pencil part attached to the shortest link, as shown in Figure 6–12.

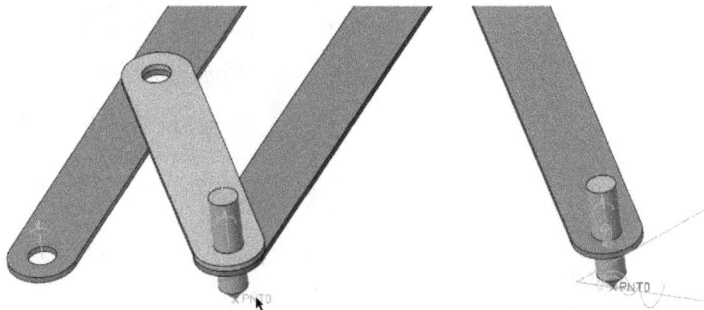

Figure 6–12

5. Maintain **2D** as the type of curve and select **AnalysisDefinition1** in the *Results* set.

6. Select **OK.**

7. The assembly updates as shown in Figure 6–13.

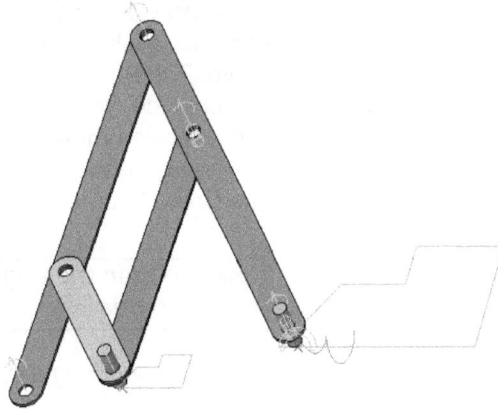

Figure 6–13

8. Save the assembly.

9. Open **paper-curves.prt.**

10. Click **Don't Save** when prompted regarding Play Backs.

11. Review the trace curve shown in Figure 6–14, and close the part, then close the assembly.

Figure 6–14

Practice 6b

Create Movie and Image Files

Practice Objectives

- View the playback of an assembly.
- Create movie and image files.

In the previous practice, you used the **Playback** tool to review a previous analysis to check for interference and create a trace curve. The **Playback** tool requires a Creo Parametric license. In this practice, you will use the same tool to export the analysis into a movie or image file. Capturing the analysis in either of these ways enables you to share results with users that do not use Creo Parametric.

Task 1 - Open the engine assembly and access Mechanism mode.

1. Set the working directory to the *Movies* folder.

2. Open **engine_6.asm**.

3. Set the model display as follows:

   - ⚒ *(Datum Display Filters)*: All Off

   - ⤲ *(Spin Center)*: Off

   - ⬚, *(Display Style)*: ⬚ (Shading With Edges)

4. Activate Mechanism mode.

5. Click ◀▶ (Playback). No result set is present because the results were not saved when Mechanism mode was previously closed. Close the Playbacks dialog box.

Task 2 - Recreate the analysis set.

1. Select **AnalysisDefiniton1** under **ANALYSES** in the mechanism tree and click ⚒ (Edit Definition) in the mini toolbar. The Analysis Definition dialog box opens.

2. Click **Run**. Creo Parametric creates the motion run.

3. Click **OK** in the dialog box.

Task 3 - Create movie and image files.

1. Click ⏮ (Playback) in the *Mechanism* tab.

2. Click 🖫 (Save Result Set) and click **Save**. The results are now saved as **AnalysisDefinition1.pbk**. They can be retrieved for future reference.

3. Click ⏮ (Play Result Set) in the Playbacks dialog box. Display the playback results. Stop the motion when you have finished viewing it.

4. Click **Capture**. The Capture dialog box opens.

5. Verify that **MPEG** is selected. Enter **engine_6.mpg** in the *Name* field.

6. Maintain the remaining default options in the Capture dialog box.

7. Click **OK**. Creo Parametric creates the MPEG. Note that the file is generated frame by frame. The processing information is available in the message window.

8. Click **Capture** a second time.

9. Select **JPEG** to create jpeg images for each of the frames.

10. Enter **engine_6.jpg** in the *Name* field and click **OK**. Creo Parametric creates the JPEG files. As with the MPEG file, the processing information is available in the message window.

11. Close the dialog boxes.

Task 4 - Open the files on the hard drive.

1. Examine the contents of the *Trace_Curves* folder in the File Explorer. All 100 JPEG files and the MPEG file are stored in this location. Open some of the files using the default viewer.

2. Return to Creo Parametric, save the assembly, and erase it from memory.

Practice 6c

Analyze Measures and Motion Envelopes

Practice Objectives

- View playback results.
- Create a motion envelope.
- Analyze measures.

In this practice, you will open the tractor assembly and display the playback results. You will begin the practice by creating motion envelopes for the assembly. This will enable you to display the full extent of the motion at the same time by displaying the envelope. In addition, you will use an analysis measurement to verify that the defined motion does not interfere with a defined location that is offset from **ASM_TOP**.

Task 1 - Open the hydraulic boom assembly and display the playback results.

1. Set the working directory to the *Motion_Envelope* folder.

2. Open **hydraulic_boom_6.asm**.

3. Set the model display as follows:

    - $\overset{\times\prime}{\sim}$ *(Datum Display Filters)*: All Off

    - $\succ$ *(Spin Center)*: Off

    - $\square$ *(Display Style)*: $\square$ (Shading With Edges)

4. Activate Mechanism mode.

5. Expand **ANALYSIS** in the Mechanism Tree, click on **AnalysisDefinition1 (POSITION)**, and select click $\overset{\triangledown}{}$ (Run) in the mini toolbar as shown in Figure 6–15.

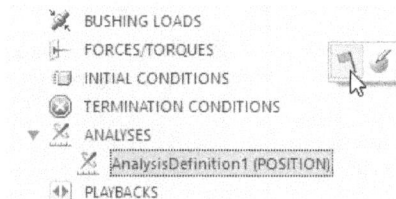

      BUSHING LOADS
      FORCES/TORQUES
      INITIAL CONDITIONS
      TERMINATION CONDITIONS
    ANALYSES
        AnalysisDefinition1 (POSITION)
    PLAYBACKS

Figure 6–15

6. In the ribbon, click $\boxed{\leftrightarrow}$ (Playback).

7. Click ⊟ (Save Result Set) and save the analysis definition in the current folder.

8. Click ◁▷ (Playback) and display the motion.

9. Once you have played back the motion, click ◁◁ (Reset to Beginning).

10. Click **Close** to close the Animate dialog box but leave the Playbacks dialog box open.

Task 2 - Create a motion envelope.

Design Considerations

In this task, you will create a motion envelope to record the swept volume that the assembly moves through for one of its analysis sets. You can customize the quality and components that will be captured in the envelope.

1. Click ◁ (Motion Envelope) in the Playback dialog box. The Create Motion Envelope dialog box opens.

2. Set the quality level to **3**. Click **OK** in the Motion Envlp Alert dialog box to disregard the note regarding memory usage.

3. Click **Preview**. The model displays similar to the one shown in Figure 6–16.

Figure 6–16

4. Change the quality to **8** and preview a new envelope. Higher quality settings produce better results, similar to the ones shown in Figure 6–17.

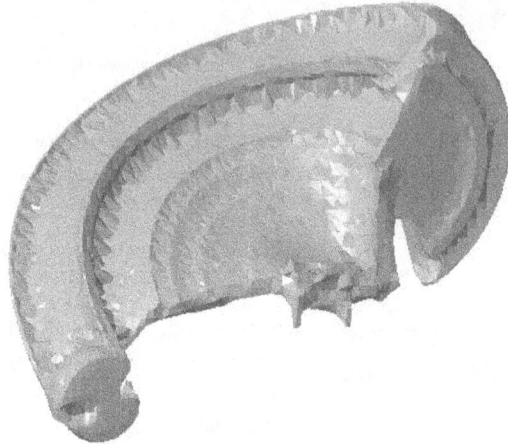

Figure 6–17

5. In *Components* area, click ▷ (Select) and select **BUCKET-1.PRT** in the graphics window (do not use the Model Tree), as shown in Figure 6–18.

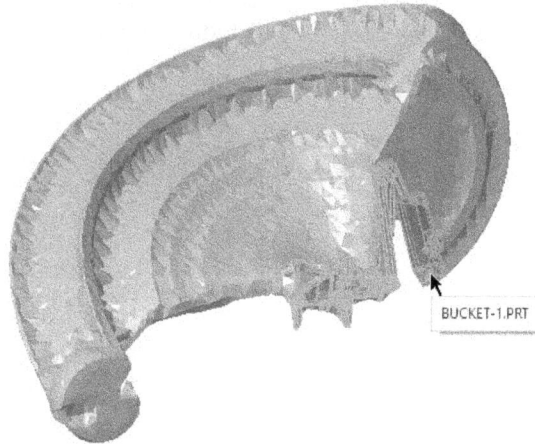

Figure 6–18

6. If required, click **Replace** in the Confirm Selection dialog box.

7. Press the middle mouse button to accept the selection. The number of selected components changes from *14* to **1**.

8. Click **Preview**. The model displays similar to the one shown in Figure 6–19.

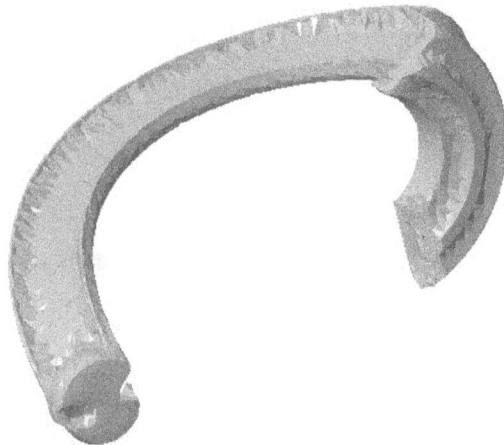

Figure 6–19

9. Click **OK**. The system saves the motion envelope as **hydraulic_boom_env0001.prt** (default) in the working directory.

10. Close the Create Motion Envelope dialog box.

Design Considerations

Once you have created the motion envelope file, it can be temporarily assembled into the mechanism assembly to help visualize the path of the components relative to the other components in the assembly.

Task 3 - Create datum plane to be used in the analysis feature.

Design Considerations

In this task, you will create a datum plane that will represent the lower extent to which the assembly can move. Once this reference has been created, you will use this reference to further study the motion of the mechanism.

1. Close the Playbacks dialog box.

2. Click ☒ (Close) in the *Mechanism* tab.

3. Create a datum plane offset from **ASM_TOP** by a value of **-1300**, as shown in Figure 6–20.

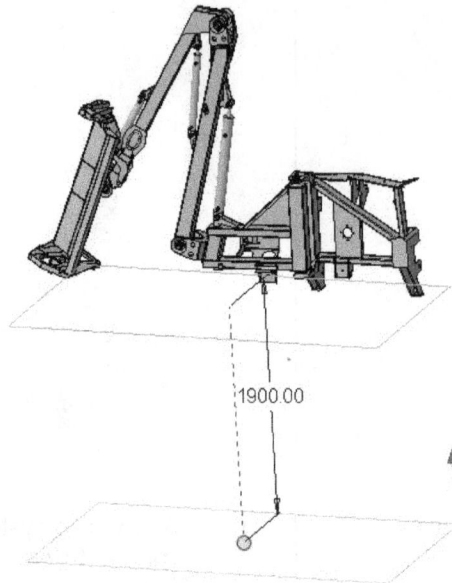

Figure 6–20

Task 4 - Create an analysis feature in the hydraulic boom assembly.

Design Considerations

In this task, you will create an analysis feature that will measure the distance between a point on the mechanism and the datum plane that was created in the previous step. Once this feature has been created, it can be used to generate a graph that will indicate the point location relative to the datum plane throughout the entire motion to ensure that it does not extend past it.

1. Click on the screen to clear any references.

2. Select the *Analysis* tab, expand (Measure) and select (Distance).

3. Click ⊞ (Expand The Dialog) to expand the Measure: Distance dialog box, as shown in Figure 6–21.

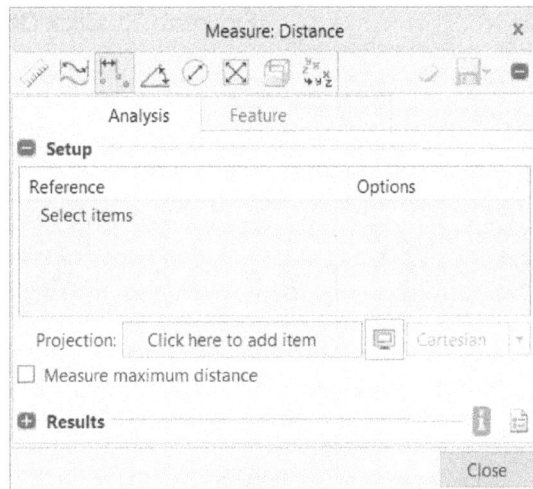

Figure 6–21

4. Select **PNT0** from **BUCKET-1.PRT** as the first reference.

5. Hold <Ctrl> and select **ADTM1** (the newly created datum plane) in **hydraulic_boom.asm** as the second reference. The model displays as shown in Figure 6–22.

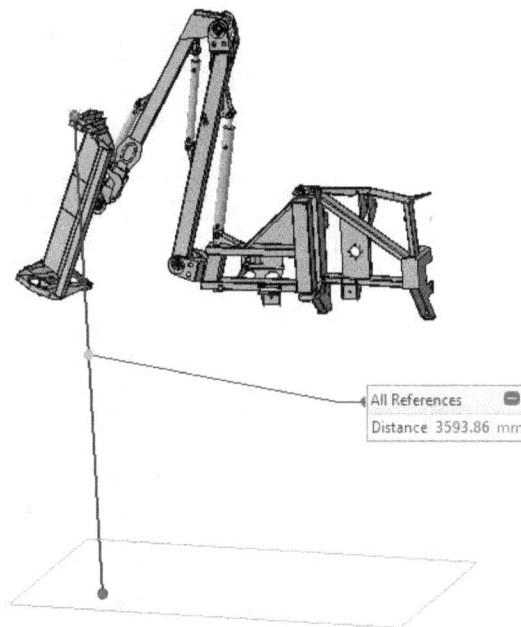

Figure 6–22

6. If the *Feature* tab is not visible in the Measure: Distance dialog box, click ⬚ (Open Options) and select **Show Feature Tab** in the Options dialog box, as shown in Figure 6–23. Click **OK**.

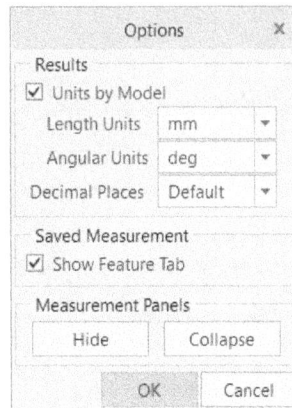

Figure 6–23

7. Select the *Feature* tab.

8. Verify that the **DISTANCE** parameter is selected in the *Parameters* area. Once the distance parameter has been created it is reviewed throughout the entire range of motion for the analysis.

9. Click ⬚▾ (Save Analysis), enable the **Make Feature** option, and click **OK**.

10. Click **Close**.

Task 5 - Analyze the measurement.

---

1. Activate Mechanism mode.

2. Click ⬚ (Measures).

3. Select **MEASURE_DISTANCE_1_DISTANCE** in the selected measures area.

4. No result sets are currently in session. Click ⬚ (Load Result Set) to retrieve the saved analysis playback file that you saved earlier.

5. Click ⬚ (Graph Selected Measures). Creo Parametric generates a graph of the distance that the point is from the datum plane throughout the entire range of motion.

6. Click **Close** in the Measure Results dialog box. Do not close the graph.

7. Click ⏩ (Play Result Set) and play the animation. A vertical tracking bar in the graph window changes position as the playback progresses. Note that the point does not intersect the datum plane as was required for the design.

8. Close all playback dialog boxes and close the graph window.

9. Save the assembly and erase it from memory.

Practice 6d | Analyze Measures

Practice Objective

- Analyze a measure as an assembly runs through a range of motion.

In this practice, you will create a distance measurement and analyze how the that measurement changes as the assembly moves through its range of motion.

Task 1 - Open a model.

1. Set the working directory to the *Analyze_Measures* folder.

2. Open **pause_slider.asm**.

3. Set the model display as follows:

   - ⚡ *(Datum Display Filters)*: All Off

   - ⚡ *(Spin Center)*: Off

   - ⬜ *(Display Style)*: ⬜ (No Hidden)

Task 2 - Create a measurement and analyze it.

4. Select the *Analysis* tab, expand ⚏ (Measure) and select ⚏ (Distance).

5. Hold <Ctrl> and the planar side surfaces of the track and **sliding_block** parts as shown in Figure 6–24.

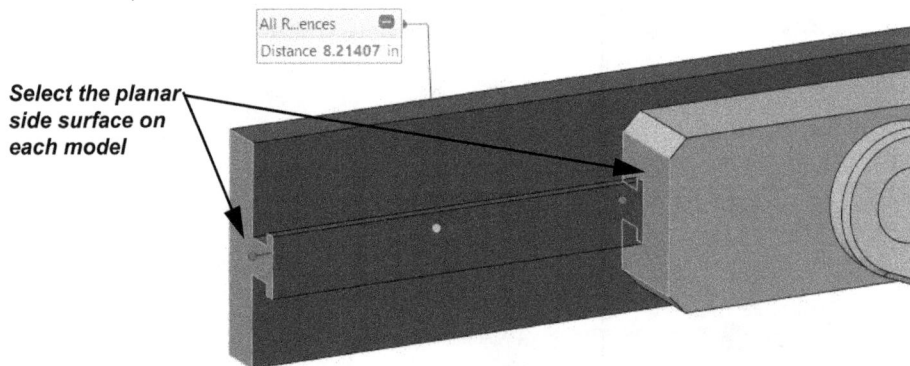

Select the planar side surface on each model

Figure 6–24

6. Save the Analysis as a feature, as shown in Figure 6–25.

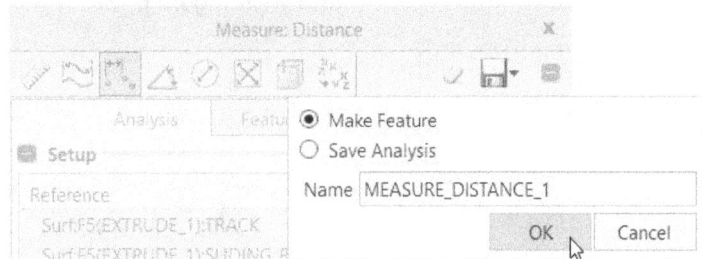

Figure 6–25

7. Close the Measure dialog box.

8. Activate Mechanism mode.

9. Expand **ANALYSIS** in the Mechanism Tree, click on **AnalysisDefinition1 (POSITION)** and select click ⚑ (Run) in the mini toolbar as shown in Figure 6–26.

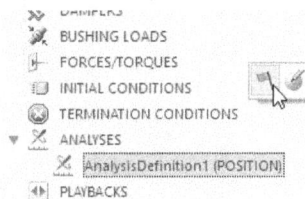

Figure 6–26

10. In the ribbon, click ⌒ (Measures).

11. Select **MEASURE_DISTANCE_1_DISTANCE** in the selected measures area.

12. Select **AnalysisDefinition1** in *Results set* area.

13. Click ☒ (Graph Selected Measures). The graph displays as shown in Figure 6–27.

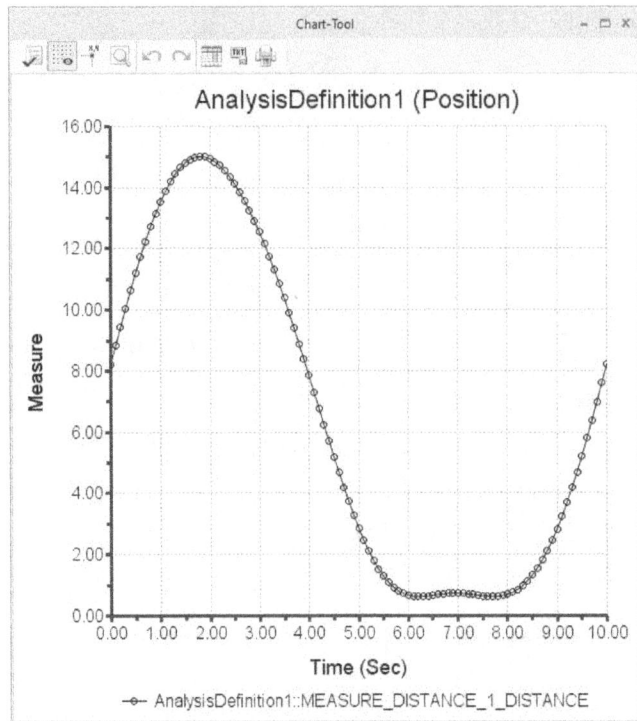

Figure 6–27

14. Close the graph window and close the Measure Results dialog box.

15. Click ◁▷ (Playback) and use the playback tools to view the motion of the assembly. Although the **sliding_block** seems to stop at the left end of the track before changing directions, the graph in Figure 6–27 shows us there is still a small amount of movement.

16. Save the assembly, and erase it from memory.

Chapter Review Questions

1. Results of an analysis in mechanism cannot be viewed outside of Creo Parametric.

   a. True

   b. False

2. What function can be used to view the results of an Analysis Definition and generate an external video file (MPEG/AVI).

   a. Joint Axis Settings

   b. Motion Viewer

   c. Servo Motor

   d. Playback

3. What are the two locations where you can set the options for interference checking between components? (Select all that apply.)

   a. Clicking **Collision Detection Settings** in the Playbacks dialog box.

   b. Select **File>Options** and select the *Assembly* category.

   c. Select **File>Prepare>Model Properties** and select **change** beside Collision Detection.

   d. Select **Tools>Environment>Collision Detection**.

4. Which of the following is created to define the volume of space that a mechanism claims in space throughout its motion.

   a. Trace Curve

   b. Playback

   c. Motion Envelope

   d. Cam Synthesis curve

5. Which of the following statements is true for a motion envelope? (Select all that apply.)

   a. The higher the quality level, the longer it takes to generate.

   b. The higher the quality level, the better the geometry is rendered.

   c. The lower the quality level, the longer it takes to generate.

   d. The lower the quality level, the better the geometry is rendered.

6. Which of the following options is used to capture the movement of a point or vertex, with respect to a component in the assembly?

   a. Trace Curve

   b. Playback

   c. Motion Envelope

   d. Cam Synthesis curve

7. The selected component in which a trace curve is stored is called the Paper Part.

   a. True

   b. False

8. Which of the following options can be used to capture the motion of a curve or edge with respect to a component in the assembly?

   a. Trace Curve

   b. Playback

   c. Motion Envelope

   d. Cam Synthesis curve

Answers: 1b, 2d, 3ac, 4c, 5ab, 6a, 7a, 8d

Design Animation

The Design Animation Option (DAO) enables you to create an animation sequence. This animation sequence can be used to visualize assembly operations similar to MDX. It can also be used to display the assembly or disassembly of models.

Learning Objectives in this Chapter

- Learn to activate the Animation application and how to use the commands in the ribbon.
- Learn the general steps to create and view an animation.
- Specify the type of animation and define the animation using the appropriate tools.
- Use servo motor in the Animation mode to force a specific motion in the assembly.
- Learn to use locked bodies to fix a component over a specific period during the animation sequence.
- Learn to change the orientation of the assembly, transparency, and the style options to use in the animation sequence.
- Use the animation timeline to display events, body locks, and visibilities for the animation and drag the items to new positions on the timeline.
- Learn to complete and start the animation sequence in the timeline.

7.1 DAO Interface

To access Animation mode, select the *Applications* tab and click 🎬 (Animation). The animation timeline displays at the top of the display window and the *Animation* tab activates, as shown in Figure 7–1.

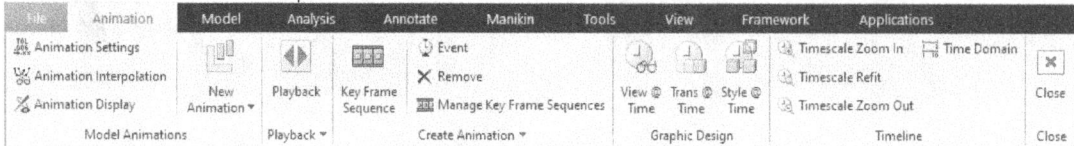

Figure 7–1

The *Animation* tab commands are described as follows:

Icon	Name	Description
	Animation Settings	Enables you to specify options for running the animation sequence.
	Animation Interpolation	Enables you to specify the interpolation options.
	Animation Display	Enables you to control the visibility of the Animation icons in the display window.
	Explode	Enables you to create a simple explode animation.
	Snapshot	Enables you to create a simple snapshot animation.
	Import From MDO	Enables you to import a mechanism animation.
	Playback	Enables you to display the Animate dialog box, which contains the playback controls.
	Key Frame Sequence	Enables you to open the Key Frame Sequence dialog box, in which you can define when an action is going to occur.
	Event	Enables you to create an event.
	Remove	Enables you to delete the selected item(s).
	Manage Key Frame Sequences	Enables you to create, edit, remove, or include a key frame sequence.

	View @ Time	Enables you to open the View @Time dialog box. The model can be displayed in any saved view orientation at a specified time.
	Trans @ Time	Enables you to open the Transparency @Time dialog box. You can specify transparency settings for any component at a specified time.
	Style @ Time	Enables you to open the Style at Time dialog box. The saved component display can be accessed at a specified time.
	Timescale Zoom In	Enables you to zoom in on the time scale.
	Timescale Refit	Enables you to refit the time scale.
	Timescale Zoom Out	Enables you to zoom out on the time scale.
	Time Domain	Enables you to change the time domain.
	Close	Closes the *Animation* tab.

7.2 Design Approach

How To: Create an Animation

1. Activate Animation mode.
2. Create a new animation.
3. Define the bodies.
4. Drag the bodies and create snapshots.
5. Create a key frame sequence and verify that it is on the timeline.
6. Create servo motors and verify that they are on the timeline.
7. Define locked bodies for specific time periods, if required.
8. Define the view orientation and magnification of the model.
9. Define the component displays of the model.
10. Edit the animation timeline.
11. Create the animation frames.
12. View the animation.

7.3 Creating an Animation

Animations can be created to do many different things. Different steps can be used depending on the goal for the animation. The first step is to specify what type of animation you wish to create.

Once the animation has been specified to be Explode or Snapshot it cannot be changed

Expand ▥ (New Animation) and select one of the three options described as follows:

Icon	Name	Description
▥	**Explode**	Enables you use exploded views to create the animation sequence.
📷	**Snapshot**	Enables you to use snapshots to create the animation sequence.
📂	**Import from MDO**	Enables you to use a mechanism playback file as the animation.

Once the type of animation has been selected, the Define Animation dialog box opens as shown in Figure 7–2. The dialog box is slightly different depending on which option has been chosen.

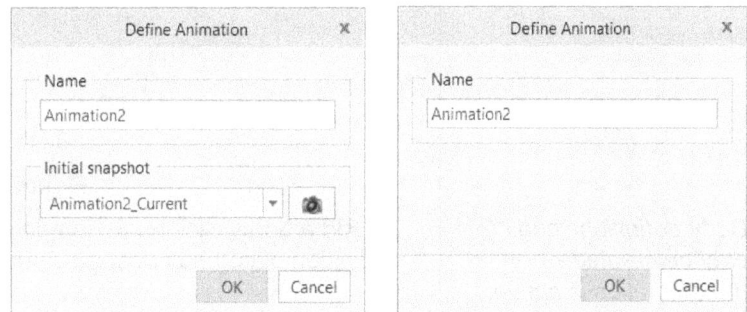

Explode option is selected   **Snapshot option is selected**

Figure 7–2

Animations can be created, opened, or removed from the model. Animations can also be renamed by double clicking on the animation and typing a new name.

If a Snapshot animation is defined, the *Animation* tab updates with several Mechanism Design options, as shown in Figure 7–3.

Figure 7–3

Body Definitions

A body is one or more components that do not move relative to each other. By default, a mechanism transferred to Animation mode includes body definitions. Body definitions can be redefined in Animation mode. To access body definitions, click ⊹ (Body Definition). The Bodies dialog box opens as shown in Figure 7–4.

Bodies that are created in Animation mode are not transferred back to Mechanism.

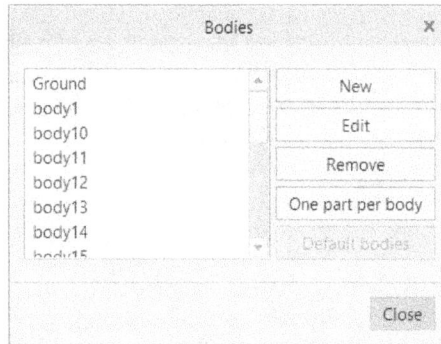

Figure 7–4

Body definitions can only be created when the animation is active.

To add a body, click **New**. To edit a body, click **Edit**. The Body Definition dialog box opens as shown in Figure 7–5.

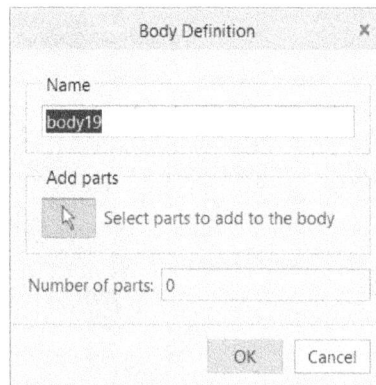

Figure 7–5

To create bodies that only create one part, click **One Part per Body**. Creo Parametric creates bodies out of all of the parts in the assembly. This is cumbersome with large assemblies.

To create bodies based on the current mechanism, click **Default Bodies**.

Drag and Snapshots

You can drag the components and take snapshots of specific positions by clicking 🖐 (Drag Components) and dragging the bodies to the required position. Once the bodies are in the correct position, click 📷 (Take Snapshot) to create the snapshot (you can assign the user name to the snapshot). Snapshots can be added to the key frame sequence.

Key Frame Sequence

A key frame sequence (KFS) is an ordered series of exploded views or snapshots placed at specific times on the timeline. Design animation interpolates the motion of the bodies between the snapshots to produce a smooth animation.

You can reuse a KFS in a single animation.

To open the Key Frame Sequences dialog box, click ▦ (Key Frame Sequence). To create a key frame, click **New**. The Key Frame Sequence dialog box opens as shown in Figure 7–6.

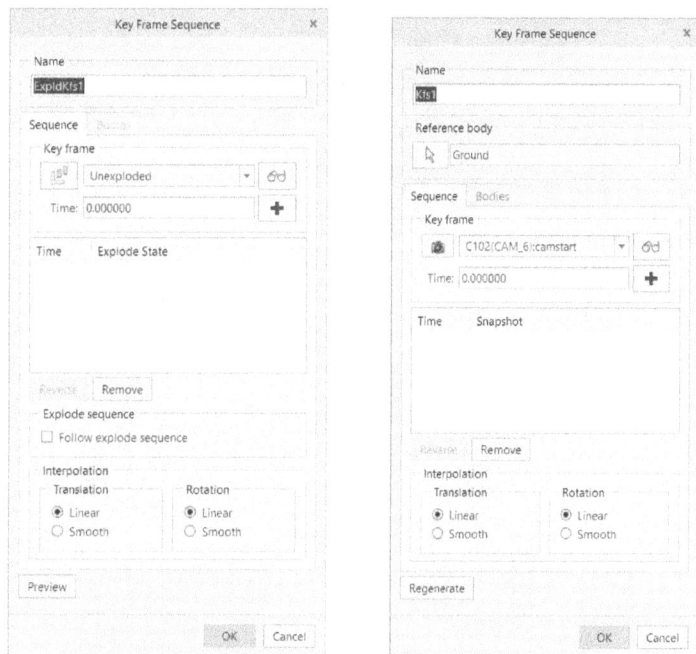

Explode animation   **Snapshot animation**

Figure 7–6

The Key Frame Sequence dialog box areas are described as follows:

Area	Description
Name	Enter the name of the KFS in this field.
Reference Body	The default reference body is ground. A different reference body can be selected.
Key Frame	Select the snapshots that you want to use in the drop-down list in this area. Specify the time for the snapshot to be displayed in the *Time* field.
Interpolation	Select the interpolation that occurs between key frames in the animation.

After the KFS is defined, it displays on the timeline.

7.4 Servo Motors

Available with a Snapshot animation, Servo Motors in Animation mode are used for the same reason as Servo Motors in Mechanism mode; they force a specific motion in the assembly.

Click ✐ (Manage Servo Motors). The Servo Motors dialog box opens as shown in Figure 7–7.

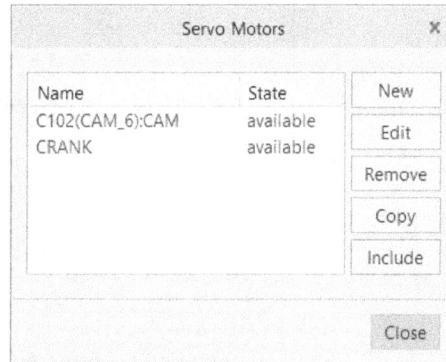

Servo Motors		✕
Name	State	New
C102(CAM_6):CAM	available	Edit
CRANK	available	Remove
		Copy
		Include
		Close

Figure 7–7

Click **New** to create new Servo Motors. To use a specific Servo Motor in the animation, select it and click **Include**. The Servo Motor displays in the animation timeline. It might be required to redefine the start time for the servo motor depending on the animation.

7.5 Lock Bodies

Available with Snapshot animations, bodies can be fixed to a component over a specific period during the animation sequence. Once fixed, movement does not occur between the bodies. To lock bodies, click ⬛ (Lock Bodies). The Lock Bodies dialog box opens as shown in Figure 7–8.

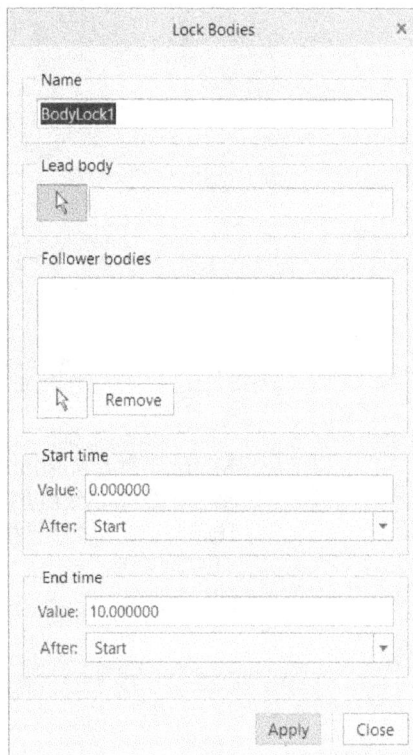

Figure 7–8

The areas in this dialog box are described as follows:

Area	Description
Name	Enter the name of the body lock in this field.
Lead Body	The lead body specifies the relative orientation and position of the follower bodies.
Follower Bodies	Select the follower bodies.
Start Time	Enter the start time that the bodies are in a locked state.
End Time	Enter the end time that the bodies are in a locked state.

7.6 Visibilities

An animation can change in orientation and display the components in a different display mode. The three available display modes are **View @ Time**, **Transparency @ Time**, and **Style @ Time**.

View @ Time

View @ Time mode enables the design animation to interpolate between different saved view orientations during playback. To use View @ Time, click ⚙ (View @ Time). The View at Time dialog box opens as shown in Figure 7–9.

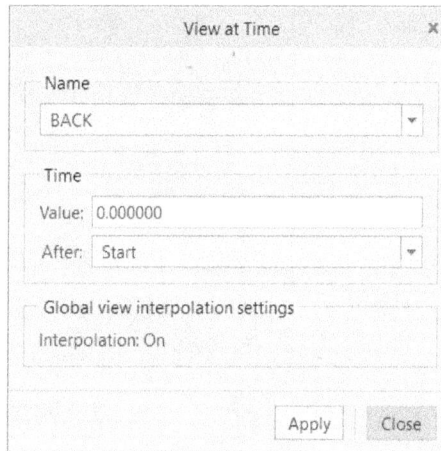

Figure 7–9

The View at Time dialog box areas are described as follows:

Area	Description
Name	Select a saved view in the drop-down list.
Time	Specify the time that the view should be available in the *Value* field. You can specify after which event the view should be available in the After drop-down list.

Click **Apply** to apply a View @ Time event to the timeline.

Transparency @ Time

Transparency @ Time mode enables the design animation to set components to be transparent or invisible. To use Transparency @ Time, click ⚏ (Trans @ Time). The Transparency at Time dialog box opens as shown in Figure 7–10.

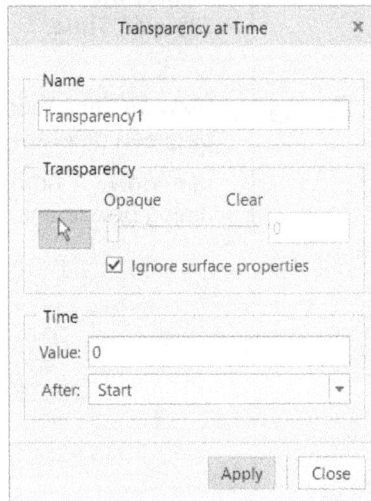

Figure 7–10

The Transparency at Time dialog box areas are described as follows:

Area	Description
Name	Enter the name of transparency event.
Transparency	Select the components to assign transparency. Set the transparency value between 0 (opaque) and 100 (clear).
Time	In the *Value* field, specify the time when the transparency event should be available. You can specify after which event the transparency should be available in the After drop-down list.

Click **Apply** to apply a Transparency @ Time event to the timeline.

Style @ Time

The Style @ Time mode controls the display of the assembly components during playback. You can use it when the internal parts of an assembly need to be displayed when a cover is present. To use Style @ Time, click ⬚ (Style @ Time). The Style at Time dialog box opens as shown in Figure 7–11.

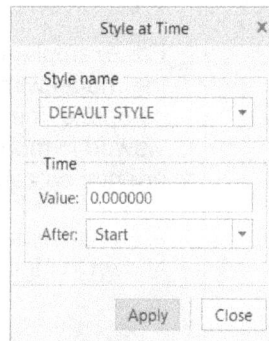

Figure 7–11

The Style at Time dialog box areas are described as follows:

Area	Description
Style Name	Select the saved component display in the drop-down list.
Time	Specify the time that the component should change in the *Value* field. You can specify after which event the component should change in the After drop-down list.

Click **Apply** to apply a Style @ Time event to the timeline.

7.7 Animation Timeline

The animation timeline displays all events, KFS, body locks, and visibilities for the animation. These items can be selected and dragged to new positions. Instances of the item can also be copied to new positions.

For example, the first KFS is created displaying the assembly of the model with a specific view orientation. After the first KFS is complete, the model is assembled. If the assembly needs to be viewed in more than one orientation, a second KFS with a new orientation can be copied to a new position.

A sample timeline with the item names and instance numbers is shown in Figure 7–12.

If an animation has been defined in a subassembly, it too can be referenced in the top-level animation.

To access the animation, select **Create Animation> Sub-animation**. *The animation displays in the timeline.*

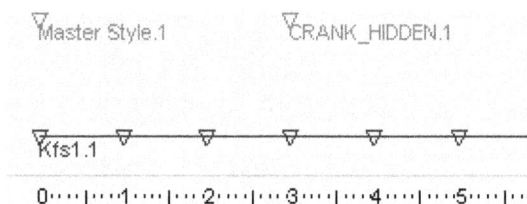

Figure 7–12

7.8 Finishing the Animation

If you are only interested in the motion of the mechanism, click

🔁 (Playback) in the tab to display the playback controls. The Animate dialog box opens.

After you have configured the timeline, you can create the frames of the animation. Click ▶ (Play) in the timeline or click

🔁 (Playback) in the *Animation* tab. Once the frames have been created, you can display the animation and check it for interference by clicking **Playback** in the timeline. The Playbacks buttons display in the timeline as shown in Figure 7–13. Click **Create** to remove the additional buttons in the timeline.

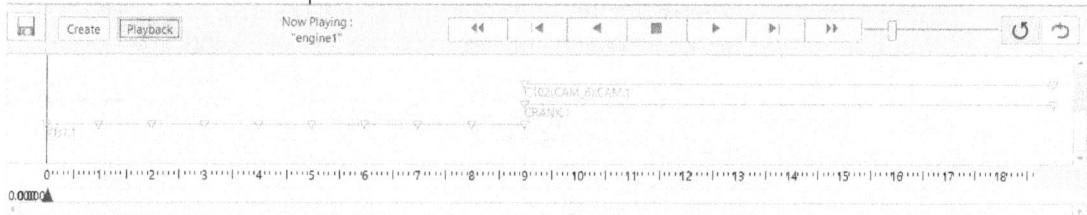

Figure 7–13

Practice 7a | Create an Animation

Practice Objective

- Create an animation.

In this practice, you will create an animation that will capture the process of assembling the engine assembly. You will begin by using the Drag functionality to separate the components and capture snapshots as each component is separated. You will then separate the components by disabling the constraints. When all of the snapshots have been created, they will be added to the animation timeline to create the animation.

Task 1 - Open the engine assembly.

1. Set the working directory to the *Create_Animation* folder.

2. Open **engine_6.asm**.

3. Set the model display as follows:

    - ⅍ *(Datum Display Filters)*: All Off

    - ⅌ *(Spin Center)*: Off

    - ▢ *(Display Style)*: ▢ (Shading With Edges)

Task 2 - Create the animation definition.

1. Click 🎬 (Animation) in the *Applications* tab.

2. Expand 🎞 (New Animation) or 📷 (New Animation) in the *Animation* tab and select 📷 (Snapshot), as shown in Figure 7–14. This option enables you to use snapshots instead of exploded views to create the animation sequence.

The New Animation icon will be whatever was selected the last time the Animation application was used.

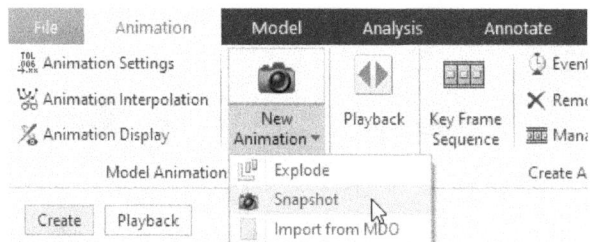

Figure 7–14

3. The Define Animation dialog box opens as shown in Figure 7–15.

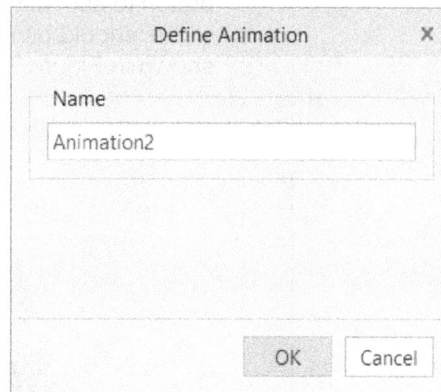

Define Animation	✕

Name

Animation2

OK   Cancel

Figure 7–15

4. Enter **engine1** in the *Name* field in the dialog box.

5. Click **OK** to close the Define Animation dialog box.

___

Task 3 - Create the initial position using the Drag/Snapshot function.

___

Design Considerations

You can create snapshots in both the Mechanism mode or the Animation mode.

1. Click 👆 (Drag Components).

2. Expand the *Snapshots* section, if required, and click 📷 (Take Snapshot) to create a new snapshot of the initial position. Set the snapshot *Name* to **1** and press <Enter>. This snapshot will be the final position in the animation sequence.

___

Task 4 - Position the camshaft away from the engine.

___

1. To move the camshaft away from the engine, the pin connection used to assemble the camshafts must be disabled. Select the *Constraints* tab in the Drag dialog box.

2. Click ⓘ (Enable/Disable Connections). Select the pin connection icon for the camshaft and press the middle mouse button to accept the selection. Once selected, the connection status should be active in the list. The model displays as shown in Figure 7–16.

Select this pin connection.

Figure 7–16

3. Expand the *Advanced Drag Options* area in the Drag dialog box and click ⓛ (Translation In Y) to restrict movement to the Y-direction.

4. Select the camshaft and drag it to the position shown in Figure 7–17. The valves move with the camshaft because the cam connections are not disabled.

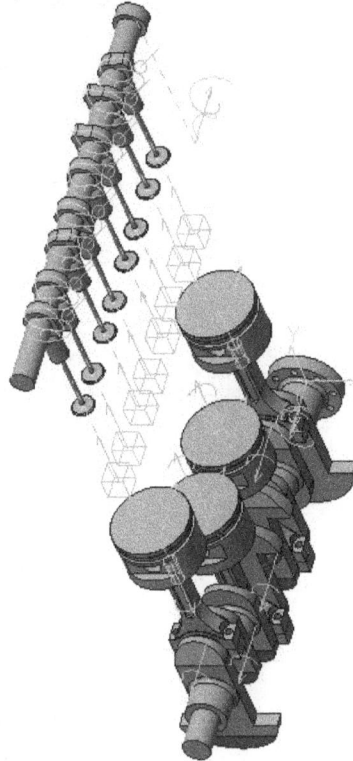

Figure 7–17

5. Select the *Snapshots* tab and create a snapshot of the new configuration. Set the *Name* to **2** and press <Enter>.

Task 5 - Position the pistons away from the connecting rod one at a time.

1. Select the *Constraints* tab.

2. Click ⁱ▷ (Enable/Disable Connections) and disable the four pin connections for the pistons. The model displays as shown in Figure 7–18.

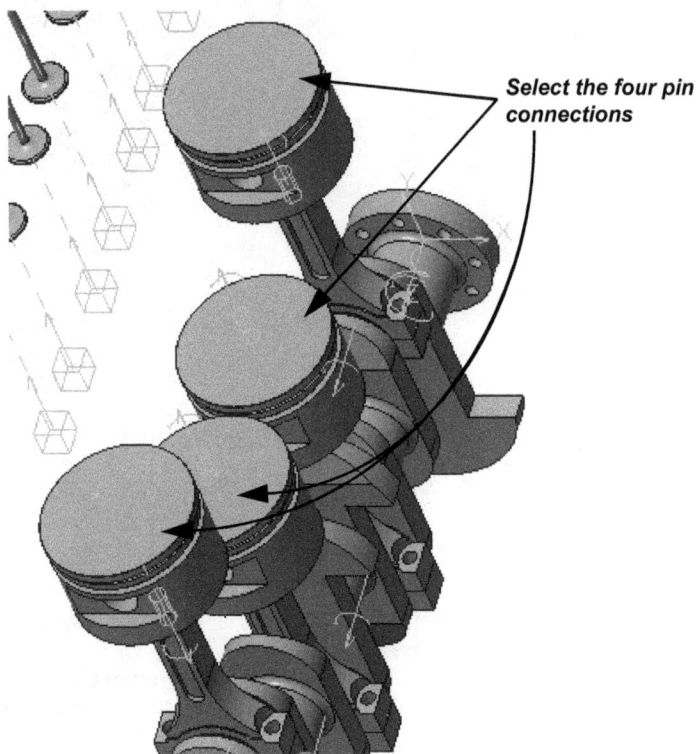

Select the four pin connections

Figure 7–18

3. Click ▱ (Select Coordinate System) and select any piston.

4. Click ⬛ (Translation In Y). Select the first piston and drag it to the position shown in Figure 7–19.

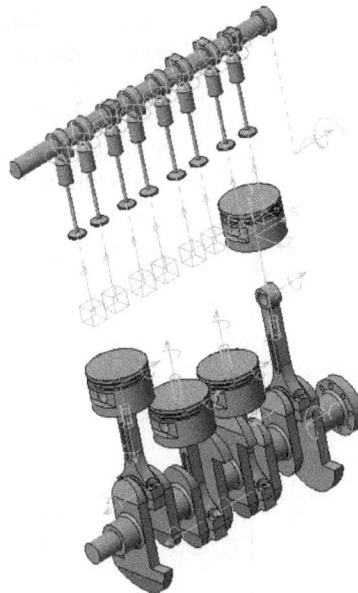

Figure 7–19

5. Create a snapshot and set the *Name* to **3**.

6. Repeat Steps 4 to 5 for the three remaining pistons. Name the three new snapshots **4**, **5**, and **6**, respectively. The snapshots display as shown in Figure 7–20.

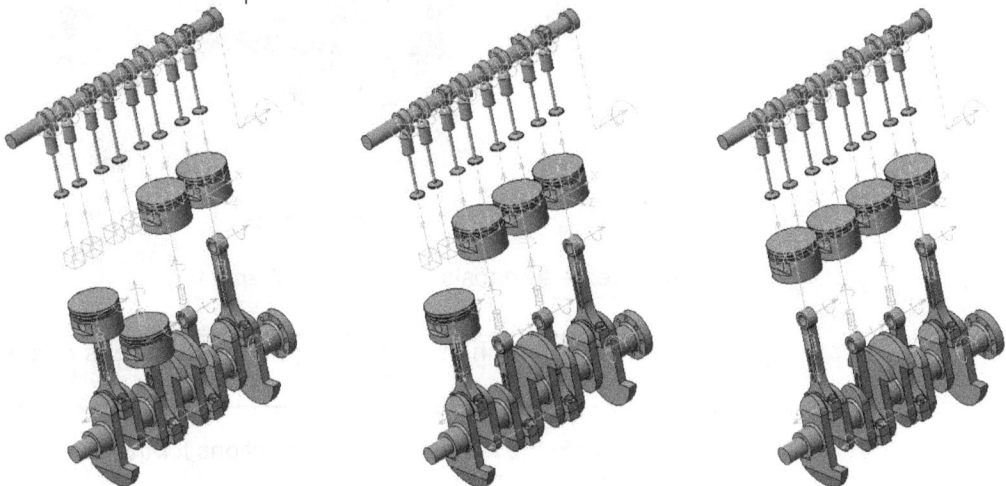

Figure 7–20

Task 6 - Position two of the connecting rods in one movement.

1. Select the *Constraints* tab and disable the first two pin connections for the connecting rods.

2. Create a body-body lock constraint between the two connecting rods. Click ⬚ (Body-Body Lock) and select the two connecting rods. Click the middle mouse button to complete.

3. Translate the connecting rods in the X-direction, as shown in Figure 7–21.

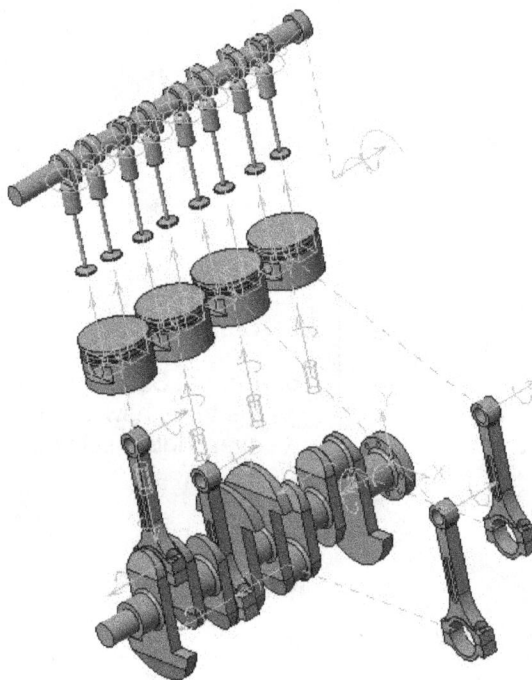

Figure 7–21

4. Create a snapshot and set the *Name* to **7**.

Task 7 - Position the remaining connecting rods one at a time.

1. Disable the remaining pin connections for the connecting rods.

2. Translate the third connecting rod in the negative X-direction, as shown in Figure 7–22.

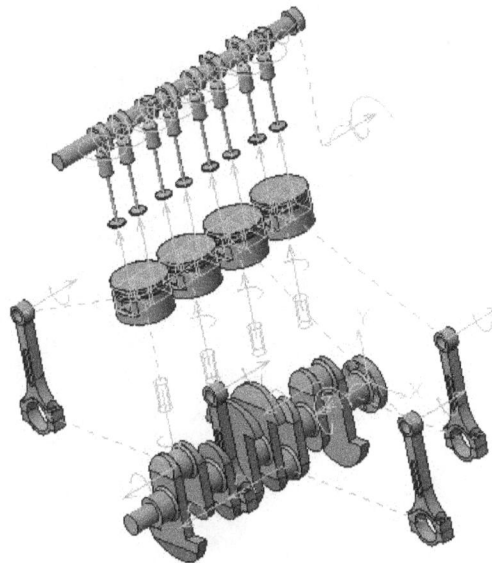

Figure 7–22

3. Create a snapshot. Set the new name for the snapshot to **8**.

4. Translate the final connecting rod in the Z-direction, as shown in Figure 7–23. Save the snapshot with the *Name* of **9**.

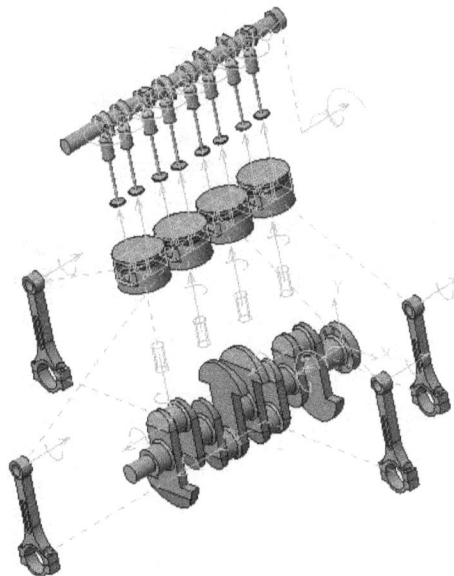

Figure 7–23

Task 8 - Position the crankshaft.

1. Select the *Constraints* tab and disable the pin connection for the crankshaft.

2. Translate the crankshaft in the Z-direction to the position shown in Figure 7–24.

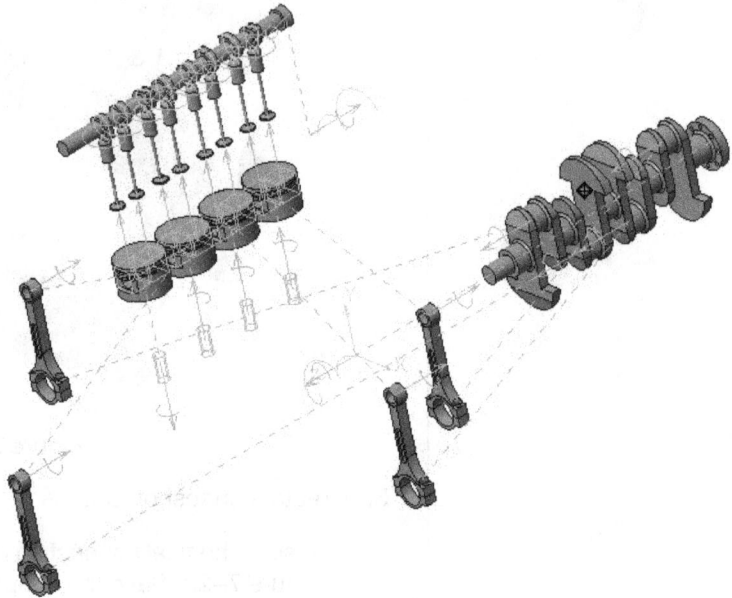

Figure 7–24

3. Create a snapshot and set the *Name* to **10**.

4. Click **Close** in the Drag dialog box, and save the assembly.

Task 9 - Create a key frame sequence.

1. If you did not complete the previous task, open **engine_6_task_9.asm**.

2. Click 🎞 (Key Frame Sequence).

3. Select snapshot **10** in the *Key frame* drop-down list.

4. Click ✚ (Add Key Frame). The Key Frame Sequence dialog box updates as shown in Figure 7–25.

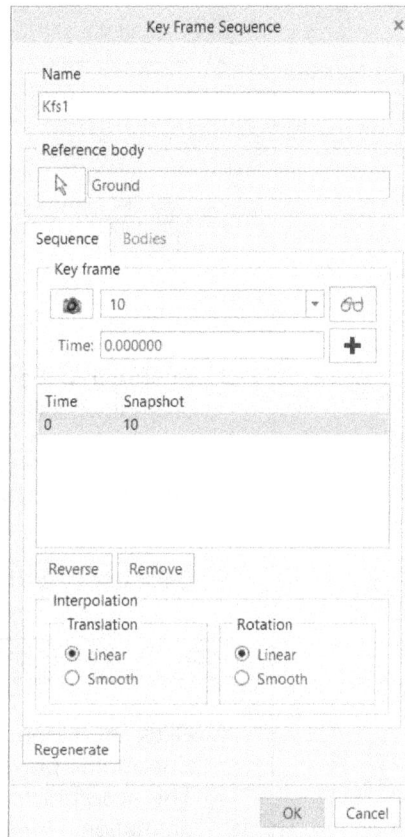

Figure 7–25

5. Repeat Step 3 and add snapshots 9 through 1. The snapshots are added in reverse order so that the animation can display the assembly of the mechanism.

6. Click **OK**.

Task 10 - Edit the timeline to correspond to the required animation length.

---

1. Verify that the key frame sequence display in the timeline. The timeline length is 10 seconds.

2. Hover the cursor over the timeline, right-click and select **Edit Time domain**, as shown in Figure 7–26.

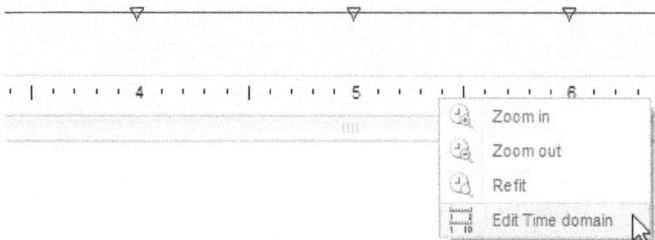

Figure 7–26

3. Ensure that the **Length and Rate** option is selected in the drop-down list.

4. Enter **19** in the *End Time* field. The Frame Count value is automatically changed to **191**, if the *Rate* field contains a value of 10.

5. Click **OK** to close the Animation Time Domain dialog box.

Task 11 - Create the animation and view the playback.

---

1. Click ▶ (Generate) at the top of the timeline. Creo Parametric plays the frames and generates the animation. The assembly only moves for the first 9 seconds of the animation.

You can also click

⬦ *(Playback) in the Animation tab.*

2. When the animation has been created, display the playback by clicking **Playback** and use the buttons to play the sequence.

3. After displaying the sequence click **Create** to collapse the playback buttons in the timeline.

4. Save the assembly. Close and erase all files.

Practice 7b | Apply Servo Motors

Practice Objective

- Apply servo motors in an animation sequence.

Similar to MDX, you can use Servo Motors in the design animation. In this practice, you will apply Servo Motors to use during the animation sequence.

Task 1 - Open the engine assembly.

1. Set the working directory to the *Apply_Servos* folder.

2. Open **engine_6.asm**.

3. Set the model display as follows:

   - ⅍. *(Datum Display Filters)*: All Off

   - ⅗ *(Spin Center)*: Off

   - 🗋. *(Display Style)*: 🗇 (Shading With Edges)

4. Click 📷 (Animation) in the *Applications* tab.

Task 2 - Add the created servo motors to the animation sequence

1. Click 🔗 (Manage Servo Motors). The Servo Motors dialog box opens.

2. Select the **crank** servo motor and click **Include**.

3. The servo motor is now included in the timeline.

4. Include the cam servo motor.

5. Click **Close**.

Task 3 - Edit the starting times for the servo motors.

Design Considerations

When the servo motors are added to the timeline, they are inserted at the beginning of the timeline. Because you want the servo motors to start after the assembly is complete, you can change their location in the timeline. Their location can be changed manually by dragging their position or you can edit the time using a dialog box.

1. Select the triangle next to **CRANK.1** Servo Motor and drag it to **9.00** on the timeline, as shown in Figure 7–27.

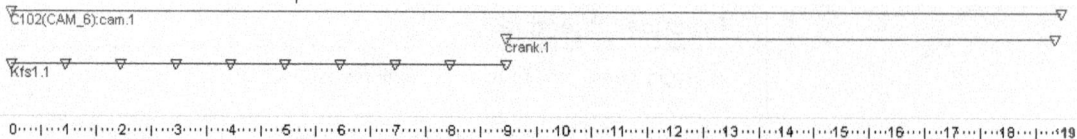

Figure 7–27

2. Select the cam servo motor timeline. It changes from blue to red. Right-click and select **Edit Time**, as shown in Figure 7–28. The Servo Motor Time Domain dialog box opens.

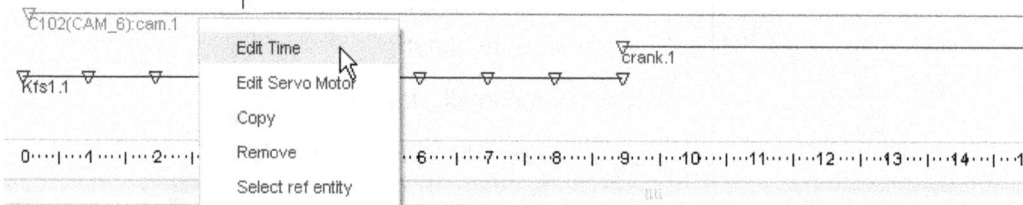

Figure 7–28

3. Enter **9.00** in the *Time* field in the *Start Driver* area, as shown in Figure 7–29.

Figure 7–29

4. Click **OK**.

Task 4 - Recreate the animation frames.

---

1. Recreate the animation frames by clicking ▶ (Play). If prompted, click **Yes** to overwrite the result.

2. Save the assembly. Close and erase all files.

Practice 7c

Specify Component Displays & Views

Practice Objective

- Specify component displays, views and transparency in an animation.

In this practice, you will use the **Style @ Time**, **View @ Time**, and **Transparency @ Time** options to further customize the timeline for an animation. Using these options, you can apply display styles that are created in the View Manager, set view orientations throughout the timeline, or set components in the assembly to fade in or out using transparency settings. All of these options will be used in this practice and incorporated into the animation for the engine.

Task 1 - Open the engine assembly.

1. Set the working directory to the *Display_In_Animation* folder.

2. Open **engine_6.asm**.

3. Set the model display as follows:

   - *(Datum Display Filters)*: All Off

   - *(Spin Center)*: Off

   - *(Display Style)*: (Shading With Edges)

Task 1 - Create a display representation for the crankshaft.

1. In the In-graphics toolbar, click (View Manager). The View Manager dialog box opens.

2. Select the *Style* tab.

3. Click **New**. Set the *Name* to **crank_hidden** and press <Enter>.

4. Click **OK** to close the EDIT dialog box.

5. In the View Manager, click **Properties>>** and select **crankshaft.prt** in the Model Tree.

6. Click ⬚ (Hidden Line) in the dialog box to assign the hidden line display to the crankshaft.

7. Click **<<List** to return to the list of styles. While this style is active, the crankshaft displays as hidden line, regardless of which setting is used in the In-graphics toolbar, as shown in Figure 7–30.

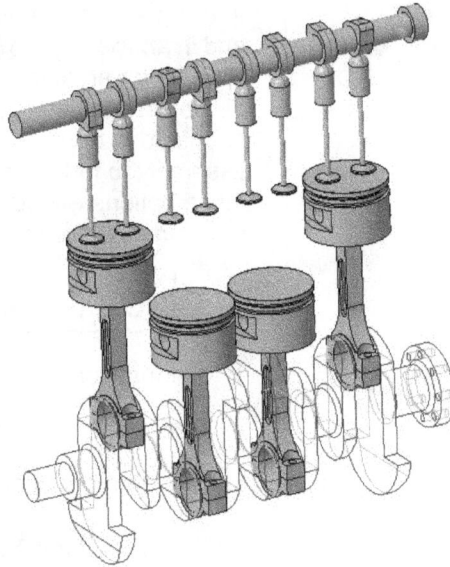

Figure 7–30

8. Right-click and select **Save** to update the new style. Click **OK**.

9. Double-click on **Master Style** in the *Names* area to return to the master style. The model returns to the display that is controlled by the environment settings.

Task 2 - Create a display representation for the cam assemblies.

---

1. Click **New**. Set the *Name* to **cam_no_hide** and press <Enter>.

2. Click **OK** to close the EDIT dialog box.

3. Click **Properties>>** and select **CAM_6.ASM** in the Model Tree.

4. Click ▱ (No Hidden) in the View Manager. Click **<<List**. The crankshaft displays without hidden line, regardless of which Display Style is used, as shown in Figure 7–31.

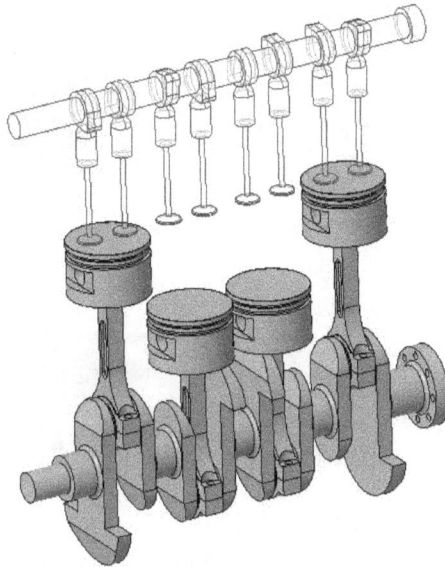

Figure 7–31

5. Right-click and select **Save** to update the new style. Click **OK**.

6. Double-click on Master Style to return to the master style.

Task 3 - Create another display representation for the crankshaft.

---

1. Click **New**. Set the *Name* to **cam_blank** and press <Enter>.

2. Click **OK** to close the EDIT dialog box.

3. Click **Properties>>** and select the **CAM_6** assembly in the Model Tree.

4. Click ✎ (Blank) in the dialog box. Click **<<List**. The crankshaft is not displayed, as shown in Figure 7–32.

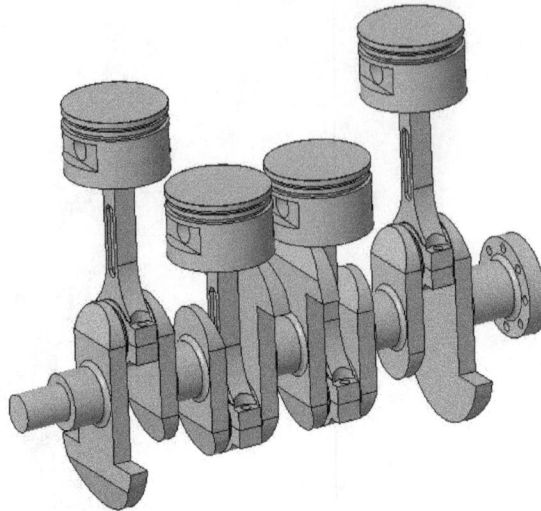

Figure 7–32

5. Right-click and select **Save** to update the new style. Click **OK**.

6. Double-click on **Master Style** to return to the master style.

7. Click **Close**.

Task 4 - Specify a time for each component display to take effect.

Design Considerations

In this task, you will incorporate the display style states that you created in previous tasks into the animation timeline. Doing this enables the display to be incorporated with the snapshots and the Servo Motors.

1. Activate the Animation application.

2. Click 🗒 (Style @ Time) in the *Animation* tab.

You might have to drag
the border to increase
the height of the timeline
section of the window.

3. Select **Master Style** in the *Style name* drop-down list and click **Apply**. The Master Style display representation displays in the timeline. By default, without changing the Time settings in the Style at Time dialog box, it is added to the beginning of the timeline, as shown in Figure 7–33.

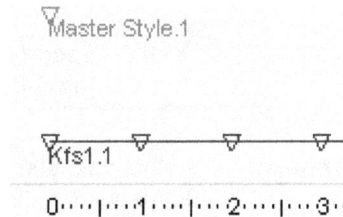

Master Style.1

Kfs1.1

0 · · · | · · · 1 · · · | · · · 2 · · · | · · · 3 · ·

Figure 7–33

4. Select **CRANK_HIDDEN** in the Style Name drop-down list.

5. This display representation should take effect three seconds after the start. Set the *Time Value* to **3** and click **Apply**. The Style at Time and the timeline display as shown in Figure 7–34.

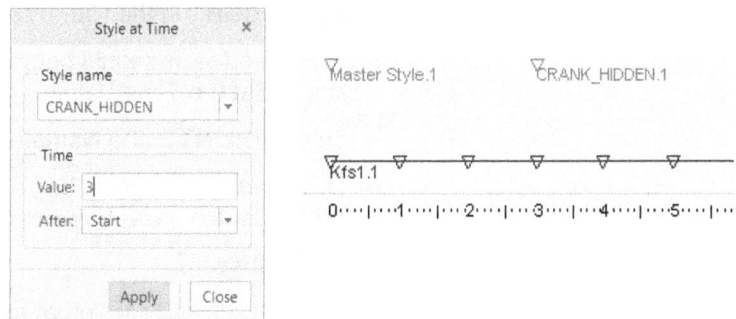

Style at Time ✕

Style name

CRANK_HIDDEN ▾

Time

Value: 3

After: Start ▾

Apply   Close

Master Style.1   CRANK_HIDDEN.1

Kfs1.1

0 · · · | · · · 1 · · · | · · · 2 · · · | · · · 3 · · · | · · · 4 · · · | · · · 5 · · · | · ·

Figure 7–34

6. Select **CAM_BLANK** in the Style Name drop-down list.

7. The display representation should begin nine seconds after the animation starts. Set the *Time Value* to **9** and click **Apply**.

8. Select **CAM_NO_HIDE** in the Style Name drop-down list.

9. This display representation should begin 15 seconds after the animation starts. Set the *Time Value* to **15** and click **Apply**.

10. Select **Master Style** in the Style Name drop-down list.

11. This display representation should begin 18 seconds after the animation starts. Set the *Time Value* to **18** and click **Apply**.

12. Click **Close**.

Task 5 - Recreate the animation and view the playback.

1. Click ▶ (Generate) to recreate the frames for the animation.

2. Click **Create**.

Task 6 - Specify saved views for the animation to use during playback.

Design Considerations

In this task, you will incorporate view orientations into the animation timeline. Doing this enables orientations to be incorporated with the snapshots, style states, and the Servo Motors.

1. Click 🜨 (View @ Time) in the *Animation* tab.

2. Select **TOP** in the Name drop-down list.

3. This saved view should begin five seconds after the animation starts. Set the *Time Value* to **5** and click **Apply**.

4. Select **RIGHT** in the Name drop-down list.

5. This saved view should begin 11 seconds after the animation starts. Set the *Time Value* to **11** and select **Apply**.

6. Select **FRONT** in the Name drop-down list.

7. This saved view should begin 17 seconds after the animation starts. Set the *Time Value* to **17** and select **Apply**.

8. Click **Close**.

9. Press <Ctrl>+<D> to return to default orientation.

10. In the In-graphics toolbar, click ⬛ (Saved Orientations)> ⤢ (Reorient).

11. Enter **stand** as the Name of the orientation, as shown in Figure 7–35.

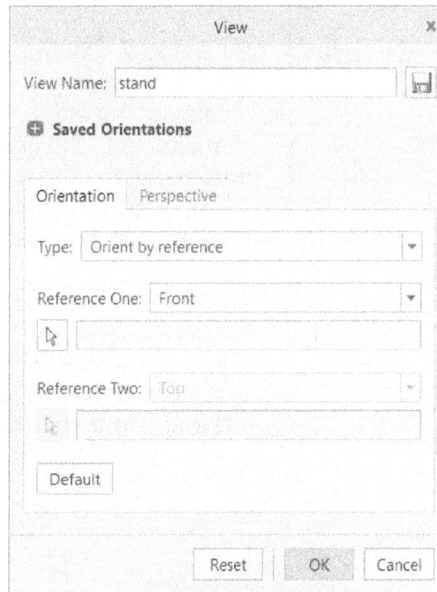

Figure 7–35

12. Click 🖫 (Save) and click **OK**.

13. Click 🜨 (View @ Time) to return to the View at Time dialog box.

14. Select **STAND** in the Name drop-down list.

15. Enter **0** after **Start** for this view to be displayed.

16. Click **Apply** and click **Close**.

Task 7 - Recreate the animation and display the playback.

---

1. Click ▶ (Generate) to recreate the frames for the animation.

2. Click **Yes** if prompted to overwrite an existing result set.

3. Click **Create**.

4. Save the assembly and erase it from memory.

Task 8 - (Optional) Apply Transparency @ Time to the animation.

Design Considerations

Similar to the **Display** and **View @ Time** options, the **Transparency @ Time** option enables you to customize the display of the animation. In this task, add two **Transparency @ Time** items to the timeline so that, between times 0 and 1, the transparency of the entire assembly goes from being completely Clear (100) to completely Opaque (0). This will enable you to fade into the animation before anything begins to move.

To accomplish this, you must begin by changing the current timeframe entities so that they begin one frame later. Once this is done, you can add the two new **Transparency @ Time** entries using similar techniques that were used for the **Display** and **View @ Time** entries.

1. Save the assembly and erase it from memory.

Chapter Review Questions

1. Once an animation has been created, it can be renamed but not deleted.

   a. True

   b. False

2. Snapshots that are created in the Mechanism application cannot be used in the Animation application.

   a. True

   b. False

3. What are the available display modes? (Select all that apply.)

   a. View @ Time

   b. Trans @ Time

   c. Display @ Time

   d. Style @ Time

4. The events in the timeline cannot be dragged to new positions.

   a. True

   b. False

5. Which of the following options are available for the Interpolation of a Key Frame Sequence? (Select all that apply.)

   a. Fast

   b. Smooth

   c. Straight

   d. Linear

   e. Slow

6. Snapshots are used to define a Key Frame Sequence in an Explode animation.

   a. True

   b. False

7. Servo motors that are created in the Animation application are available in the Mechanism application.

   a. True

   b. False